Myth and Society

in Ancient Greece

Translated by Janet Lloyd

Myth and Society

in Ancient Greece

Jean-Pierre Vernant

ZONE BOOKS · NEW YORK

1988

ZONE BOOKS
611 Broadway Suite 838
New York, NY 10012

Originally published in France as *Mythe et société
en Grèce ancienne*
© 1974 by Librairie François Maspero.
Published 1988 by Éditions la Découverte.

Printed in the United States of America

Distributed by The MIT Press,
Cambridge, Massachusetts, and London, England

Library of Congress Cataloging-in-Publication Data

Vernant, Jean-Pierre.
    [Mythe et société en Grèce ancienne. English]
    Myth and society in ancient Greece /
    Jean-Pierre Vernant; translated by Janet Lloyd.
        p. cm.
    Translation of: Mythe et société en Grèce ancienne.
    Bibliography: p.
ISBN 0-942299-16-7. ISBN 0-942299-17-5 (pbk.)
1. Greece—Social life and customs. 2. Greece—Social
conditions—To 146 B.C. 3. Mythology, Greek. I. Title.
DF78.V4713 1988   87-33786
938—dc19   CIP

Contents

Introduction   7

I   The Class Struggle   11

II   City-State Warfare   29

III   Marriage   55

IV   Social History and the Evolution of Ideas in China
and Greece from the Sixth to the Second Centuries B.C.
(with Jacques Gernet)   79

V   The Society of the Gods   101

VI   The Pure and the Impure   121

VII   Between the Beasts and the Gods   143

VIII   The Myth of Prometheus in Hesiod   183

IX   The Reason of Myth   203

Notes   261

Introduction

Following *Myth and Thought* and *Myth and Tragedy*, here is a collection of studies under the title of *Myth and Society*, the most recent of which have never been published before. The reader has every right to question this triple coupling of myth with something else, all the more so since in French (and in English) the "copular" *and* can carry more than one meaning and may infer not simply juxtaposition but also association or contrast.

While I was writing *Myth and Thought* I had in my mind one of Henri Delacroix's fine books, entitled *Language and Thought*, which appeared when I was a young man. His title conveyed not only that language already contains thought, that language is thought, but also that thought consists of more than just language: It is never completely contained by its linguistic expression. The papers I had collected in that volume [*Myth and Thought*] seemed to me to lend themselves, in a similar way, to a double reading. On the one hand, I was trying to reveal the intellectual code peculiar to myth and to distinguish the mental aspects of myths concerned with, for instance, memory, time, and Hermes and Hestia, but on the other hand, I also wanted to indicate how far Greek thought, as it developed historically, broke away from the language of myth. In *Myth and Tragedy* the problem was quite similar. Pierre Vidal-Naquet and I aimed to throw some light upon the interconnections between legendary traditions and certain new forms of thought — in particular in law and politics — in fifth-century

Athens. The works of the tragedians seemed to us to offer a particularly favorable field in which the texts themselves allowed us to seize upon this confrontation, this constant tension as expressed in a literary genre which used the great themes of legend but treated them in accordance with its own specific demands so that the myths are both present and, at the same time, challenged. Our desire to respect the equivocal and ambiguous character of the relationship between myth and tragedy was no doubt affected by the double methodological orientation of our studies: We used a structural analysis of the texts — the works themselves — to detect the system of thought within them, but, at the same time, followed a method of historical inquiry, as this alone could explain the changes, innovations, and restructuring that took place within any system.

With this third volume one might be tempted to suppose the connection between myth and society to be a looser, more accidental, and less significant one, and to suspect that this time I have simply juxtaposed a number of studies on the subject of Greek society and its institutions alongside a number of others on the subject of myth. And in fact this book does open with three articles on the subject of the class struggle, war, and marriage, and closes with the mythology of spices, the myth of Prometheus, and some general reflections on the problems of myth as they appear to Greek scholars of today. I would certainly not deny that my choice of this or that theme has often been affected by the various circumstances, requests, or opportunities that are bound to arise in the course of one's research. However, when I consider the question closely it seems to me that here, as elsewhere, chance has another, hidden side to it, and that the digressions made in the course of a work can often be accounted for by a kind of internal necessity. I do not think that the careful reader will have any difficulty in picking out the thread that links together these various studies and also links this book to those that preceded it.

I shall therefore make only a few brief preliminary remarks. The framework of my first article is a debate within Marxism. In examining the validity of the concepts of a slave-based mode of production, of class, and of the class struggle when applied to ancient Greece, I wanted, by returning to the ancient texts, to give Marx his due for his acute sense of historical reality and his understanding of the specific characteristics of different types of social forms. In emphasizing what was — in many respects — the decisive role of the city's institutions and political life in the functioning of the social system, I also intended to make the point that economic factors and relationships do not, in the context of the ancient *polis*, have the same effects as they do in that of modern capitalist societies. In order to present the economic facts accurately it is necessary to take account of the attitudes and behavior of the social agents, for these show that the religion and economics of the society are still very closely interconnected. In this respect the starting point and background of this paper is Louis Gernet's study, "La Notion mythique de la valeur en Grèce."[1]

"City-State Warfare" was written as the introduction to a collective work, *Problems of Warfare in Greece*. It is no mere chance that so much of this preliminary study is devoted to the reciprocal relations that can be established between the religious and the military spheres. They were bound together by complex and, once again, equivocal relationships whose development can be traced through time.

The study of marriage and the transformations it underwent between the archaic and classical periods was specifically undertaken to solve a problem which had been posed by a particular work of mythological analysis. When Marcel Detienne studied the corpus of texts relevant to Adonis and widened its scope to embrace the whole of the mythology of spices, he turned up a new problem: how to account for the manifest disparity between the picture myth gives us, in which the wife is diametrically opposed to the concubine, and the much more vaguely defined institutions of fifth- and fourth-century Athens. To my mind, the historical study of the customs of marriage and the inquiry into the structural analysis of the corpus of myth collected by Detienne are two aspects of a single piece of research. The aim of this double approach is to distinguish more clearly the reciprocal effects of society and myth and to define both the similarities, and, at the same time, the divergences between these two levels that illuminate one another and now reinforce, now check and counterbalance one another.

Our remarks on the Greek gods consider the pantheon from two points of view: first, as a divine society with its own hierarchy, in which each god enjoys his own particular attributes and privileges, bearing a more or less close, more or less direct relation to the structure of human society; and second, as a classificatory system, a symbolic language with its own intellectual ends.

In "The Pure and the Impure," an examination of the thesis of Louis Moulinier, we attempt to show that while this author has successfully discovered what these concepts mean in psychological and social terms, they can only be fully understood through their relation to a coherent body of religious representations.

Then there are the last two studies: "The Myth of Prometheus in Hesiod" and "The Reason of Myth." They seem to us to speak for themselves, and both refer so clearly to the book's central theme that there is no need to labor the point: to what extent and in what forms is myth present in a society and a society present in its myths? In fact, expressed in this way, the question is perhaps too simple. In this set of works, originally published by my friend François Maspero, it is not, despite their titles, a matter of conjunction between *two* terms. Three terms, myth, thought, and society, form as it were a triangular framework in which each to some extent implies the other two while remaining at the same time distinct and autonomous. Piece by piece, hesitantly and incompletely, our research, in collaboration with others, has attempted to explore the field of study that this framework defines.

CHAPTER I

The Class Struggle[1]

In his study on the problem of class struggle in classical antiquity,[2] Charles Parain tried to define the specific characteristics of forms of social life that underwent profound changes in the period between pre-Homeric Greece and Imperial Rome, and that also present marked spatial variations. Parain is well aware of the diversity in the historical material. He is, however, interested in a more abstract level of analysis and attempts to define the fundamental characteristics that gave a unique structure to this whole period of human history in the Mediterranean West and constitute a particular mode of production.

For Marxists, the ancient world is a class society which in its typical form can be defined as a slave mode of production. But does it follow inevitably that the whole history of classical antiquity can be seen in terms of an opposition between the two conflicting classes of slaves and slave owners? If Marxist theory has to be reduced to such a brief, rigid, and anti-dialectical formula, it will scarcely be capable of illuminating the work of historians.

First of all, slavery has its own history. Its birth and development are inevitably linked to certain modes of land appropriation. As a result, its spread, its importance, and its forms (in the family, agriculture, manufacturing, state administration) are not the same in different places nor at different times. Thus, all ancient classical societies cannot be classified indiscriminately as slave societies. Several of Marx's texts themselves underline the point that

11

the spread of slavery within ancient civilizations undermines and ultimately destroys the forms of property characteristic of the ancient city. In *Capital*, for example, Marx states:

> Peasant agriculture on a small scale and the carrying out of independent handicrafts... form the economic foundation of the classical communities at their best, after the primitive form of ownership of land in common had disappeared, and before slavery had seized on production in earnest.[3]

Marxists should therefore consider slavery dialectically as a process, both in so far as it determines the specific characteristics, after a certain stage, of the social relations of antiquity, and insofar as, in the course of its development, it destroys the original forms that these social relationships assumed in the context of the city. Historians of ancient Greece and Rome will not, therefore, have exactly the same perspective. As far as Greece is concerned, the perspective, again, will not be the same for the whole of antiquity. It will be different for the archaic period when the city developed its original structure and slavery, which still existed only on a small scale, retained its patriarchal character, and for the classical age and the subsequent period of dissolution, which were marked by the expansion of servile labor in different branches of economic life.

These preliminary comments can be usefully supplemented by reference to Parain's work. He underlines the difference between a fundamental contradiction, which corresponds to the specific character of a mode of production in its typical form, and the principal or dominant contradiction, which indicates which social groups have actually been opposed at any definite moment in history in the concrete context of a particular situation. But there is a fundamental and essential problem, which goes beyond this question of vocabulary, that I want to discuss very briefly, less to try to answer the question than to try to define it better and locate its multiple implications.

We can talk of basic and principal contradictions only because Marxist analysis, while seeing each social formation as a whole, distinguishes within it various levels, each with its own structure and dynamic. Contradiction in a social system can exist within any one level or between different levels. The well-known Marxist schema corresponds to this: productive forces, economic relations of production, sociopolitical relationships, forms of thought and ideology. In the capitalist society studied by Marx, the class contradictions that at the sociopolitical level oppose the workers and the capitalists, correspond to the contradictions that at the base of society oppose the increasingly collective process of production (forces of production) to the private and increasingly concentrated ownership of these means of production (relations or system of production). Class conflict, manifested in the social and political conflicts that are the concrete material of history, coincides with what is seen, in the abstract analysis of political economy, as the fundamental contradiction of the capitalist mode of production. This is why the definition of classes and class conflict must show how these human groups and their evolution are rooted, at all levels of social reality, in contradictions that in general terms, coincide. This correspondence of the contradictions at different levels explains why within the working class there is the possibility of a new society. Its struggle, its political victory, and its takeover of the state all entail, according to Marx, a radical transformation of social relations, and thus a new advance at the level of the productive forces. To demonstrate that the situation in the ancient world was not the same, and that this clear-cut theoretical model cannot be applied directly to ancient societies, it is enough to note that the slave class did not carry within itself the possibility of a new society. The political victory of the slaves, if such a hypothesis had ever been meaningful, would not have undermined the relations of production nor changed the way in which property was held. All historians agree that even when slave revolts took the form of an organized political or military struggle (something that never occurred in the Greek city-states) they had neither program nor prospects and could not have brought about a transformation of the social system of production. They were incapable of changing the society because the fundamental contradictions developing between the forces of production and the relations of production, which were eventually to threaten their necessary articulation, were not completely expressed in the antagonism between the slaves and their owners at the level of social and political conflict.

To grasp the complex interplay of the antagonism between social groups in antiquity, historians, whether Marxist or non-Marxist, must first define more precisely the various contradictions active in the ancient economy, locate them within society as a whole, and specify — as far as possible — their hierarchy and their relative importance during the different periods of ancient history. Marx has given some indications of the contradictions that seemed to him to be fundamental in the earliest period, when the *polis* was established. According to him, we have to deal with an opposition between two forms of landownership, the coexistence of which constituted the uniqueness of the Greco-Roman city-state.[4] The first was state landownership — communal, in principle; the second, private property in land which was originally obtained through the medium of state appropriation. It was this dual land-tenure system that made the landowner a citizen and turned the old village cultivator into a town dweller. The destruction of the equilibrium between these two forms of landholding to the advantage of the latter — that is, the gradual consolidation of private landholding within the framework of the city-state — seems to be the necessary condition for the development of slavery and a monetary economy. Essentially Marx based his analysis on Niebuhr's work on Roman history. Historians of the archaic economy of Greece, who are not themselves necessarily working in a Marxist framework, are currently concerning themselves with the same issues. Recent work suggests the possibility that there were two different forms of citizen land-tenure in the ancient Greek world.[5] On the one hand, there was family property belonging to a household (*oikos*) and not to individuals, who had no right to dispose freely of their *patroa* (ancestral possessions) outside the family by sale. Even in city-states like Athens, it appears that up to the last third of the fifth century most landholdings (probably those around the urban area, that, properly speaking, was what was meant by the term "city land") retained their character as inalienable family possessions, allotments (*kleroi*), each belonging to one of the households making up the state, and not to a private individual. On the other hand, alongside these inalienable landholdings (sometimes coexisting with them in the same state, but localized in more outlying regions) there may have been areas where ownership was further developed and where it was easier to buy and sell land.

A detailed study of land law with its various forms and historical changes is indispensable since, throughout this period, while the economy remained essentially an agricultural one, class struggles were rooted in problems connected with land tenure. In the beginning, the town (*astu*) was opposed to the country (*dēmoi*) as the place where *a certain type of landowner* lived (in Athens, the *Eupatridai*). These landowners monopolized the state, controlling both political offices and military functions. It was only later (in Athens, from the sixth century onward), that the area within the city walls came to provide a framework for independent industrial and commercial activity that was entirely cut off from agriculture. It was this situation that prompted Marx to write:

> The history of classical antiquity is the history of cities, but of cities founded on landed property and on agriculture.[6]

In the same text he defined economic life at the beginning of the city-state in this way:

> Concentration in the towns, with the land as territorium; small-scale agriculture working for direct consumption; manufacture as a domestic side-occupation of wives and daughters

(spinning and weaving) or independent in specific branches (smiths...) only.[7]

The city-state can thus be defined as a system of institutions which allows a privileged minority (the citizens) exclusive access to landed property within a definite area. In this sense the economic basis of the *polis* was a particular form of land appropriation.

The later development of slavery, the separation of artisan manufacturing from the domestic economy, the growth of a limited market sector both within and, to use Marx's own term, in the interstices of these agricultural societies, the spread of money — all these phenomena indicated that new contradictions were becoming dominant. These contradictions could arise only in conditions specific to the city-state. But, at the same time, their development challenged the very structures within which they had evolved. For Marx, the generalization of slavery and the spread of domestic exchange and maritime commerce, along with the establishment of commercial production and the concentration of landownership in fewer hands, broke down the forms of land tenure and the sociopolitical structures that characterized the city-state. At its apogee, the community in effect depended "on the preservation of equality among its free self-sufficient peasants," using surplus not for market production but for the communal interests (real or imaginary) of the group that made them simultaneously citizens and landowners: war, politics, and religion.[8] Conversely, we can characterize the Hellenistic period, when the nature of Greek economic and political life was no longer defined by the traditional framework of the city-state, in terms of the following factors: expansion of slavery, uninterrupted circulation of money throughout the Mediterranean basin, and growth of the role of the market (although in antiquity commodity production always remained limited to certain sectors and, in general terms, dependent on agriculture).[9]

It is therefore fairly easy to see why industry and commerce, which were to become increasingly important in economic life, developed in every case more or less on the periphery of the city-state, being somehow extraneous to the civic community. Those who were occupied full-time in such activities and played the main part in maritime commerce, banking, and commercial production were typically non-citizens (*metics*). Marx wrote:

> In classical antiquity, manufacture appears already as a corruption (business for *freedmen*, clients, aliens, etc.). This development of productive labor (not bound in pure subordination to agriculture as a domestic task, labor by free men for agriculture or war only, or for religious observance and manufactures for the community — such as construction of houses, streets, temples), which necessarily develops through intercourse with aliens and slaves, through the desire to exchange the surplus product, etc., dissolves the mode of production on which the community rests and, with it, the *objective individual*, i.e., the individual defined as Roman, Greek, etc.[10]

Marx's brief references to the antagonisms within the relations of production in the city-state anticipate and clarify the most recent research done on the ancient economy.[11] Following Friedrich Oertel and Richard Laqueur, Erb has emphasized that the basic driving force in ancient Greece was, in Greek terms, the opposition between *oikonomia* and *chrēmatistikē*. *Oikonomia* referred to the agrarian economy based on the family, upon which the city-state as such was constructed. This system corresponded to a political ideal of autarchy and was supported by primitive artisan production that provided for minimum needs. *Chrēmatistikē* referred to an economy that developed out of the growth of the city-state with its need for a food supply and for financial resources, particularly as a result of the demands of warfare. The growth of maritime trade, credit banking, and bottomry loans (providing capital and insurance for traders) were all manifestations of *chrēmatistikē*. On the one hand, there was a very short-range agricultural economy which was inward-looking and autarchic in character, and was associated with craft or activity geared to consumption rather than production, or to satisfying the needs of the political community (war and the upkeep of the city). On the other hand, there was a wider ecomomic system with active, developed, and outward-looking commerce, and maritime exchange. This system was built up essentially for personal gain. As M.I. Finley remarks, one of the most striking characteristics of the Greek economy is that, to a very great extent, land and money continue to be organized in two separate spheres.[12] This fundamental separation is characteristic of economic development in the ancient world.

Marxists should bear in mind these features of economic history if they wish to analyze, in each period, the concrete manifestations of class conflict and the economic structures which determined their form. In a note in *Capital* Marx replies to an objection made against the *Critique of Political Economy*. It is certainly true, so the criticism went, that in modern society, which is ruled by material interests, all development of social, political, and spiritual life is dominated by the mode of production of material life and derives, in the last analysis, from economic structures. But this was not so in the Middle Ages "when Catholicism reigned" nor in Athens and Rome "where politics reigned." Marx's reply is doubly interesting from our point of view. On the one hand, he does not make the last attempt to deny that politics ruled over social existence in ancient times. He tries to show why this is so and why it was within the framework of political life that class conflict took shape and was acted out, just as it was within the framework of political life that Greek civilization created in philosophy, science, and the arts its distinctive ways of thinking. On the other hand, Marx indicates yet again, and in the clearest terms, in what area of economic reality the fundamental contradiction of antiquity was to be found – the contradiction that gives us the key to the general process of development. Having observed that antiquity could no more live by politics than the Middle Ages by Catholicism, Marx wrote:

On the contrary it is the mode by which they gained a livelihood that explains why here politics, and there Catholicism, *played the chief part*. For the rest, it requires but a slight acquaintance with the history of the Roman republic, for example, to be aware that the key to its history is 'the history of *landed* property.'[13] *(our italics)*

As far as archaic and classical Greece are concerned – I will not venture into a discussion of the Hellenistic and Roman periods – I would say that Marx's formulation appears to have perfectly defined the area in which the fundamental contradiction emerged and developed. I believe, with him, that it concerns the structures of landed property. To use Parain's terminology again, the principal contradictions at the beginning of the city-state opposed a class of landowners of the type of the *Eupatridai*, living in the town, controlling the state and undertaking its military functions, to the village farmers who made up the rural *dēmos*. Later on, as a direct result of the social evolution which has been outlined, the principal contradictions shifted with the emergence of new antagonisms, resulting from the development of the division of labor.

With this in mind, one should emphasize the decisive importance for a state like Athens of the shift which occurred in the second half of the fifth century. It was at this point that the whole social and economic equilibrium, upon which the régime of the *polis* rested, was called into question. Three features, which can be said in the main to have given the social life of the city-state its special character, were equally affected. These were, first, the unity of town and countryside (the built-up area was initially and in principle only the center which united the countryside because it contained all the *public* buildings in which the communal life of the group was centered; *private* interests and individual family households were distinct from this); second, the unity of citizen and soldier (military duties shared by and exclusively reserved for citizens being considered an integral part of

19

political duties); third, the close bond between citizenship and landownership. Toward the end of the fifth century there was a whole series of changes which were to have decisive effects. The countryside had been devastated by war, and fields and rural farms deserted; at the same time, in the town a truly urban milieu had already developed, a city existence whose way of life, occupational patterns, and mentality now made a clear contrast to the old traditions of the rural dwellers. In response to the demands of war, mercenaries reappeared and professional military leaders began to gain power. Finally, land ceased to be inalienable as in the past. It was drawn into the sphere of the monetary system from which it had previously been separated, and was also granted more easily to non-citizens as a reward for their services.[14] There is an additional significant factor: at about the same time, the influence of a new commercial form of law began to be felt that, for the purposes of maritime trade, elaborated a notion of contract relatively modern in inspiration that, contrary to all Greek legal custom, made use of written documents.[15] We might say, following Louis Gernet, that the economy – in the sense that we nowadays give to this term – had done its work.[16] From the fourth century onward everything was to be measured by money. But now we are talking of the fourth century, the period of the collapse of the city-state, not the seventh or sixth, the eras during which it was founded and consolidated. Moreover, we are referring to Athens, a maritime and commercial city-state, and not to the whole of Greece. Finally, although Aristotle wrote: "We call goods [chrēmata] all things whose value is measured in money," it is nevertheless a fact that, even when he reflected upon economics, he continued to set his face stubbornly against the commercial way of thinking.[17] Was this a biased attitude, or a false perception of the economic realities of his age? On the contrary; I believe, with Marx, that Aristotle was a faithful recorder of the social world of his period. In Aristotle's time, the largest sector of economic life remained outside the market economy. This was particularly true since there was no paid labor force.[18]

What was class struggle like in fourth-century Greece? Claude Mossé has recently studied the different aspects and ramifications of this question for fourth-century Athens.[19] She has demonstrated very usefully the difficulties involved in such a study. We can here only refer the reader to the picture she has painted of class relations and their evolution through the phase of the collapse of the classical *polis*.

Clearly, class struggle has never (at any time in history) taken a simple form. But Marx believed, apparently correctly, that in ancient times it was far more complex in character. There are various reasons for this complexity, some of which Claude Mossé has clarified. I would like, as a working hypothesis, to note what seems to be essential in this context. The conflicts that toward the fourth century involved the different social groups within the framework of the city-state were neither baseless nor purely ideological: They were rooted in the economy of these societies. Human groups came into conflict because of their material interests. But these material interests did not derive either directly or exclusively from the position the individuals occupied in the process of production. They always stemmed from the position that these individuals occupied in political life, which played the dominant role in the system of the *polis*. In other words, the economic function of different individuals — which determined their material interests, fashioned their social needs, and oriented their social and political behavior in alliance with or in opposition to other groups — was mediated via political status.

A few very simple examples will be enough to make this clear. Between a metic and a citizen, both in charge of a manufacturing establishment with 15 or 20 slaves, or active in maritime commerce, or dealing in bottomry loans, there was no difference in economic status, that is, in their positions in the process of production. Nevertheless, it would be impossible to consider them as members of the same class. Between them there were antagonisms and conflicts, including conflict of interest. The institutions of the *polis* system gave to all citizens privileges to which non-citizens could not hope to aspire (some of which were economic, such as the right to own land). The solidarity that drew all the citizens of the same city together and made them a relatively united group in opposition to non-citizens despite their internal divisions, no doubt reflected their common interest. But this community of interests among the citizens of a single city, and the divergence of interests between citizens and non-citizens, can be understood only when the mediating role played by the structures of the state has been taken into account. These points can be made more precisely through a second example.

Claude Mossé has demonstrated that it would be rash to speak as though a commercial and industrial class were opposed to a landowning class even in the fourth century (and *a fortiori* even more rash in the case of earlier periods). Certainly there existed in Athens a category of traders who were only traders – true middlemen – in addition to all those who sold part of the production of their agricultural and artisan labor directly. But these middlemen were generally engaged in retail trade, small shopkeepers with booths or stalls in the *agora*. In contrast, all the evidence about the large fortunes of those whom we call (with Parain) the slave-owning entrepreneurs indicates that they almost always included real estate in addition to workshops, liquid assets, and funds out on loan. Given the importance assumed by landholding in terms of civil status, it is highly unlikely that a citizen who controlled huge financial resources was not a landowner as well. If he did not have land at the outset we can be sure that he would buy it, since land carried both prestige and intrinsic worth and endowed the citizen with a dignity, importance, and status that monetary wealth could not provide.

We have to remember, moreover, what happened to most of the profits of the slave-owning entrepreneur in the city-state system. There was no industrial capital in antiquity. Profits were not reinvested in business. Technology remained primitive since the basic productive force was the human labor of the slaves. Under these conditions the greater part of the entrepreneur's surplus returned to the civic collectivity in the form of liturgies, filling the treasury and paying for the communal expenditure of the state. This included the costs of civic and religious festivals, military expenses, and the construction of public buildings. Marx has demonstrated that in societies where the productive forces are at an early stage of development and commercial production is still limited, money has neither the same role nor the same forms as in a more developed economy. While monetary circulation remains confined to coins, and money itself conserves its local and political character (functioning as money of account and currency — as an instrument of circulation[20] — and not yet as credit[21] or universal money[22]) wealth can only be accumulated in the domain of mere monetary circulation and specifically in the form of hoarding: "The activity which amasses hoards is, on the one hand, the withdrawal of money from circulation by constantly repeated sales, and on the other, simple piling up, *accumulation*."[23]

Although it is true that in antiquity everyone hoarded — hoards were scattered and dispersed over a whole area, and not centralized in banks as nowadays[24] — this continuous and widespread practice of taking money out of circulation was compensated for by a counter-movement which Marx analyzed as usual from both an anthropological and an economic viewpoint. Because economic facts are to Marx relations between men (relations that endlessly transform themselves), their study must be accompanied by what one might call a comparative typology of economic behavior.[25] The hoarder who tried to save his money by hiding it, by burying it, who accumulated it incessantly, was also the man who was driven to show it off in front of others and spread it before the public.[26] A lot of money found its way back into circulation in the form of conspicuous consumption and, in the city-state, where personal indulgence was in principle forbidden, this took the form of generous gifts to the civic community. A certain redistribution of the surplus between the citizens took place through the intermediary of the city-state, whose treasury paid the salaries of legal and political positions that were available to everyone, and even financed some cash gifts to the poorest in the community.

One can understand, therefore, why Parain and Claude Mossé interpreted the class struggle between citizens as a conflict between rich and poor. At first sight such a formulation is surprising, and hardly seems Marxist in spirit. Membership in a class depends neither on property nor on income levels but on a man's place in the system of production. How then can a Marxist speak of a class of rich men or a class of poor? Yet if this formulation appears to be inapplicable to contemporary society, nevertheless it seems to be the only one that accurately defines the situation that existed during the decline of the Greek city-state. At that time conflicts between citizens all revolved around the same problem: Who should benefit from the redistribution of surplus by means of the institutions of the city-state? The mass of citizens, whatever the diversity of their economic status, were polarized into two opposed camps. Those who had nothing or very little sought to use the structures of the state to tax the rich as much as possible, while the owners — whatever the origins of their fortunes — were determined to resist this.

Within this general model, where should we situate the conflict between the slaves and their free owners? What form did the struggle of the former take and how much influence did it have on social evolution? On the factual level, one observation must be accepted without hesitation by the Greek historian, at least as far as it concerns the archaic and classical periods, to which this analysis is limited. The opposition between slaves and their owners never emerged as the principal contradiction. In the social and political struggles of this period, with their violent clashes, the slaves never once appear as a unified social grouping; they never acted as a class playing its own role in the succession of conflicts that were a permanent feature of the city-states. No wonder, since class struggles were generated and acted out within a sociopolitical framework from which the slaves were by definition excluded. Throughout this period the slaves' opposition to their masters was never directly expressed in terms of social and political struggle.

In this respect, we need to consider what exactly is implied by the formula of Aristotle, a witness to whom Marx paid particular attention. Aristotle saw the slave as a "living tool." In other words, to the Greek mind, the humanity of a man was inseparable from his social nature; and man was social in so far as he was a political being, a citizen. Because he was outside the city-state, the slave was outside society, and therefore outside humanity. He had no identity apart from being a productive instrument. There is a dialectical connection between this image of the slave, reduced to the simple condition of a living tool, and the minor role actually played in history by the slaves. As long as the system of the classical city-state remained alive — in its economic structures, in its institutions, and in its ways of thinking — the slaves could not form an active, unified social force, a united body of men intervening on the historical stage to direct the course of events in a way that reflected their interests and their aspirations. Furthermore, it is known that the slaves as a whole were not as unified as a group, as we are sometimes led to imagine. In addition to the variety of their ethnic origins and the differences of language, which in themselves raised obstacles, it is evident that considerable differences in their actual conditions of work lay behind their apparently uniform legal status. What did domestic slaves like those being presented in New Comedy, or the slave who ran an artisan business for and in the name of his master, have in common with those who sweated in chains in the mines of Laurion? What was there in common between an agricultural slave, a tutor in a wealthy family, or an employee of the state administration?

Does this mean that the opposition between the slaves and their masters did not play a crucial role in the evolution of ancient societies? Not at all. But this opposition did not take the form of an organized struggle occurring at the level of the social and political structures. It came out in individual expressions of revolt; sometimes, when external conditions or the vicissitudes of war permitted it, by mass escapes; but it was always a question of escaping from the condition of enslavement, and not of changing the social system to the advantage of the group of which the slave felt himself to be a member. In fact, the collective opposition came into play, and had a decisive effect, in other terms: It was at the level of the forces of production that the slaves, as a whole and as a social class, manifested resistance to their masters — the same forces of production of which the slaves were precisely the central factor in the economic and technical context of ancient Greece. At this level, as the use of slave labor became general, the conflict between the slaves and their owners became the fundamental contradiction of the slave mode of production. In this system, in which overall technical progress was blocked or at least markedly held back, the spread of slavery was clearly the only way to develop the forces of production. But at the same time the slaves' opposition to their masters, their resistance, their inevitable reluctance to perform the tasks allotted to them, impeded progress and imposed tighter and tighter limits on output. Moreover, when it came to increasing productive capacity, multiplying the numbers of slaves could not be continued indefinitely without endangering the stability of the social system as a whole. Thus we can say that, after a certain point, the conflict between the slaves and those who used them became the fundamental contradiction of the system, even though, as Parain pointed out, it did not appear as the principal contradiction.

These preliminary remarks have been both too long-winded and inadequate. But they were above all intended to remind ourselves that we cannot take the conceptual apparatus that has been developed out of a study of contemporary society and apply it directly and without modification to the ancient world. Arguing against classical economics, Marx asserted the historical character of the economic categories that he distinguished in his study of modern society; it was in *modern* society that they acquired the developed form we recognize today. Marx believed that these categories provide keys to an understanding of social development as a whole, but he stated at the same time that they are not timeless. They have not always existed. One must therefore beware of projecting them purely and simply on non-capitalist societies, in which they will perhaps not be found, or in which they have taken forms very different from those that they have assumed under industrial capitalism. To the same extent, whenever we use the notions of class and class struggle in application to the ancient world, we should beware of anachronism and remain faithful to the historical spirit of Marxism.

CHAPTER II

City-State Warfare[1]

War was quite natural to the Greeks of the classical period. Organized, as they were, into small cities, all equally jealous of their own independence and equally anxious to affirm their supremacy, they saw warfare as the normal expression of the rivalry that governed relations between different states, so that times of peace, or rather truces, seemed like dead periods in the constantly renewed web of conflict.

Moreover, the spirit of strife that set the city-states against each other was simply one aspect of a much vaster power at work in all human relationships and even in nature itself. In individual relationships and between families, as between one state and another, in the competitive Games, in lawsuits, in the debates of the Assembly, and on the battlefield, the ancient Greeks recognized under various names — *Polemos, Eris, Neikos* — that same power of confrontation that Hesiod places at the origins of the world and Heraclitus celebrates as the father and king of the whole universe.

This agonistic view of man, of social relations, and of natural forces is deeply rooted not only in the heroic ethos of the epic but also in certain institutional practices in which we can detect, as it were, the prehistory of this "political" conflict in which city-states engaged.

At a period when there was still no legal organization, such as the *polis*, to set up, arbitrate, and regulate the relations between the various family groups in the name of the State, there was no distinct boundary between private vengeance and warfare in the proper sense of the term. The difference between a band setting out to take vengeance for bloodshed, a raid for cattle or women, and an expedition of war, was a matter of scope and the size of the group mobilized, but in all these cases the social mechanisms and psychological attitudes are identical. Thus Glotz writes: "The vendetta is a war just as war consists of an indefinite series of vendettas."[2] So in this context war does not yet appear as the type of institution that regulates power relations between states, but rather as one aspect among others of exchanges between different families — just one of the forms taken by the dealings between different human groups that both associate with and oppose each other.

The use of certain words still current during the classical period is significant in this respect. The enemy, *echthros*, is the opposite of the friend, *philos*, which is close to the Latin *suus* in that it has a possessive sense. The *philos* is first and foremost an individual's close relative;[3] and the model of *philia* is realized in the close family circle where children, parents and siblings feel themselves to be in some way identical to each other, each one belonging to all the others.[4] The enemy is the stranger, *xenos*. Yet this same term *xenos* also applies to the guest who is welcomed to the hearth to establish a link of hospitality between one house and another.[5] There is a similar ambiguity in the term *othneios*. It means "the stranger" as opposed to "the relative." Thus Plato was later to make a distinction between two kinds of conflict: discord, *stasis*, and war, *polemos*. *Stasis* concerns that which is *oikeion kai xuggenes*, related and of common origin; *polemos* concerns that which is *allotrion kai othneion*, different and foreign.[6] However, *othneios* also means a link of alliance between two families. It is the word Euripides several times uses to refer to the status of Alcestis within the family of her husband.[7]

Thus Ares and Aphrodite, *Polemos* and *Philia*, *Neikos* and *Harmonia*, *Eris* and *Erōs* also appear in the organization of the pantheon, in legends and in the theories of the philosophers, as pairs of powers that are opposed yet closely linked, presiding over the complementary institutions that war and marriage represented so long as private revenge and the exchange of women took place within the same framework of interfamily relations. The gift of a daughter is a means of paying off the price of bloodshed, the *poinē*. Marriage puts an end to a vendetta and changes two hostile groups into allies united by a private peace pact of *philotes*. The procedure for *philotes* rests upon a solemn exchange of vows between the two parties. *Horcoi* or *spondai* institutes, as it were, a fictitious family relationship between two groups that had, until then, stood in opposition to each other. An exchange of women has the same effect. To become reconciled with Amphiaraos, Adrastos gives him his sister Eriphyle, "ὅρκιον ὡς ὅτε πιστόν."[8] Moreover, the term *philotes* – which can still be used during the classical period to refer to a public pact of alliance between two cities[9] – applies in particular to the union between a man and a woman. As a religious power, *Philotes* presides, at Aphrodite's side, over sexual relationships.

When Ares, the god of war, pardons Cadmos, the murderer of his son, he gives him as a wife Harmonia, his own daughter by Aphrodite. All the gods attend this marriage, bringing gifts. Their presence gives a cosmic dimension to this reconciliation from which the city of Thebes is born.[10] However, in the account of the wedding of Cadmos and Harmonia, as in that of the marriage between Peleus and Thetis, which is in many ways so similar, the theme of the gift of discord (Eriphyle's necklace or the apple of *eris*) shows that, although war may end in marriage, marriage may also be at the origin of war and may cause it to spring up again. In the eyes of the Greeks it was not possible to isolate the forces of discord from those of union either in the web of human relationships or in the constitution of the world.

Religious practices that persisted throughout the whole of Greek history testify to this intimate connection between confrontation and association. The so-called ritual battles do very often have a warlike significance, but some of them are not confined to the strictly military domain and appear to have a wider significance: On the very occasions when the group, gathered together at some festival, affirms its unity, these ritual combats express the tensions on which its equilibrium depends and the opposition that exists between the various elements which constitute it.[11] A Greek festival does not only give expression to feelings of communion between its participants; conflict is also one of its essential social and psychological components. The combats sometimes feature women, sometimes men, sometimes women against men,[12] sometimes one age group against another, and sometimes territorial, tribal, or family units within the same age-group, especially when, at puberty, it was about to leave childhood behind and become integrated within the social community. These combats – which were not always altogether sham ones, since in some of them blood had to be shed[13] – made use of arms that were different from those of war, usually sticks and stones. Depending on the religious context and the human and divine agents involved, these combats might have an apotropaic and purificatory purpose; or, as in the case of the *lithobolia* of Troezene and Eleusis, they might serve as fertility rites;[14] or, again, have a warlike significance as, for example, in the battles in which the two *moirai* of Spartan ephebes grappled, unarmed, against each other at the Platanistas, after sacrificing a dog to Enyalios.[15] But in every case, whatever its particular purpose, the role of the ritual was to promote social integration and cohesion. It was through battles and competitions that the group became aware of its unity, as if the social links that bound it together were the same as those stressed by the rivalries between the different groups. After the death of Alexander, in the reign of Philip V, at a difficult time when the Macedonian army was divided against itself, two kinds of rituals were performed, the purpose of which was at the same time purification and unification.[16] First the entire army had to file through a space bounded by the head and the hindquarters of a sacrificed dog that had been cut in half. Then, under the leadership of the *regii juvenes duces*, the sons of the king, a ritual battle was organized in which the army was divided into two sides. Livy, following Polybius, notes that it was so violent that it resembled a true battle except that the use of the sword was forbidden. Although the circumstances may have lent a heightened drama to the ritual battle by reason of the rivalry between the two young princes, this was apparently an annual ceremony known as the *Xanthika* and celebrated during the month of *Xanthikos*.[17] So one is tempted to compare it to the combat between *Xanthos* and *Melanthos* that the Athenian *Apatouria* were believed to commemorate each year during the month of October. All the information that can be gleaned from the sources concerning the *Apatouria* has been carefully collected by Pierre Vidal-Naquet.[18] It was a festival celebrated by the phratries during which, at puberty, the Athenian adolescents were enrolled as members of the group by their fathers, following the vote of approval of the *phrateres*. However, it would seem that this integration into the phratry came about at the end of a period of "latency" during which the ephebe was, in the company of the rest of his age-group, segregated from society and sent to the "wild" frontier regions, where he underwent a military training that constituted a kind of initiation into the status of a warrior, as well as into that of a member of the community.

Did these male adolescent rituals with their ritual battles invariably carry this double significance of warrior initiation and social integration in ancient Greece, so that a boy would, as it were, with the same step enter both military and public life? Or should we, with Louis Gernet,[19] also acknowledge that, among the peasants, young people underwent initiation ceremonies of a different type directed toward marriage rather than warfare? Two points may, in our view, be made on this subject. First, we should note that at different times, especially during the period of hoplite reforms, when the warrior function was extended to take in new strata of the peasant population, ancient agricultural rites were adapted to the purposes of military initiation and training. This was clearly the case in Sparta, where the cult of Artemis Orthia, in which young boys underwent flagellation, appears to have become an integral part of the whole system of trials in the Spartan

agōgē that was aimed at selecting skilled warrior citizens. This
example is all the more striking in that, in Sparta, as well as
Artemis Orthia, an Artemis Korythalia was a patroness of youth,
although she clearly had nothing to do with the domain of war.[20]
Secondly, if for a boy the significance of the rites of passage was
to mark his accession to the condition of a warrior, for the girl
who took part alongside him in these same rites, and who was
also often subjected to a period of seclusion, the initiatory trials
had the force of a preparation for marriage. Here again both the
link and the polar opposition between the two types of institution are noticeable. Marriage is for the girl what war is for the
boy: For each of them these mark the fulfillment of their respective natures as they emerge from a state in which each still shared
in the nature of the other. Thus a girl who refuses marriage,
thereby also renouncing her "femininity," finds herself to some
extent forced toward warfare, and paradoxically becomes the
equivalent of a warrior. This is the situation in myth of females
like the Amazons[21] and, in a religious context, of goddesses such
as Athena: Their status as warrior is linked to their condition as
a *parthenos* who has sworn everlasting virginity. It could even
be said that this deviation both from the normal state of women,
who are destined for marriage, not warfare, and from the normal
state of warriors, who are men, not women, gives a special inten-
sity to warrior values when these are embodied in a girl. They
cease, in a way, to be merely relative or confined to a single
sex, and become "total."

In this way the ritual battles in which adolescent girls of the
same age group confront each other as warriors do not simply have
the effect of putting them at the disposal of the social group from
the point of view of the intermarriages that must take place within
it. They also serve as a test of virginity: The girls who are overcome in these combats reveal themselves not to be true virgins.
In one of the spots where Greek tradition situated the birth of
Athena Tritogeneia[22] — Lake Tritonis, in Libya — there was an
annual festival in which, in homage to the goddess, one girl, always

the most beautiful, was dressed in the hoplite panoply with a Corinthian helmet and Greek armor. Thus representing the warrior-virgin Athena for the young generation that had just reached maturity, she was ritually driven right round the lake in a war chariot. After this the entire band of *parthenoi*, divided into two camps, fought against each other with sticks and stones. Those who died from their wounds were called *Pseudoparthenoi*, false virgins.[23] If the false *parthenoi* can thus betray themselves in the warrior trial in which they are overcome, the young warrior may reveal his truly warlike nature by taking on the appearance of a *parthenos*. Achilles is one example, brought up as a girl among girls and dressed as a girl. Another is the warrior who worshipped his lance so tenaciously, swearing by it and revering it more than the gods themselves: his name, Parthenopea, indicates clearly enough that he looked like a young virgin.[24] Moreover, for both sexes the initiation through which a young man or woman is confirmed in his or her specific nature may entail, through a ritual exchange of clothing, temporary participation in the nature of the opposite sex, whose complement he or she will become by being separated from it. Warrior initiation ceremonies of young boys usually employ feminine disguises just as, in Sparta, on the first day of her marriage, the young bride wears men's clothing.[25]

This complementarity between war and marriage, which is expressed in religious thought and which we have also detected in the institutional practices connected with private vengeance, disappears with the advent of the city-state. There are a number of reasons to account for this. In the first place, marriages are usually arranged between families belonging to the same city; the *polis* normally reserves its women for its own citizens. For example, a law passed by Pericles laid down that to qualify for citizenship one had to be of Athenian birth on both the father's and the mother's side. Thus confined within the limits of a single state, the sphere of matrimonial exchange no longer coincides with that of war, for this is waged between different states. Second, in the *polis*, family units are regrouped within a community that not only extends beyond them but also defines another level of relationship. The political links that unite the citizens are different from family relationships and have a different purpose. Marriage is something private, left to the initiative of the head of the family acting within the framework of the recognized matrimonial rules. War belongs to the public sector and is the exclusive prerogative of the State. It cannot be decided upon or waged by individuals, families, or separate groups within the city-state. It is the responsibility of the city-state itself, acting as such, namely as a political entity. Politics can be defined as the city seen from the inside, the public life that the citizens share within the domain of whatever is common to them above and beyond their individual family differences. War is the same city facing outward, the activity of this same group of citizens now confronting something other than themselves, something foreign to them, in other words — as a rule — other cities.

In the model of the hoplite city-state the army does not constitute a specialized body with its own particular techniques and its own form of organization and command; nor does warfare represent a separate domain calling for different abilities and rules of action from those of public life. There is no professional army, there are no foreign mercenaries and no categories of citizens specially devoted to the profession of arms. Military organization is continuous with, and an extension of, civic organization. The *strategoi* who exercise command are the highest civil magistrates, elected like all the others without any particular experience in the art of warfare being demanded of them. A hoplite's training no doubt involves some skill in maneuvering, which presupposes a certain apprenticeship. But this is acquired earlier, in the gymnasium, in the context of a *paideia* the scope of which is more general. Pericles could assert as self-evident that Athenians did not need to undergo any training or learn any military techniques in order to make war.[26] According to him, success on the battlefield depended on the same virtues as those that ensured the prestige of the city of Athens in peacetime. All decisions were taken in the Assembly by the whole body of citizens according to the normal procedures and after public debate, whether they were concerned with engaging in war, mounting a warlike expedition, or drawing up a plan of campaign. The fact that the enemy was thus alerted and the advantage of surprise lost mattered little. The concept of military secrecy,[27] so important in our own eyes, was something lacking in Greek "strategy," to use the term in the modern sense. This was because it belonged to the same universal discourse that comprises the whole of political thought in ancient times. Thus, it would not be correct to say that city-state warfare during the sixth and fifth centuries was an extension, using other means, of the politics of these states. The warrior and the man of politics are completely identified together. Several of the essays in *Problèmes de la guerre en Grèce ancienne* quite correctly stress this point: The army is the popular assembly in arms, the city out campaigning, just as conversely the city is a community of warriors, for only those who can equip themselves as hoplites at their own expense qualify for full political rights. To hold that the circumstances of war can be freely and openly discussed in this way, that men can reason about them or — which comes to the same thing — can present an intelligible history of them after the event, as Thucydides did, is to apply to military operations the model of the logic of debate and to represent confrontations between city-states in the same terms as the rhetorical struggles of the Assembly. In the political arena a faction ensures its predominance by its superior powers of persuasion. If, in the context of war, the force of arms can replace the force of argument, this is because they are considered as the same type of power, both aimed at compelling and dominating others, the former concretely effecting on the battlefield what the latter achieves in the minds of men in the Assembly. A well-argued speech can save one a war, just as, in Thucydides, a victory on the battlefield settles a debate that was begun in the antithetical speeches of opposed *strategoi*.[28]

There is another reason why warfare should be intelligible to rational political enquiry, the only exception being the element of change, or *tuchē*. It is the fact that each of the cities waging war seeks not so much to annihilate its adversary, or even to destroy its army, but rather to force it to acknowledge its superior strength as the outcome of a test as rule-bound as a tournament. The war has a time limit set upon it, for a campaign normally takes place during the summer and ends before the onset of winter. Apart from minor operations of harassment on enemy territory, raids to destroy their crops, or sieges, for which the infantry is not well-equipped, the decisive battle is fought on chosen ground, a *pedion* where it is possible to deploy the two phalanxes of heavy infantry. In the clash between their hoplite lines the two hostile armies, through the energy, discipline, and staunchness of their respective fighting men, are the measure of the power and cohesion, the *dunamis*, of the two civic communities confronting each other. It is not, in principle, necessary to give pursuit to the enemy. It is sufficient that their line should not have held, that one should remain in control of the field, that they should have sought permission to gather up their dead, and that a trophy should have been set up. The peace treaty then has only to ratify the superior power of *kratein*, or mastery, that one side has demonstrated to the other on the field of battle.

Of course, this is an idealized schema that the historians will not fail to modify in detail. Nevertheless, as a theoretical model it establishes the peculiar features and character of warfare as waged between the city-states. For the war game to be played according to these rules a number of conditions are necessary that historically were not fulfilled all at the same time except during a short period. Nevertheless, the coherence of the system and its character as a part of the social and intellectual world of the *polis* give it the role of a model that persisted in the minds of men even when everything, or almost everything, about these conflicts — namely the techniques, the social and national framework, and the aims of the war — had changed.

One of the essential elements of this political warfare is the almost complete predominance, as a military weapon, of the heavy infantry deployed in the phalanx. In *Problèmes de la guerre en Grèce ancienne*,[29] Marcel Detienne shows, on the basis of the archaeological evidence of Paul Courbin, that the hoplite reform of the army was not the result of a sudden transformation in combat techniques, nor did it stem from the use of infantry deployed in a close formation formerly totally unknown. There is, in this respect, an undeniable continuity with the Homeric world. Nevertheless, there is a striking contrast between, on the one hand, the complex texture of the duels described in Homer between the chariot-borne fighters, the champions of the two armies, and on the other the collective discipline that governs hoplite combat. The reason is that military reforms cannot be separated from all the social, political, and mental changes that accompanied the advent of the city-state. We are dealing here with a break with the past, inaugurating a new system of collective life and at the same time introducing a new pattern of warfare. By extending the military privileges of the aristocracy to the entire body of small-scale peasant landowners who made up the civic community, the city itself took over the warrior function. It integrated into its own political world the sphere of war, which heroic legend exalted by separating it from ordinary life. The activities of war now lost their specific functional characteristics, and the figure of the warrior, seen as a human type, disappeared. Or rather, to be more precise, he became merged with the figure of the citizen who inherited the prestige that had been his and took over, and modified, some of the values that the warrior had embodied. At the same time, all the disturbing aspects of this figure, such as his *hubris*, which is so marked in, for example, the myths about warriors studied by Francis Vian,[30] are rejected. These aspects were a compound of frenzy and arrogance in a man who, by devoting himself entirely to war and wishing to know of nothing but war, deliberately places himself outside his own society.

Yet even if the city refused to endow the military art with a special prestige, warfare nevertheless continued to entail its own particular exigencies. The use of violence has its own logic. The suitability of the phalanx was strictly limited to one type of terrain and one specific form of combat. The practice of requiring the soldier-citizen to equip himself as a hoplite set a dangerous limitation upon the number of available infantrymen. It became necessary to extend recruitment for the heavy infantry so as to mobilize all the manpower the city could provide. Military armament also had to be diversified to suit different terrains, and so light infantry and bowmen came into being. Above all, naval warfare, whose development and types are described by Jean Taillardat,[31] was of crucial importance for a city such as Athens, and this made it necessary to consider warfare in a new light. What is most important in naval warfare is maneuverability of the craft and all that this entails in the way of training, experience, and inventiveness, and adequate state funds; for it is the state that, together with the trierarchs, bears the expense of building and equipping the ships and paying the wages of the crews. Siege warfare as it developed called into question not only the equipment, organization, and tactics of the army, but also the very concept of warfare. This takes different forms depending on whether the city considers it more important to defend its rural territory or the urban center, and that choice has in its turn important implications for the balance of social power and the orientation of its economic policies.[32] In an urbanized *polis* such as Athens, directed outward toward the sea on which it depends for its supplies and power, the spirit of enterprise shown by the citizens and exemplified in the building of the Long Walls, the importance attached to the fleet, and the control exercised over the islands and sea routes stand in contrast to the military traditionalism of cities like Sparta, where the emphasis was on their territory as a whole. In the former circumstances, the importance of the financial and economic aspects of war looms larger, and *technē*, which Pericles could afford to ignore so long as only the hoplite battle was concerned, comes into its own in the new domains of warfare. Everything thus combines to produce a higher degree of technicality and specialization within the military sector. War now tends to become a separate activity — an art with its own ends and means, a profession that needs its own specialists at every level, both in the area of command and in that of execution. As early as the fourth century the mercenary reappears. War ceased to be "political" in the full sense of the term even before the *polis* disappeared from the historical scene.

The mere existence of the city-states was not enough to make war political. It was also necessary that all the states should together form a single organized system in which each unit, free to choose its own allies and adversaries, could advance its own interests in the general competition toward hegemony. It was in the context of this framework that conflicts took place; war was waged in the setting of a Greek world in which, in their very confrontation with one another, cities were brought together in a community united by its language, religions, customs, forms of social life, and ways of thought. The *xenos* was not someone radically different, to be fought as one hunts an animal simply because it is foreign to everything that goes to make civilization and because it is outside the pale of humanity. Not even the barbarian was considered thus by the Greek. The *xenos* was a partner in social intercourse; even in the hatred they bore him he remained close to the Greeks, through the gods that he worshipped, the sanctuaries he visited, and the ways and customs that he shared with them. The city-states at war are "rivals" and rivalry can only exist between those who are similar, who recognize the same values, use the same criteria of judgment, and play the same game. To consider no more than the religious aspect of these conflicts, it should be noted that the Greeks could not, as the Jews did, desire to destroy the gods of the enemy, nor, in the manner of the Hittites or the Romans, take them over as exiles so that the religious powers of the enemy could be assimilated. Since the gods were common to both camps they were invoked as arbiters who would guarantee the rules that both sides had to observe. To this extent the wars between the city-states were an extension of the family confrontations of the vendetta. This warfare was a compound of antagonism and fellowship, and of conflict and agreement.

War in classical Greece is an *agōn*. It takes the form of an organized competition that rules out both the fight to the death to annihilate the enemy as a social and religious being, and conquest designed to absorb him totally. It is related to the Great Panhellenic Games in which rivalries are played out peacefully in a framework of rules that are in many respects similar. Those who take part in the Games confront each other in the name of the same city-states as those that go to war against each other. The fact that the protagonists are the same, as is the structure of these two institutions, makes warfare and the Games as it were the two opposite sides of one and the same social phenomenon. All military operations had to be suspended for the duration of the Games. There is sufficient continuity between the following four types of confrontation for it sometimes to be possible to pass from one form to another: (i) the ritual battles which give a formalized expression to the aggression felt within a group; (ii) the competitions in which various elements of a single civic community are opposed; (iii) the Great Games that bring all the Greek city-states together in one competition; and (iv) war.[33] If we are to believe the Greek historians, during the sixth century it was possible to resolve a number of inter-city quarrels by common consent, by organizing duels between champions, or tournaments between select groups each comprising the same number of fighting men.[34] No doubt this was an echo of "Homeric" times, but it also underlines the close relation between the warlike joust, the Games, and practices of the law, or, to be more precise, of the "pre-law" (*prédroit*), to adapt the expression of Louis Gernet. In these circumstances the confrontation only uses the force of arms as a kind of test or trial in which the supernatural powers are entrusted with the responsibility of pronouncing judgment. Like the legal *agōn*, the most archaic forms of which it adopts, the contest between warriors presupposes, if not a tribunal and laws, as in the legal system of the city-state, at least in the first place a judge – even if a divine one – whose authority is recognized by both parties,

42

and second, procedures of judgment that they both agree to accept. In the quarrel that divides them, the city-states demonstrate themselves to be all part of the same system that places them in exactly symmetrical positions, just as if they were plaintiffs before the tribunal, or families bringing their dispute to arbitration. To be sure, there exists nothing that resembles any international law, the domain of law being by definition internal to each city-state. However, the religious beliefs and social traditions of the Greeks — which can be referred to by the same term, *nomoi*, which is applied precisely to civil laws — are sufficiently strong to impose their criteria in war as in peace. From this point of view, war and peace do not represent such radically opposed states that the opening of hostilities introduces a total break with the state of law that prevailed hitherto, an abandonment of the rules recognized in dealings between the different groups, and accession to an entirely different religious world. The state of war is not and cannot be *anomia*, an absence of rules. On the contrary, it unfolds in the context of norms accepted by all the Greeks, precisely because these norms are not derived from law, which applies to each *polis* separately (and because, unlike in Rome, there is no judicial framework for war), but stem from the common body of customs, values, and beliefs. It was this body of beliefs that constituted the unity of the Greek world insofar as it comprised a single whole, composed of different city-states that were always more or less in a state of rivalry and confrontation in peacetime, but that in war remained always more or less united or associated with one another.

Here again, the picture we have drawn is true only given extreme circumstances. This is because, in the first place, war never remained confined within the frontiers of the Greek world, and because the Persian invasion, in particular, by provoking such a large-scale alliance to resist it, prepared the way for the hegemony of Athens, which rapidly developed into a domination imposed by force. From that time on Greece was divided into two enemy camps and engaged in a struggle whose aim, scope, and form were quite different. As Mme. de Romilly notes,[35] the whole system of ancient rules gave way in the Peloponnesian War. Even before it the balance was necessarily an uneasy one; it rested upon the tension between the will to leadership of the various states and the ideal of self-sufficiency that no city could renounce without denying its very nature. Apart from the occasional alliance, the states regrouped into amphictyonic partnerships centering, as at Delphi, around a sanctuary. Union was possible on a religious but not on a political level. The same tension expressed itself in strictly ideological terms. There were, on the one hand, those laws that were common to the whole of Greece, *ta tōn, Hellēnōn nomima*; on the other, the idea, more or less clearly formulated, that since each city was a sovereign state, the *archē* acquired through victory gave it the quasi-absolute power of *kratein* over the enemy — the power to treat it as a master, doing as one would with it, if necessary reducing it to servitude. All the same, as M. Ducrey has observed,[36] despite the acts of violence that were often perpetrated, the unwritten rules were on the whole strong enough to confine the treatment meted out to the vanquished within certain bounds. The rules were not always respected. However, their influence can be detected in the very violations that were done them. The unease, and sometimes repentance, of the guilty parties and the general indignation aroused by such crimes are sufficient testimony to the enduring power of the rules of the game that, by tacit consent, presided over the conflicts between city-states.

We have thus seen Greek war both as a system with its own deep coherence and as an historical phenomenon strictly localized in both space and time and linked to too many internal tensions for the balance on which it rested to be maintained for long. The system disintegrated and gave way to the Hellenistic wars which have been described by Pierre Lévêque.[37] The word is the same, the gods invoked have not changed, the phalanx still exists, and the military traditions of Greece still appear to be alive. Nevertheless, warfare is now quite a different matter, and it takes place in a world that is quite transformed. Mercenary armies in the service of princes, recruited to carve out and keep a hold on empires that now include peoples of the most disparate origins, characterize this kind of warfare that, being quite separate from politics, has lost the status that it had in the hoplite city-state. Its place in social life as a whole is quite different from what it used to be.

We can follow the process that brought about the destruction of this system through the testimonies of the ancient historians and other written documents, but how did the system itself come into being during the seventh century? From what warlike institutions did it emerge? What technical and social changes had undermined the more ancient military traditions of the Greeks to give rise to this type of political warfare and to the warrior-citizen, the model of which we have attempted to describe? The sources available for consultation to answer these questions are indirect, fragmentary, and equivocal. We can now consult linear B tablets, some of which are concerned with the military organization of Knossos and Pylos. But the light that they shed upon various aspects of Mycenaean warfare gives rise to more problems than it solves. It forces us to consider with a new and critical eye evidence as venerable as the Homeric poems without, however, authorizing us to come to any definite conclusions. Is there any congruence or even any real continuity between the world of the Mycenaean warrior and that which Homer describes for us? If not, where do the discontinuities lie, and how great were the transformations? The problem is all the greater in that we must be very wary in making a comparison between documents relating to administrative matters, on the one hand, and a work of epic poetry on the other. The Homeric world owes its unity to its being a literary creation. Once it is submitted to a historical analysis, different, more or less compatible layers become apparent, betrayed first and foremost in the language but also detectable — to consider only the areas that most concern us — in the weaponry, the modes of combat, and the varying social and psychological status of the warrior. Any attempts to locate these on a time scale

45

must depend precisely upon one's idea of how the Homeric epics relate to the Mycenaean world – the world that is both the immediate subject of the poems and at the same time a historical backdrop separated from the author by several centuries of oral tradition. M. Lejeune has assessed the Mycenaean evidence as well as anyone could have done, and so too has G.S. Kirk for the complex of Homeric evidence.[38] This two-pronged enquiry clearly needed to be supplemented by an archaeological viewpoint, and all the factual evidence at our disposal has been collected in a most clear and convincing study by Paul Courbain.[39] We would, however, have judged this difficult investigation incomplete if we were not able to add a fourth perspective by which to check it. Marcel Granet has remarked, on the subject of ancient China, that in a sense legend is truer than history. Francis Vian is the scholar who has examined the warrior myths that developed around the great Achaean centers and that have lived on in the minds of Greeks ever since.[40] In focusing upon the figure of the warrior of legend and establishing his place in fraternities that were sometimes integrated into social life as a whole and sometimes existed on the periphery of communal life, Francis Vian came up against the problem of the role and the precise character of the military class in social thought and contemporary collective representations.

Bearing in mind the evidence produced by these four separate approaches, Marcel Detienne tackled the crucial problem of the hoplite reform: the practice of fighting in close formation that, to start with, seems to have been the prerogative of a military elite and that led, in the new framework of the city-state, to the integration of war and politics and to the identification of the figure of the warrior with that of the citizen.[41] Two other to some extent symmetrical studies carry this investigation further. M.I. Finley shows how, in Sparta, the appearance of the hoplite, the passing of the military function of the *laos* to the Equals as a whole, is one aspect of a reorganization of the social system of Sparta that is so total and profound that it can be described as a sixth-century revolution. The *agōgē* was the keystone of the system. It put the ancient initiation rituals to new purposes. This was how the whole city of Sparta became an organization engaged in selecting and training warriors and fostering, at every level, a spirit of conflict and rivalry alongside obedience and discipline. However, this army, which is kept in a constant state of tension and preparedness, is directed inward rather than outward. It is not so much an instrument for conquest abroad as a vast police force whose role is to maintain internal order. The use of this instrument in war and the success it owed to its superiority in infantry combat were in the end to recoil against itself and bring about the destruction of the model warrior-state.[42]

This study is balanced by that of Pierre Vidal-Naquet, who begins with a description of Athenian military organization at the end of the fourth century. He shows how the hoplite tradition, which had manifestly outlived its usefulness in a predominantly urban democratic state, lingered on and became institutionalized at the very time when, in the theoretical thought of the philosophers, the ideology of a specialized warrior function was being promoted in an attempt to solve the problems posed by the developments of military strategy and the crisis of the city.[43]

We cannot explore in detail the complex interrelations of the various studies whose main themes we have outlined, nor assess their positions in a general inquiry into warfare in Greece. They are too rich to be briefly summarized, and their structure is too definite for such an undertaking to be necessary. We should simply like to indicate briefly the problem that represents the guiding thread to the whole of this part of the investigation.

As we have noted, the state of war is normal in the relations between city-states. However, the fact that war is a natural and necessary part of city-state life means that, in a sense, it is absent from it just as much as it is present in it. War no longer constitutes a separate domain in social life, with its own specialized institutions and agents and its own values, ideology, and religion. It is inseparable from the communal life of the group as this finds expression through the state institutions. War is not just subject to the state, at the service of politics; it is itself political, identified with the city since the warrior is the citizen and only assumes a warrior role inasmuch as he also plays a political role, exercising a power equal to that of his fellows in the communal affairs of the group.

The absorption of the domain of war into the "civic" sector is all the more striking in that it takes place among one of the Indo-European peoples who are known to have conceived a society as an integral whole in which warfare has an important though strictly limited place.[44] Among the gods as among men, everything to do with war is organized as a specialized function; the warrior appears as a particular type of man who undergoes a special training or drill; he has a character of his own, his own particular powers and mode of action, his own code of ethics; he has a special social status and a distinct psychology.

Greece does not appear to have been an exception to the rule in this respect. Consider the presence in the pantheon of a god so exclusively devoted to war as Ares, or the role played in the power struggles of the gods by mythical groups such as the Giants, to which must be compared the fraternities of specialized warriors of legend such as the Spartans at Thebes or the Phlegyens at Orchomene: These are all factors that allow one to conclude with Francis Vian that the Greeks shared the ideology of the warrior function. When, following Hippodamos, Plato declared himself to be in favor of a military class living separately on the Acropolis, segregated from the "producers" in the community in order to devote itself exclusively to the activity of war, it is no doubt in response to certain contemporary political and strategic preoccupations. At the same time, however, by favoring a certain image of Sparta, he was also going back, beyond the hoplite ideal and in some degree in opposition to it, to a traditional model of warfare that had remained alive in the legends of the heroes.

What is the historical evidence on the position of this military class during the Mycenaean period, and why was it that, in Greece, in contrast to other civilizations, the warrior function embodied by this group disappeared toward the seventh century?

Apart from the foot soldiery, the Mycenaean army comprised a force of chariot fighters which depended both militarily and economically upon the king. The palace issued to each man in command of a chariot the following equipment: one chariot, two horses, and two breastplates. There is insufficient evidence for us to define the social status of these knights who had to be sufficiently adept at controlling a light chariot to drive it over all kinds of terrain, deploy themselves in battle order, charge, pursue the enemy, and fight from the chariot, leaping down from and mounting it while it was in motion. But a comparison with other peoples who also developed the chariot for military use during the second half of the second millennium is illuminating. The broad lines of such a comparison can be found in an appendix to *Problèmes de la guerre en Grèce ancienne* containing studies on China (J. Gernet), Mesopotamia (E. Cassin, P. Garelli), and Greece (M. Detienne).[45] Despite differences in the kinds of chariots used, the composition and armament of the chariot units, and the fighting tactics, there are a number of common features linking the societies characterized by a use of chariot forces. These were powerful states, sufficiently centralized to concentrate in the same hands responsibility for all the technical, economic, and administrative means required by the construction, supply, maintenance, and distribution of a large force of chariots. The charioteers constituted an aristocracy both of the army and of the people, whose status was closely linked with their military activities. Owning horses and driving chariots implied both a way of life, essentially devoted to hunting and warfare, and high social standing. The horse was a noble, warlike beast and possessing, raising, and training it were the privileges of a minority. The chariot was a prestigious object made for show as well as battle. Furthermore, skill in handling it could only come from hard training and professional know-how. Where a warrior class already existed, the introduction of a force of chariots could only increase its specialist character; where no such class existed such a development must have

49

contributed toward its formation. The form of allegiance owed by this class to its sovereign varied considerably. However, in general it can be said that the use of massed chariots in combat always presupposed a measure of dependence of the warrior caste upon its prince. This was likely to be the more pronounced the greater the control exercised by the palace economy over the life of the country. In all the known cases the chariots were provided for the warriors by the palace, although this does not necessarily imply the existence of a permanent garrisoned army. Very often the chariot would be a gift; its presence in warrior tombs proves that the charioteer could do what he liked with it even in death. Being thus the gift of the sovereign, the chariot symbolized the privileges granted by the king to its owner; however, at the same time it represented the charioteer's obligation to serve the king who had given it to him. The oath sworn before their king by the Hittite army at the beginning of a campaign was unilaterally binding: It marked the warrior's personal bond of allegiance to one who was not only leader of the army but also sovereign of the kingdom. It is quite different from the pact of *philotes* that, as described in Homer, concluded with a reciprocal exchange of oaths, where both men swearing the oath committed themselves in their own name and in that of their *philoi*, for the duration of the expedition. Thus, at the beginning of the *Iliad*, Achilles is free to withdraw from the coalition with his whole troop of *hetairoi*, just as he had earlier joined it. There were other changes that accompanied this transformation of the military oath, or the *horcos*, which brought separate groups of warriors together in a single army. Military equipment was no longer centralized; it was no longer the palace that issued the fighting men with horses, chariots, and breastplates. These were *ktemata*, personal possessions. His horses were an owner's pride. Each warrior was responsible for the manufacture of his own chariot and breastplates, which were made for his own purposes. Thus, the old economic and military dependence of the charioteers upon their sovereign, or *anax*, did not survive the disintegration of the Mycenaean kingdoms.

50

The greater autonomy of the warrior aristocracy, no longer subject as it used to be to the power of a centralized state, is reflected, in the army, by the disappearance of the chariot force used as a combat weapon. In the picture of battle painted by Homer, not only are chariots no longer used in formation, to charge or harass the enemy, but the individual warrior no longer fights from his chariot whether it be stationary or in motion. The vehicle is no longer a weapon of combat; it is simply a means of transport and a symbol of social prestige indicating that the hero belongs to the warrior elite. The members of this elite move around by chariot and this clearly gives them an increased mobility, but they always fight on foot. In view of this there is no way of avoiding the contradiction noted by G.S. Kirk: Either the chariots did indeed play the role assigned to them by Homer, in which case they were positioned behind the lines, the purpose being to bring the war leaders to the scene of the battle, in the same way as horses were used for the *hippeis* in the archaic period (at least up to the introduction of a specialized corps of cavalry); or, alternatively, the chariots drew up in front of the lines, as Homer describes, but in that case they engaged in a mass charge in the manner of the Hittites or the Assyrians, or at least did battle, chariot to chariot, like the Chinese. They would not have been used simply to get from one point to another on the battlefield, presenting an almost defenseless target for the enemy.

The importance of these two alternatives to which the Homeric text, in its very confusion, testifies, cannot be too strongly stressed. On the one hand we have the survival of the chariot as the symbol of the privileged social status that continued to be enjoyed by an aristocracy specialized in warfare and faithful to the heroic ideal; on the other, the total disappearance of a chariot force seen as the characteristic military institution of a centralized state. If the military aristocracy fought on foot it is easy to understand how (as M. Detienne suggests) the development of the practice of fighting in close formation could have been initiated in this context. The first phalanx may have comprised a small group of élite fighting men and assured these specialists in warfare of success in the works of Ares. But the phalanx implies a radical transformation of the warrior ethos: Collective discipline takes the place of individual exploits and *sophrosunē*, self-discipline, supplants *mēnos*, the state of warrior frenzy. In the context of the social conflicts of the seventh century it also made it possible for the men who made up the former foot soldiery (the men of the *dēmos*, the *laoi agroiotai* that Homer contrasts with the *kouroi* and the *aristoi*) to accede to all the privileges which until then had been reserved for the *hippeis* and *hēniochoi* by reason of the latters' military superiority, symbolized by their chariots and horses. With the introduction of the phalanx the warrior's panoply was in fact reduced to the hoplite equipment that was within the means of the small peasant landowner as well as of those who possessed horses. Finally, the phalanx represents on the field of battle the model of the human group in which every man is equal and claims to be nothing more. The ideal of *isotes, homoiotes*, with its corollary, the right to *isegoria*, freedom of speech in the military assembly, may originally have been a feature of an elite group of fighting men united by the *pistis* which their reciprocal oaths of loyalty have sealed, but it now became possible to extend it to other social categories, to all fighting men, in other words to the citizens as a whole. So it was that the aristocratic and warrior values did not die out with the advent of the city-state. They lost certain specific features and were diluted to the extent that the entire city now became an aristocratic, military elite.

Thus before the warrior function could become integrated into, and disappear within, the *polis*, it was necessary for it to affirm its own autonomy and free itself from its subjection to a centralized type of state that implied a hierarchical order of society and a "mystical" form of sovereign power. Once this had happened, it became possible for a new development to occur within the warrior groups themselves – that of the institutional practices and modes of thought which were to lead to a new form of state, the *polis*, which simply meant *ta koina*, the communal affairs of the group settled among equals by public debate. Although every Greek remains hegemonic as regards his family and private affairs, just as a king does in relation to his subjects, in public life in the city-state he is obliged to accept that he is a different, egalitarian man, as are the fighting men in the phalanx, each one in his own place playing an equal part in the battle. Thus the introduction, with the advent of the city, of a truly political sphere that overlaid family connections and loyalties and hierarchical relations of dependence, can be seen as the extension to the whole community of a model of egalitarian, symmetrical, and reversible relationships already highly developed within warrior circles.

In saying that at the time of the city-state the military function becomes absorbed by the political we are, it is true, implying that the latter causes the former to disappear. At the same time, however, we are suggesting that the practices and spirit of the former live on in the institutions of the latter. This accounts for the tension, the oscillation that Claude Mossé illustrates by two striking historical examples: On the one hand, the army is nothing if not the city itself; on the other, the city is nothing but a troop of warriors.[46]

CHAPTER III

Marriage[1]

Why choose the subject of marriage in an inquiry concerning the archaic period? There seem to be two reasons for undertaking a study on this theme. In the first place the domain of matrimonial practices appears to offer the best opportunity to gauge the extent of the transformations introduced by the advent of the city-state and – more precisely – by the establishment, in Athens, of the democratic city-state at the end of the sixth century. Second, marriage as we see it functioning in Athens during the classical period, that is during the fifth and fourth centuries, cannot itself be understood properly unless account is taken of the historical background from which, it is true, it marked a departure, but from which, at the same time, it inherited a number of characteristics.

We tend to speak of Greek marriage during the classical period as if there existed such a thing as the institution of marriage with a single well-defined legal form. We have only to read the texts of the orators to see that in a city such as Athens the situation was by no means so simple. The status of a legitimate wife – whether she was referred to by the old word of *damar* or the more technical expressions of *gametē gunē* or *gunē enguētē* – involves a number of factors not one of which, taken on its own, constitutes a decisive, unequivocal criterion.

The essential element of marriage at this time is the *enguē*. The *enguē* turns the union between a man and a woman into a social action whose effect reaches beyond the two individuals involved to seal, through them, a commitment between two domestic households, two "houses." The *enguē* binds them to each other by a mutual, public, and solemn agreement sworn in the presence of witnesses who can act as its guarantors. Demosthenes cites a law that defines the *gnēsioi*, or legitimate children, as those "who are the issue of a woman given through *enguē* by her father, blood brother or paternal grandfather."[2] And yet the *enguē* does not, in itself, have the force of constituting a marriage. It is a necessary element in marriage but not its sufficient condition. In this connection we need only recall the well-known example of Demosthenes' father: Before his death he promised his wife by *enguē* to one of his nephews and his daughter, aged five, to another. Neither of these marriages was ever consummated and the *enguē* by itself provoked no legal consequences. In neither case was it necessary to nullify or break the link it was supposed to have established. If the *enguē* was not followed by cohabitation between the woman and her husband it had no effect. Similarly, we notice that the act of handing over the daughter by her *kurios*, the relative who has the authority to arrange her marriage, is not definitive. The act of handing over, or *ekdosis*, consists in the transfer of the woman from one *kurios* to another, from the qualified relative to the husband. The nature of this transfer is not absolute; it does not sever once and for all the links between the daughter and her family of origin; it is valid for the duration of the period of cohabitation and for predetermined purposes, in particular the procreation of children.[3] The act of giving the daughter is associated with presentation of the dowry, the *proix*, a practice introduced after the time of Solon that, in the classical period, had the force of a legitimation, testifying that the daughter had truly been settled by her *oikos* in the family of her spouse. However, the dowry was no more irreversibly made over to the husband than was the daughter. It was composed of movable chattels, usually in the form of cash the value of which was decided in the presence of witnesses, and, although it was presented to the husband, it remained attached to the daughter throughout her matrimonial career, acting as a kind of link with her original home. If the marriage broke down the dowry was returned, together with the daughter, to the man who gave her away, or, failing this, to his representative. In a sense, it remained at the disposal of the daughter to be used for a new marriage.[4]

This system may, at first sight, appear quite strict. A legitimate wife was one who, after an *enguē*, had been given together with her dowry by her *kurios* to her husband. The *proix* was the tangible sign of the alliance between the two houses. In contrast, the woman became a concubine if she installed herself on her own responsibility, no intervention being made by her *oikos*. In this case there was, strictly speaking, no marriage. However, a text from Isaeus shows that a girl could be installed with a man as a concubine, *pallakē*, by the member of her family who had authority over her, and this relative fixed in advance the payments that had to be made to him in return.[5] The opposition between legitimate wife and concubine was not as clear-cut on this point as it seemed.

Furthermore, the *ekdosis* and the *proix* are no more sufficient conditions of a legitimate union than is the *enguē*. Marriage is first and foremost a state of fact, the fact being *sunoikein*, lasting cohabitation with the husband. In his speech *Against Neera*, Demosthenes cites the law (dating from 451) that forbids a foreigner to *sunoikein* and *paidopoieisthai* with an Athenian woman and have children by her.[6] But a clear distinction is made between the concubine and the courtesan, *hetaira*, the difference being that the concubine cohabits with her man. But how was a cohabitation that was legitimate to be distinguished from one that was not? It cannot have been an easy task: At 51 Demosthenes uses this very term, *sunoikein*, to describe the position of Neera, who lives with Stephanos and the legitimacy of whose marriage Demosthenes is contesting.

True, one can use expressions such as *sunoikein kata tous nomous* or *kata ton thesmon* (to cohabit legitimately) as opposed to *sunoikein para ton nomon* (to do so against the law).[7] But this *nomos* boils down to a declaration that Neera is not the *gunē* of the man whose house she shares, that he took her in as a *pallakē* ("παλλακὴν ἔχειν ἔνδον").[8] This is precisely what ought to be capable of proof by law but can only be inferred from the evidence, *tekmēria*. Demosthenes' remarks in this same speech indicate better than anything both the desire to establish a clear demarcation, or even a positive opposition, between the legitimate wife and the concubine, and at the same time the impossibility of so doing. Demosthenes declares: "The state of marriage consists in procreating children that belong to one [τὸ γὰρ συνοικεῖν τοῦτ᾽ ἔστιν, ὅς ἂν παιδοποιῆται],"[9] and he goes on to say, "We have courtesans for pleasure, concubines for one's day-to-day needs τῆς καθ᾽ ἡμέραν θεραπείας τοῦ σώματος, and wives in order to have legitimate children by them παιδοποιεῖσθαι γνησίως, and as the faithful guardians of the household goods." It is a purely rhetorical distinction that has no meaning in terms of the existing institutions. Courtesans for pleasure – it is easy enough to see what Demosthenes means. Legitimate wives for the procreation of children – that is equally clear. But what about the *pallakē*? How is one to understand this *therapeia tou sōmatos* that she is supposed to fulfill? In the *Gorgias*, Plato uses this expression to refer to gymnastics and medicine.[10] This cannot be what Demosthenes means by it, and one gets the feeling that, in default of any valid definition of the concubine, he has chosen this formula precisely because it has no precise meaning. Furthermore, in his *Against Aristocrates*, he cites a law of Solon or Dracon declaring that one has the right to kill a man caught in one's own house, "in *flagrante delicto* with one's wife *(damar)*, mother, sister, daughter or with the *pallakē* that one has taken for the purpose of procreating free children [ἐπ᾽ ἐλευθέροις παισίν]."[11] The text of this law has been the subject of many commentaries. We will note three points from it. First, the *pallakē* is put on the same level as the *damar* and all the other closely related women over whom the head of the family has full authority in his own *oikos*. Second, the *pallakē* lives in one's house for the purpose of *paidopoieisthai* (having children), which was used just now to define the status of marriage. It is true that these children are not *gnēsioi*, but neither are they defined as *nothoi*; they are referred to as *eleutheroi*, free. There is every reason to believe that, under Solon, unlike in the fifth

58

century, children born from a marriage without *enguē*, from a union which we would today describe as unofficial, had a status which did not radically exclude them from the *anchisteia*, or inheritance, or from the right to take part in the religious and political life of the city.[12] It should further be pointed out that during the Peloponnesian War, between 411 and 403-2 (when Euclid was *archōn*), there was no doubt a return to the earlier state of affairs. This would explain Diogenes Laertius' remark about Socrates' double marriage. The philosopher would appear to have had two wives, the second of whom, Myrto, had no dowry (*aproikon*). Diogenes Laertius notes: "Some people say that he had them both at the same time, for there was apparently a decree, prompted by the lack of men, allowing a citizen both to marry an Athenian woman and to have children by another woman [γαμεῖν μὲν ἀστὴν μίαν, παιδοποιεῖσθαι δὲ καὶ ἐξ ἑτέρας]."[13] The status of children born from such unions was no doubt comparable to that of the *eleutheroi* of Athens in the period before Cleisthenes. If he wished to, their father could ask that they should be enrolled in the phratry, the latter having the right to grant or refuse his request. The same permission was given to Pericles during the fifth century, in quite exceptional circumstances, in connection with the son he had had from Aspasia. This boy was doubly *nothos* since his mother was neither a legitimate wife nor an Athenian. Pericles obtained the right to present him as his son to the phratry, giving him his own name.[14] Thus, we do not find the institution of marriage perfectly defined in fifth-century Athens. Rather, there were several types of union to one of which the democratic city attempted to give a privileged status, to the exclusion of the others. It did not, however, succeed in giving it an altogether clearly defined legal character, and alongside it there continued to exist different types of union whose implications for the woman and her children varied according to the historical circumstances.

We should therefore give full weight and attach due social significance to Aristotle's remark that, in Greek, there existed no word to denote the union between a man and a woman ("ἀνώνυμος ή γυναικος καὶ ἀνδρὸς σύζευξις").[15] It is a remark that is illuminated by Emile Benveniste's general observation that there is no Indo-European word for marriage.[16] This vagueness, or rather, these contradictions make it necessary for us to examine the past, where we find not monogamous or polygamous marriage but a number of different matrimonial practices that can coexist with one another because they all fulfill different ends and purposes in a context where the network of matrimonial exchanges operates according to very flexible and free rules. The framework is that of social interchange between the great noble families, with the exchange of women seen as a means of creating links of union or dependence, of acquiring prestige or confirming vassaldom. In this interchange the women play the role of precious objects; they can be compared to the *agalmata* that Louis Gernet has shown to have been so important to the social practice and thought of the Greeks during the archaic period.[17]

In this respect one can speak in terms of a break between archaic marriage and marriage as it became established within the framework of a democratic city, in Athens, at the end of the sixth century. In the Athens of the period after Cleisthenes, matrimonial unions no longer have as their object the establishment of relationships of power or of mutual service between great autonomous families; rather, their purpose is to perpetuate the households, that is to say the domestic hearths that constitute the city, in other words to ensure, through strict rules governing marriage, the permanence of the city itself through constant reproduction.

It is agreed that the measures which established the supremacy of this type of "legitimate" marriage should be dated to the period of Solon or just after. These to some extent gave it an "official" status by attempting to provide a stricter legal foundation for it. The *enguē*, considered as a necessary condition for official marriage, may have been introduced by Solon. Aristotle tells us that before this certain magistracies — and he cites, no doubt quite mistakenly, those of *strategoi* and *hipparchoi* — were reserved for those who had legitimate children born from a married wife, a *gametē*.[18] If the children born from a non-legitimate wife had, on that account, been excluded from citizenship, it would have been superfluous to make the point. Besides, as is noted again by Aristotle, at the time of Peisistratos there were, among the Dacrians who made up his following, many whose birth was not pure (in other words, *nothoi*).[19] After the expulsion of the tyrants the lists of citizenship were revised because of the large number enjoying political rights although not qualified to do so. It would thus seem to be after Cleisthenes that the civil marriage was actually established. At this point *nothoi* found themselves excluded from the *anchisteia*; they were not considered as belonging to their *oikos* and their father could no longer integrate them into it. Thus they no longer belonged to the city on either a religious or a political level.[20] They remained free men and they were not *xenoi*, foreigners, in the strict sense, but their status was comparable to that of the metics. It is to be supposed that in earlier times they sometimes succeeded their fathers, at least if there were no legitimate children, as was still happening at Tegea in the mid-fifth century, where the order of succession was as follows: first the legitimate sons, then the legitimate daughters, then the *nothoi* and, only after that, collateral relations.[21] If the *nothoi* had been entirely excluded from the *oikos* in the time of Solon, it is difficult to see why the latter should have relieved them from the obligation of looking after their parents in their old age.[22] It is a measure which implies their belonging to the paternal family. After Cleisthenes a clearer distinction is made between the *gunē gametē* and the simple *pallakē*, and between the *gnēsioi* and the *nothoi*. The second distinction follows systematically from the first, for to be a *gnēsios* it was necessary to be the child of a *gunē gametē*. Hans Julius Wolff has pointed out that the key to the entire marriage system of Attica lies in the clearcut distinction made between the *nothoi* and the *gnēsioi*,[23] marriage being considered in the framework of the city as the means of ensuring that a house should have a legitimate line of descent, the father's existence being continued through a son who is "like him," his own issue, *gono gegonōs*.[24] This ensured that none of the limited number of matrimonial hearths that go to make up the city was at any time left deserted. By giving to marriage founded upon the *enguē* and *proix* the exclusive privilege of procuring a legitimate line of descent by having legitimate sons, the city was attempting to guarantee the permanence of its own institutions and form across the generations.[25]

It has often been noted that in the Homeric world, as in that of heroic legend, the opposition between the legitimate wife and the concubine appears much less marked than in the classical period. Linguistic usage and the matrimonial customs attested in the great families of the legendary past are equally telling in this respect. A wife, *alochos* or *kouridiē alochos*, is a woman who is led to a man's home in order to share his bed there. There are several ways of leading a woman to one's home. The most official way is to obtain her from her parents by offering them, in return, the *hedna* that — in principle at least — consist of a certain number of head of livestock, in particular cattle. This constitutes a noble marriage that, through the daughter, seals the alliance between two families. In such a marriage the daughter, just like the herds for which she is exchanged, is an important item of exchange in the network of gifts and counter-gifts. However, one may also obtain a woman without *hedna*,[26] in return for some exceptional exploit or for some service done for the girl's parents, or by winning her by armed force in some warlike expedition, or carrying her off in a foray or piratical raid. True, there are differences of status between the women acquired by these various means, but these depend upon the way that they are treated and "honored" in the husband's house, by the man whose bed they share, as much as upon the actual process of marriage. To express his preference for Chryseis over his *kouridiē alochos*, his legitimate spouse, Clytemnestra, Agamemnon says that he wishes to "keep her in his house."[27] Achilles uses the same term, *alochos*, to refer to Briseis,[28] a captive of war and thereby, by definition, if one abides by the clear-cut categories we have referred to, a woman whose status is that of a slave concubine. Now, in a speech recalling the memory of the husband given her by her father and mother and killed by Achilles, Briseis points out that, according to Patrokles, Achilles himself intended to make her his *kouridiē alochos* and to celebrate the wedding as soon as they returned to his homeland.[29] In Priam's palace, which houses in neighboring apartments not only all his sons with their wives but also many of his daughters, together with the sons-in-law chosen for them, Hecabe certainly enjoys pride of place. She is the queen. But it would not be true to say that she is Priam's only legitimate wife, and none of the king's other companions is called *pallakē*. The daughter of the king of the Lelegoi, Laothoë whom Priam introduces as the most noble of women ("*κρείουσα γυναικῶν*"), is certainly no concubine.[30] No more is Castianeira who, we are told, came to Troy "*ἐξ Αἰσύμηθεν ὀπυιομένη*," having been married from Aisyme.[31] In such conditions, the opposition between the *nothos* and the *gnēsios* is in no way an absolute one. Priam's bastard sons live in the palace just as do their legitimate brothers; they fight alongside each other, the bastard often as the driver of the legitimate son's chariot and, as such, associated with him. This is the case for Isos and Antiphos[32] and also for Cebrion, Hector's driver, whom the hero calls his *adelphos* even though, being born from a different mother, he is in fact no more than his bastard half-brother.[33] Furthermore, Imbrios is married to one of Priam's bastard daughters, Medesicaste. When the Achaeans attack Troy, he feels it his duty to come to Ilium where he distinguishes himself with warlike deeds. He lives with the bastard daughter, his wife, in Priam's own palace and we are told that the king "honors him equally with his own sons."[34]

The situation among the Greeks is similar. Menelaos celebrates the marriage of both his children at the same time: They are Hermione, the daughter of his wife Helen, and Megapenthes, his son *ek doulēs*, by a slave. For this bastard child "who is dear to him," the poet tells us, Menelaos has chosen the daughter of a Spartan noble, Alector.[35] Odysseus, in one of his lying stories, claims to be the son of a "*παλλακὶς ὠνητή*," a bought concubine, his father having had legitimate sons ("*γνήσιοι*") from a wife ("*ἐξ ἀλόχου*"). But, he goes on to say, his father "*ἶσον ἰθαγενέεσσιν ἐτίμα*" ("held him in as high regard as his legitimate children"). At his father's death he was not entirely excluded from the inheritance; he was given a house and a little property. Although he feels he has been unfairly provided for compared with his brothers, he will be able to make a rich marriage, taking a wife from a very wealthy family.[36]

These cases make it easier to understand the exact position, at first sight a strange one, of Eurycleia in relation to Laertes. Eurycleia is the daughter of Ops, and the granddaughter of Pisenor who acts as herald of Ithaca. While still a child she was obtained by Laertes, who gave twenty oxen from his own possessions in order to have her in his house. Like the mother Odysseus falsely claimed, she was a *doulē ōnētēr*, a slave bought to be the *pallakē* of her master, but at the same time, by reason of her birth and the exceptional price he has had to pay for her, a sort of second wife. It is she who is in charge of the running of the palace and who is nurse to the son of the house, whom she has brought up, and it is she who asked Autolycos, Odysseus' maternal grandfather, to choose a name for the child. Laertes "honors her, in the house, equally with his legitimate wife"; nevertheless, to avoid displeasing his wife, he has abstained from taking her to bed with him.[37] Was it simply that he feared her jealousy for a rival? Or was it that the *cholos*, or resentment, of his wife would be aimed, through the woman whom Laertes honored as her equal, against the son she might have borne and who might have rivaled the child from his wife's own bed in the affections of his father? On this point of family psychology we should recall the story of Peisistratos and the daughter of the Alcmaeonid, Megacles. At the time when Peisistratos married her for political reasons, he already had two adolescent sons from a previous marriage. If the tyrant refused to have normal sexual relations with his new wife this was not simply through a quirk in his nature, nor in order to humiliate her, but rather because sons from such a union, being the children of a woman of such high rank, might be prejudicial to the line of descent from the first marriage bed, or even eclipse it entirely, to the greater profit of the Alcmaeonid clan.[38]

The status of women, like that of their sons, whether legitimate or bastard, thus depended to a large extent upon the *time* or honor in which they were held by the head of the family. And he was, in all probability, not entirely free to behave as he wished in this respect. A woman of high birth who had had to be won at the expense of *hedna* of exceptional value and who, in terms of the interchange of gifts and counter-gifts brought about by marriage, represented a commitment to an alliance between two powerful families, could not with impunity be treated in the same way as some girl who had been bought or captured in war. Nevertheless, even if certain norms and rules of behavior obtained, a wide margin of choice still remained, and the range of possible attitudes was so great that we cannot speak in terms of a single model for the institution of marriage. The range in the kinds of status women could enjoy and the scale of different positions that could be held by the companions of the head of the family were such that they formed a hierarchy too subtle to be forced into our simple categories of monogamy or polygamy. In *Mariages de Tyrans*, Louis Gernet notes a number of matrimonial customs peculiar to the aristocracy of legend, customs that had lived on into the classical period and that for practical political purposes, had become identified with those exceptional figures, the tyrants, who were not strictly speaking a part of the city-state. He describes cases that we should be tempted to call bigamous were it not that for us the term carries too precise legal implications.[39] We are told that at the end of the fifth century the Elder Dionysus of Syracuse married two women at the same time, on the very same day. One was a Syracusan, the other came from Locri. It was the son of the wife from Locri who later succeeded him, and Dionysus had him marry the daughter of his other wife, the Syracusan woman. Similarly, before Peisistratos took the daughter of Megacles as his wife, he also contracted a double marriage, with an Athenian and with a woman of noble birth from Argos, whose name was

Timonossa. We are told that only the Athenian woman was *gametē*, legitimately married; but the woman from Argos was certainly not considered as a concubine nor her children as bastards. The two marriages, one with a woman from the same city, the other with a foreigner, were equally valid and equally official but they belonged to different types. The second was a matrilocal marriage. The children from it, and probably their mother too, stayed in their maternal grandfather's house; they were Argive, not Athenian. At Pallene, one of them was in command of group of a thousand Argives who had come to fight on Peisistratos' side. As Louis Gernet points out, the two marriages were equally "noble." It was not so much that they were of unequal rank; rather, their purpose was different. Similar cases of double marriages can be found in legend. Alcmaeon marries Arsinoë, the daughter of Phegeus, and offers her, as presents and symbols of their union, the necklace and dress of Harmonia, which are family talismans. Subsequently, while on this travels, he marries Callirhoe, the daughter of a river god of the land he is in. She demands the same presents and pledges as Arsinoë received, and Alcmaeon is obliged to use false pretenses to get his first wife to part with them.[40] Even Helen's status is not without ambiguity. In respect of Priam, Hecuba, and their sons, she uses the terminology of kinship *hekuros* and *hekura* (father-in-law and mother-in-law), *daēr* and *einateres* (brother-in-law [*brother of the husband*], sisters-in-law [*wives of the brothers of the husband*]), but she also uses the same terms of her Achaean family-in-law. She is thus involved in a double network of legitimate alliances, through her union with Paris and also through her union with Menelaos. Although somewhat different, certain customs of Sparta reported by Xenophon and Plutarch follow the same tendency.[41] A Spartan citizen has the right, given the agreement of the husband, to have children by a woman who is already legitimately married. These children will not belong to the husband but to him. As *gnēsioi* they will carry on the line of his house and family. This *gunē gametē* or matron thus finds herself straddling two lines of descent, providing legitimate scions for both.

As we have seen, the dowry represents an essential part of the marriage system of the classical period. The *proix* represents more than a mere break with the earlier practice of marriage by *hedna*: It is a kind of reversal of it. The *hedna* were gifts presented to the father of the girl by her husband. The *proix* is given to the husband by the girl's father. There is no doubt that the expression "marriage by purchase" which has sometimes been applied to this type of institution is open to criticism.[42] It was not a matter of a purchase in the true sense of the term and, as M.I. Finley has shown very clearly, the *hedna* was part of the system of reciprocal loans between two families.[43] Nevertheless, the word *hedna* has a precise technical meaning: It is not normally used to refer to the gifts offered to the husband by the girl's family; these are referred to as *dōra* or *meilia*. The term *phernē*, which appears in the *Laws of Solon*, also refers to something other than the dowry. It applies rather to what we, today, would call the bride's trousseau, and it consisted in particular of rich materials and precious garments. So it is easy to understand why the sumptuary laws attempted to restrain the ostentation of the *phernē* that gave the noble families a chance to parade their opulence. The generalized practice of providing a dowry, considered as a necessary element of legitimate marriage introduced a radical change. Louis Gernet notes that such an innovation could not be explained in terms of "a spontaneous, gradual development but only by the substitution of one régime for another." He goes on to conclude that it was the establishment of the city that was the determining factor here. "It imposes a definite type of marriage, an exchange made within the city as opposed to the earlier system followed by the noble families, in which marriages were made with foreigners."[44] The law passed in 451 that officially prohibited marriage between Athenians and foreigners was simply legalizing a state of fact. The practice had already for some time been for marriage to take place between citizens, and there was, furthermore, a marked tendency toward family endogamy.

Herodotus' account of how Cleisthenes of Sicyon set about arranging the marriage of his daughter Agariste shows clearly how important marriage with a foreigner could be for the aristocracy.[45] The tyrant invited the elite of eligible young men, who flocked to his house from every corner of Greece. He put them all to the test, submitting them day after day to trials of masculine excellence. This lasted for a whole year during which, in order to observe them well, Cleisthenes accommodated them under his own roof, fed them and showered generosity upon them. His fame and the prestige of his house were spread abroad all the more effectively given that the suitors had come from far and wide. When they returned home they were all in his debt, all beholden to their host, who had dazzled them with his ostentatious wealth and had compensated all the unlucky suitors by giving them presents. As we know, Cleisthenes' choice fell upon the Athenian, Megacles, of the Alcmaeonid family. And without a doubt, the influence and renown of the father-in-law must have redounded to the glory of his new son-in-law and all his line of descent through this marriage that so notably demonstrated them. Herodotus concludes his account with the remark: "It is thus that the Alcmaeonids became famous."[46]

This system of marriage with a foreigner may have been subject to certain rules, but it is very difficult to reconstruct them. The evidence is fragmentary and thin. The most we can do is put forward a few tentative suggestions. There may, at an early period, have existed a definite network of alliances in Attica. In his *Life of Theseus*, Plutarch indicates that the people of Pallene are not allowed to marry those of Hagnous.[47] This negative fact, that is, the absence or prohibition of marriage between the two groups, implies its positive counterpart: that there were regular matrimonial exchanges between two or more groups. Pallene and Hagnous are situated close to each other but belong to different demes. It seems likely that systems of organization involving three or four different groups existed. One thinks, for instance, of Tetrapoleis, groups of four villages such as that in which Marathon was associated with Oenoe, Probalinthus, and Tricorythus. Even after the synoecism this type of grouping was still important from a political and, above all, a religious point of view, and it may have been of some significance in the domain of matrimonial customs.

In aristocratic circles the models for exchanges of women can be more clearly defined. Here again the example of the tyrants is illuminating. At the beginning of the fifth century a restricted system of marital interchange, operating in two directions, was established between the family of Gelon in Syracuse and that of Theron in Agrigentum. Each family took its wives from the other.[48] Gelon married Damareta, the daughter of Theron. When Gelon died, his brother Polyzalos took his place in the widow's bed, and married her. Gelon's other brother, Hieron, took as his wife one of Theron's nieces (the daughter of his brother). Meanwhile, Theron married the daughter of Polyzalos and Polyzalos thus became both his father-in-law, having given him his daughter, and also his son-in-law, since, following Gelon's death, he had married the woman whom Theron had given his brother. Relations of a similar kind existed at one time between the Cypselids of Corinth and the Philaids of Athens from whom Miltiades was descended.

Sometimes the circle of exchange was much wider and, as in the case of the Bacchiades in Corinth, embraced a total of two hundred noble families who reserved their daughters for one another. In such cases it was considered equally scandalous if the daughters were married outside the circle or if they were not found marriages within it.

It is also clear that there could be a system of regular exchange involving two lineages but operating only one way (which obviously implies the existence of a wider system of exchange as well). In his sixth *Olympian* Pindar uses the phrase μάτρωες ἄνδρες to refer to one particular *genos*, the Iamides.[49] The word *mētrōs*, which is not Indo-European, is formed on the analogy of the word *patrōs*, brother of the father. It may refer to the maternal grandfather or to the uncle, the brother of the mother.[50] But it may also, as in the expression *matroes andres*, refer to the entire lineage whose part in relation to the paternal *genos*, in the matrimonial exchange system, is simply to provide wives.[51] It seems possible that certain legendary episodes might be interpreted in this way, notably those in which the brothers in an exclusively male lineage aspire to the hands of, or in fact marry, the sisters of an exclusively female lineage. Thus, the fifty sons of Aigyptos pursue the fifty daughters of Danaos, wishing to be united with them. And then there is the case of the Leucippids. Leucippos has two daughters, his brother Tyndareos has two sons and a third brother, Aphareos, also has two sons. The sons of Tyndareos and those of Aphareos compete with each other for the hands of the two daughters of Leucippos. In Thebes two of the sons of Cadmos marry the daughters of the surviving Spartoi and this double union is the origin of the Theban aristocracy.

Whatever the various forms of these types of union may have been, it is clear that, however far back we go in our attempts to trace this matrimonial system, it always appears to reflect a state of crisis. Anthropologists have noted that, in a system where the exchange of women is the rule, tendencies toward endogamy are often a sign, if not of the system being completely blocked, at least of difficulties in its functioning. It is our belief that it is in this light that we should interpret the many instances, in legend, of unions within a single family, marriages between close relatives, and exchanges of daughters between brothers. It is enough, in this connection, to mention the marriages of the sons of Pandion in Athens or the case of Cretheus, the brother of Salmoneus who brings up the daughter of his brother in his own house. It is not a matter of gratuitous hospitality. Cretheus is "reserving" his niece as a wife for himself.[52] He has a number of sons by her, notably Pheres and Amythaon. Similarly, the latter marries the daughter of his brother Pheres, Eidomene. We can regard this as the mythical model of an institution which was regularized in the classical period under the title of the *ipiklēratē*. This certainly originated from certain customs peculiar to the aristocracy. Given that in the framework of the life of the nobility women were regarded as precious possessions and that, when put into circulation, they transmitted prestige and wealth, as soon as it no longer proved advantageous to exchange them with one's peers, one kept them for oneself.

In legend, endogamous unions sometimes take forms that are even more astonishing from a Greek point of view than marriage between an uncle and his niece. The nephew marries his aunt, the sister of his mother. One example is the case of Pandion who takes as his wife his maternal aunt, Zeuxippe.[53] Another is Iphidamos, whom Cisses, his *mētropatōr*, that is, his maternal grandfather, brings up in his own house in Thrace in order to give his daughter — that is to say, the sister of the young man's mother — to him in marriage as soon as he reaches the age of adolescence.[54] This could be described as a kind of inverted *epiklēratē*.

Apart from these endogamous practices we have evidence of another custom which also testifies to the existence of a state of crisis in the normal processes of matrimonial exchange. It is what the anthropologists refer to as *svayamvara*; the selection of a husband is left to the free choice of the daughter. Here again historical evidence and legendary tradition overlap and are mutually illuminating. Herodotus tells us the story of Kallias, victor at the Olympic and Pythian games and renowned for his sumptuous extravagance. However, the historian adds, he is chiefly admired for the way he behaved toward his three daughters. He settled very rich dowries on each of them and "gave each one to the man she elected to choose as a husband."[55] To leave the choice of a husband to the daughter herself, who has full powers to select the man she wants, is in some ways similar to the typically noble procedure of marriage by competition. The two themes are often presented as doublets, or are associated, in legend. In some accounts Helen is held to have been given to Menelaos following a competition, a race held between her many suitors. According to Euripedes, her father "allowed her to select as husband the man to whom she had lost her heart in love. She chose the man she should not have taken, Menelaos."[56] Idas carries off Marpessa, the daughter of Evenos, to whose hand Apollo also aspires. At Messene the man and the god fight to decide who shall marry her. Zeus intervenes, stops the fight, and asks Marpessa to decide for herself whom she will marry. Fearing that Apollo will abandon her in her old age, Marpessa chooses the mortal, Idas, as her husband.[57]

There is one further type of marriage, often attested, which is also a response to the difficulties involved in concluding, in normal conditions, an alliance that is not too unequal with one of the foreign families with which relations exist. This is marriage with a man quite unknown, an exile, all of whose connections with his country and family of origin have been severed. It is precisely his status as a man without a background that qualifies him to marry a girl of such high birth that her father cannot hope to find a suitor of high enough degree among his own circle. Giving her to a stranger is both a way of not lowering oneself and also of not losing her. Since the son-in-law has no connections he is bound to be integrated into the family of his father-in-law and there father children who will continue the line within the house.[58] This is the reason why Alkinous, knowing as yet nothing of Odysseus, except that he is entirely alone, lost on Phaeacian territory, wastes no time in suggesting that he should marry his daughter: It is precisely that the hero is entirely foreign to the normal system of alliances of the land.

The practice of endogamy, the acceptance as son-in-law of the solitary exile, and the choice of a husband being left to the daughter are three instances that reflect the ambiguity of the status of a woman in any system of matrimonial exchange in which the woman's role is that of a precious possession. To acquire a wife of high birth is to have her in one's house as a pledge of agreement with powerful allies, to win prestige and increase the standing of one's children and entire line of descent. But one also becomes indebted for her. Even if she has been fully paid for by the *hedna*, the husband is in the position of keeping in his house one who represents a different lineage and, through his wife, he contracts obligations that are all the greater the higher her value.

72

Conversely, to give one's daughter to a foreign family is to acquire influence and fame, to put others in one's debt and to make allies, as Cleisthenes of Sicyon did, but at the same time it is to lose her and forego the children she may produce. The balance of the system is unstable. When the system is threatened or destroyed as a result of the interplay of exchanges being restricted or blocked, one keeps one's women for oneself or, what amounts to the same thing despite appearing to be the opposite, one hands over one's daughter to an unknown man, a "total stranger" who, being outside society, can become one's own son as well as one's son-in-law. Alternatively, one puts into the hands of one's daughter, whose prestige and value are thereby enhanced, a decision that it is impossible for one to take oneself according to the normal rules — which is yet another way of bypassing the system.

There is one more aspect of the wife we should mention. As a daughter offered in marriage to a foreign *genos*, she fulfills the role of wealth put into circulation, weaving a network of alliances between different groups, just as do the *agalmata* exchanged at the wedding, or the herds that, in order to win his wife, the husband must present to her father. But as a mother who bears a man children that are truly his own and that directly continue his line, she is identified with the cultivated land owned by her husband, and the marriage has the significance of an exercise of ploughing, with the woman as the furrow.[59] Seen from this point of view, the wife takes on different functions. She appears intimately linked to her husband's house, soil, and hearth — at least for as long as she lives with him and shares the master's bed. She represents the husband's hearth and all that it signifies, and in particular the virtues of a royal hearth. It is as if the conjugal bed in which the king sleeps with the queen held powers which qualify the king's house to provide his kingdom with sovereigns who will make it bear fruit. To take the king's place at the heart of his house, in his bed, by becoming united with his wife, is to acquire a claim to reign after him over the land which his wife, in a way, symbolizes.

There are plenty of examples in legend, in tragedy, and even in history, to illustrate this identification of the wife with the power of her husband and the privilege which her conjugal status confers upon her of perpetuating and transmitting the sovereign power.

We shall limit ourselves to mentioning two of them, one taken from the world of the gods and the other from that of mortal men in the native land of Odysseus. As wife of Zeus, Hera is not merely the patroness of legitimate marriage. Through the intermediary of the king of the gods she is also associated with sovereign power that she can bestow, in some indirect way, because she shares the royal bed with her husband. In the myth of the judgment of Paris, each goddess promises the shepherd a gift in order to win his vote. Athena and Aphrodite offer him the very things that constitute their attributes as goddesses, the advantages connected with their functional powers, victory in war on the part of Athena, and success in erotic seduction on the part of Aphrodite.[60] Only Hera commits herself to promising something that she does not strictly speaking possess but in which she shares through her union with Zeus, namely sovereignty. Euripides puts it quite clearly: "Cypris boasted of desire, Athena of her lance and Hera of the royal bed of sovereign Zeus Ἥρα τε Διὸς ἄνακτος ἐυναῖσι Βασιλίσιν."[61]

This tale about the gods will perhaps illuminate the status and role of Penelope in the *Odyssey*.[62] Why are the suitors so determined to seek a place in her bed? How should we explain the somewhat equivocal attitude of the queen who seems not to want to come to any decision, neither dismissing the crowd of suitors *en masse*, once and for all, nor clearly committing herself in favor of any one of them? The initial situation can be summed up as follows: Telemachos, who is still a child, is not counted as a man. He remains, so to speak, tied to his mother's apron strings. In the absence of Odysseus, in the vacuum left at the hearth of his house by the departure of the head of the family, and at the center of his kingdom by the disappearance of the king, it is she who, as mistress of the house, represents the continuity of the hearth and, as wife of the prince, stands for the permanence of the royal authority. What the suitors want from Penelope is that, in the very house

74

in which she lives by reason of her marriage, she should finally accept to consider herself a widow, and take into Odysseus' bed a replacement for her husband who should, on the strength of his position, step directly into the former master's place both in the palace and the land. When Athena intervenes the facts of the situation are changed. She asks Telemachos to declare himself an adult and to behave as such. To convene the *agora* is to take up a man's position and, thenceforward, to take in hand the affairs of one's own house. Thus, if his mother truly desires a new marriage she will have to return of her own free will to the house of her father, Icaros, and if the suitors persist in their desire to marry her, they will have to win his favor by promising him more *hedna* than any of the others can give him.[63] But from that point onward Penelope will have severed the links that connected her to the house of Odysseus, which, if the hero is dead, will now become the house of Telemachos. This is precisely what the suitors fear. Telemachos accuses them, before the assembly, of fearing such a departure on the part of his mother to the house of Icaros;[64] they prefer, instead, to remain in the house of Odysseus as if he were dead and Telemachos did not count. In their reply, before the *dēmos*, the suitors present their defence and counter-attack. They claim that it is Penelope who, for years, has been leading them on, giving them reason to believe that she is ready to marry one of their number; this is the reason for their still being there, waiting for her decision. As for Telemachos, if he is no longer a child and claims to be a man, he has only himself to blame for his misfortunes. It is up to him to send his mother away from his house, back to Icaros, if he really wants the suitors to betake themselves to the old man with gifts of *hedna*.[65] This time it is Telemachos who refuses to cooperate. He says he cannot force his mother; it would be doing wrong both to her and to Icaros, who would then be justified in insisting on reparation in the form of gifts.[66] So an impasse appears to have been reached. Penelope, fearing for her son, whom she does not consider strong enough to take on the suitors, and still hoping for the return of her husband, whose death

75

has never been confirmed, spins things out without ever coming
to an irrevocable decision. The suitors refuse either to leave the
royal house or to allow Penelope to return to Icaros of her own
free will, thereby forfeiting what she represents in terms of the
continuity of power. Telemachos does not want to force his mother
to sever the links which bind her to the hearth of Odysseus. But
the young man puts forward a new proposal. He desires to put
an end to the uncertainty that reigns as to his father, an uncertainty which makes the entire situation indefinite and ambiguous. This is the case both within Odysseus' own household (where,
because it is not clear who is in authority, the suitors can install
themselves and make themselves at home) and in the country as
a whole, where nobody knows who is king. Telemachos declares
that if he finds proof that his father is no more, he will set up a
sēma for him and will offer his mother a choice between two solutions: She can either remain with him in the house of his father,
where he will then be undisputed master, or else she can depart
and occupy the house of the man she has decided to marry.[67] If she
wishes to marry, Telemachos will himself arrange for her marriage
and will, as befits his station, offer huge presents *"ἄσπετα δῶρα"*
in return for the *hedna*.[68] This solution fits in with one of the two
schemes envisaged by the suitors, namely to spare the life of
Telemachos, who would then, as master of the household, be in
a position to dispose of his patrimony as he so desired, and themselves to solicit the hand of Penelope by offering *hedna*, each suitor
this time courting her from his own home rather than in a group
in the palace of Odysseus.[69] The implication of this would be that
Penelope, by accepting such a marriage, would give up living in
her former royal residence and would leave it to become installed
in the home of another family. The second plan, suggested to the
suitors by one of their number, has similar implications regarding the ties which link Penelope, through the conjugal bed, to
royalty. It is to kill Telemachos, now that he has become a man.
The house of Odysseus would thus be left without any kind of
heir, either direct, since Telemachos would now be dead, or indi-

rect, there being no cousins or collateral relatives. The house would be left devoid of a man, "deserted." It would then be simple for the suitors to divide between themselves, in equal shares, all the food reserves and treasury, all the *ktēmata* of Odysseus. His house, however, would have to remain the property of Penelope.[70] Whomever she chose as husband would enter this royal dwelling there to act both as husband to the widow of the former monarch and also as prince over all those to whom he has been preferred by the queen.[71]

Neither of these plans is actually fulfilled. But when Penelope decides to allow the suitors to compete for her hand, it is in fact sovereignty over Ithaca that they are striving to gain through marriage to the queen. And when Telemachos himself enters the lists, competing with the suitors and setting himself up against them all, it is so that his mother should remain at his side and he should thus be clearly seen to be the one qualified to take the place formerly filled by his father, both in his own house and in the kingdom.[72] Neither Telemachos nor the suitors are successful in their attempts to bend the bow that Penelope's royal husband used to handle with ease, and that he left behind him, at home with Penelope. The exploit which reveals Odysseus, beneath the misleading disguise of a poor beggar, restores him to his rightful place: Penelope's bed and the throne of Ithaca. Besides, even before his arrow hit its mark, victory was already assured. It was all decided from the moment when, on returning to his home, he went into the marriage chamber and saw that the bed that he used to share with his wife was still in its proper place, immovable and the same as ever and with one of its legs — just like the hearth of the royal palace — rooted deep in the earth of Ithaca.

CHAPTER IV

Social History and the Evolution

of Ideas in China and Greece from the

Sixth to the Second Centuries B.C.[1]

I. *In China*

The very terms in which this discussion between a Chinese scholar and a Greek scholar was set up beg the question as to whether the history of Greek and Chinese thought can be related to the particular historical experience of the ancient Chinese and Greek worlds, and whether their modes of thought can be understood in relation to certain political institutions and practices and certain types of activity — in sum, whether mental phenomena are one aspect among others of social phenomena.

This discussion of China must inevitably be in part conjectural; it contains a number of ideas that are new, that is to say that have not yet been put to the test of criticism. However, this was unavoidable. Classicists should bear in mind how few scholars are engaged in research on Chinese history and the relatively recent date of any studies on this strange, rich, and complex world whose history stretches over more than three millennia.

The comparison seemed feasible because the general lines, at least, of the historical development of these two worlds appear to be similar. In China as in Greece we find the dissolution of an aristocratic society of warriors and this phenomenon is speeded up by changes in military techniques. In the one case it is a matter of a transition from noble *hippeis* to citizen hoplites, in the other from nobles fighting from chariots to peasant infantrymen. A profound change in mentality accompanies these transforma-

79

tions: The place and function of religion are altered, modes of action take on a more positivist character, and thought becomes increasingly secular. Nevertheless, we also find fundamental differences. The ephemeral institution of the city-state seems to have been a remarkably unique and original phenomenon, whereas the states established in China between the fifth and third centuries appear similar to a type of political constitution quite common in the history of mankind. Furthermore, it has to be recognized that, in China, social and political change takes place at the same time as a rapid development of technology and economic life, and also a sudden increase in population. This material progress, the continuity of population, and the absence of natural obstacles were no doubt not irrelevant to the establishment of the tyrannies and the appearance of a unified empire.

But let us begin at the beginning. In about the seventeenth century B.C., in the lower basin of the Yellow River, there develops a civilization that is characterized by the use of bronze, horse-drawn chariots, and writing. The centers of this civilization comprise flat sites accommodating the palaces and temples of a class of nobles whose principal activities consist of performing religious rituals, taking part in huge hunting expeditions, and raiding other communities. These centers are situated in zones of cleared land where a peasant population, under the protection of the nobility, continue to pursue the same activities as in neolithic times. Meanwhile, vast forests and expanses of marshland still cover most of the territories in which this bronze-age civilization spreads, between the seventeenth and eighth centuries. Widely diverse aboriginal populations, which are however in the process of being absorbed by the Chinese, are almost everywhere in contact with the Chinese communities. Thus, from the beginning of the first millennium, new cultures come into being as a result of interchange and fusion between the Chinese and aboriginal cultures. Certain cities, situated far away from the original centers, begin to play a locally predominant role and appear, at the moment when Chinese history begins to be better known to us (the end of the eighth century), as the capitals of different kingdoms. Increasingly bitter wars are waged between confederations of kingdoms and principalities and, at the same time, internal conflicts between the great noble families multiply (seventh and sixth centuries). At this point efforts are made to introduce a measure of centralization. They run counter to the traditions of the noble class and herald the great transformations that take place in the fifth and fourth centuries.

Meanwhile, it seems that the way of life of the noble class gradually changed between the end of the second millennium and the seventh and sixth centuries. More land was cleared, reducing the hunting grounds and pasturage, and the foundation of the nobility's wealth became agriculture. Although still a warrior nobility, it was now also a court nobility preoccupied with matters of etiquette and protocol.

One ritual, the *Li ki* (*K'iu li*, I, 1 §23), based on practices probably dating from before the period of the Warring Kingdoms (fifth to third centuries), refers to a very ancient period when the rituals were not yet standardized. It runs as follows: "High Antiquity set the highest value upon *virtue*" — that is to say competitions in generosity and vehement rivalry for prestige, for that is what the word *to* (virtue) means. This becomes easier to understand when we think of the type of life reflected in the excavations at Anyang: These revealed the remains of dozens of human and animal sacrifices, religious objects of great richness, and in particular bronzes depicting fabulous hunting expeditions and drinking parties. All are characteristic of a period when "the highest value was set upon virtue." The *Li ki* goes on to note: "But subsequently more importance was given to the exchange of gifts, for the rites value as most important of all [the balance in] relations between men: going without coming, and coming without going are both contrary to the rites."

The *Li ki* is not the only evidence of this fundamental change in customs, the transition from lavish gift-presentation of an agonistic type to a minutely organized system of exchange. There is abundant written as well as archaeological evidence to confirm

81

it. Nevertheless, the historical situation was a complex one. On the one hand we find this *ritualization* of all the activities of the noble class. The stimulus toward this attempt to systematize the ritual appears originally to have come from the ancient principalities of the Great Plain, the agents being the small group of those employed to administrate the power of the nobles — the scribes, diviners, chroniclers, astronomers, and so on. On the other hand, in contrast to the spirit of moderation which inspired the ritualists, other, more ancient types of conduct were still very much alive, involving contests in prestige and ostentation, demonstrations of generosity and wagering on the future. Concurrently, the measures taken to advance centralization in certain kingdoms during the sixth century — for example, agrarian and fiscal reforms, population censuses and the promulgation of written penal codes — appear as so many attacks against the rites. They were prompted by a widespread desire for wealth, possessions, and power, which was felt to be radically opposed both to the spirit of moderation associated with the rites and to the spirit of generosity that inspired the contests in prestige of archaic times. It was, however, toward centralization that China was to move.

In the course of the three centuries leading up to the imperial unification of 221 B.C., warfare provoked the creation of statelike structures and also resulted in a very rapid increase both in the power of the armies and in cereal production. Two factors appear to have had a determining influence on the formation of centralized states in China during the fifth, fourth, and third centuries. These were the development of an infantry recruited from among the peasantry and constituting the biggest element in the armed forces, and, from about 500 B.C. onward, the diffusion of a new technique, the casting of iron, which made possible the production in large quantities of tools for clearing the land for agriculture and for great civic and military undertakings. It seems to have been these technical innovations that precipitated the historical changes that occurred.

New ways of thinking appeared, in keeping with the needs of

organizing and directing large armies of infantrymen, and also connected with the complex problems posed by the administration
of richer and more densely populated countries. The leaders of
these kingdoms no longer needed sages of exceptional qualities
but administrators and specialists instead. A system of rewards and
punishments inspired by army life got the most out of these civil
servants. Stamped coinage came into more general use, as did commercial contracts and objective methods, and progress reports
were introduced in the administration. Quantitative calculation
became common. All these factors no doubt help to account for
the manifestation in China at this period of a spirit which it would
not be exaggerated to describe as positivist and rational. We should
note, however, that this is a practical form of rationality that does
not conflict with other forms of thought, which we find coexisting with it among, for example, the big businessmen whose
mentality probably had a considerable influence on the political
thinking of the period, and who attached great importance to the
ideas of chance, secrecy, and the auspicious moment – all of which
reappear among the professional politicians. The same is the case
among schoolteachers, diplomats, and orators, all of whom continue to set great store by the rituals and the morality of moderation, and among the promoters of anarchy and of individual
self-sufficiency.... In short, the behavior patterns and mental attitudes inherited from the archaic periods continue to operate more
or less beneath the surface. They manifest themselves, for example, in the ostentatious funerary customs, and reappear in flam-
boyant form with the first emperor, for all that he was the head
of a state founded upon *law*.

Thus, the social changes, the scale of which varied in different kingdoms, did not bring about an abrupt break with the past,
despite the fact that the men of the fourth and third centuries
were well aware that the world they lived in was very different
from that of the Hegemons of the seventh and eighth centuries.
They all accepted the fact that problems of subsistence and administration made it essential to employ objective methods of gov-

83

ernment, systems of reward and punishment, and quantitative calculation. Although there were still sovereign monarchs, their sovereignty was stripped of its mythical and autocratic aspects and became nothing more than the source of an impersonal order. The ruler no longer commanded. He simply set up a system of measures and laws. Whatever religious element the sovereign power retained was seen as part of the order of nature itself. To the educated classes, Heaven was no longer a deity, as it had been in the archaic period, but rather an expression of the cosmic order. Critics who relied on historical explanations were determined to purge the ancient myths of all that might seem strange and contrary to the accepted mores, and transformed them into nothing more than historical events. There were no more personal, creator gods; these were replaced by historical sages and impersonal religious forces. The rituals that in the seventh century were no more than forms of court etiquette now became universal procedures whose purpose was to ensure the internal order of society as a whole (for, according to the moralists, laws could only maintain this order in an external and artificial manner). This explains the importance given to example, education, and culture.

The so-called Chinese philosophers pursued many different lines of thought. However, between the fifth and third centuries B.C. the Chinese world inclined toward a type of thought that could be described as "organicist." It is rational thought, in its way, since its terms of reference apply to a human and social order and to a cosmic one, both of which are independent of any individualized power.

Nevertheless, this thought had its own particular framework and themes. It was concerned with questions that, at least until quite recently, attracted little or no interest in the West. So it would be fruitless to expect it to manifest those philosophical preoccupations which dominate the Western tradition, and unjust to use our own categories when analyzing it.

Mencius (end of the fourth and beginning of the third centuries) makes a distinction between the mind (the "heart" or seat of the intelligence) and the senses (the "ears and eyes"). But we should be quite wrong to interpret this in terms of our own familiar opposition. On close analysis it becomes clear that this distinction rests upon another: that between the productive and the administrative functions. Mencius is simply expressing a dualist hierarchy of complementary grades and values. Indeed, the radical opposition so characteristic of Greek thought, between the sensible world and the intelligible, is totally unfamiliar to the Chinese writers before the empire. No doubt they would have rejected it emphatically as artificial.

Similarly, the distinction, so important in our eyes, between a positivist and a religious attitude does not appear to have preoccupied the Chinese. The opposition does not appear in the same form in the Greek and Chinese worlds. The first emperor of China unified the administrative system of the new empire, in 221 B.C. But we should beware of regarding this simply as a positivist action to be explained purely in terms of the practical needs of the administration. Another powerful and, to our way of seeing it, irrational idea is also detectable here: that it is the emperor's own genius, his own personal "virtue" that is diffused through the world and brings it order. There were thus ritualistic and religious aspects to the system, and without these aspects the administrative action would undoubtedly have lost its essential significance and efficacy.

The Chinese authors of the three centuries before the empire were not engaged in a quest for the Truth, the non-changing and non-contradictory. We should like, in passing, to point out that in China there were linguistic obstacles, quite apart from anything else, to the development of a philosophy of being and to the elaboration of logic. Chinese thought took a quite different path: toward a more precise analysis of the factors ordering the social and the cosmic spheres.

In the work of the Chinese philosophers we often find the idea that action can be efficacious only if it conforms with the constant tendencies of man or the forces of nature, only if it exploits these natural inclinations to minimize the effort required for maxi-

85

mum effects. This is one of the major themes of Chinese fourth-
and third-century thought. It is easy to see what concept of society and nature is implied by such a philosophy: Order can never
result from the external intervention of a power of command, nor
from an arbitrary authoritarian division of functions and powers,
nor from a balance dependent upon an agreement reached between
antagonistic forces. In short, it cannot proceed from anything that
is arbitrary. The activity of the sovereign is similar to that of the
farmer who does no more than encourage the growth of his plants
and in no way intervenes in the process of germination and growth.
He acts in accordance with the orders of Heaven (*t'ien*), and identifies himself with it. The principle of order is to be found only
in the things that are. It cannot but be immanent in the world.

The concepts of influence, of patterns, of spontaneity, and of
modes of being carry more weight than that of law. This may
explain why the Chinese paid more attention to precisely those
areas of physics that were neglected by Greek science and its heirs.
They preferred to concern themselves with the study and interpretation of the phenomena of magnetism and vibration, tides,
and sonic and seismic waves. In music they appear to have been
particularly interested in the tonal quality of different instruments
and in ways to construct accurate models of chimes, whereas the
Greeks defined the musical scale geometrically.

How should we explain these fundamental differences in orientation? In our view history may provide the beginnings of an
explanation. In China, there was no violent crisis or confrontation between the *dēmos* and the aristocracy leading to a radical
change in the political constitution and a revaluation of the whole
past, but rather an evolution that, despite its great scope and the
progress it made toward rationality, allowed accommodation and
compromise. In China, there was nothing that can be compared
with the radical separation between the world of men and the
world of the gods that was the first necessary step toward the
birth of Greek rationality. In this respect one could say that Chinese thought before the empire both falls short of and goes beyond

such a distinction; it goes beyond it in the sense that the Greek gods and myths would have been considered as puerile inventions by the Chinese (in just the same way as the Christian myths were, later on). But it also falls short of making such a distinction because it was never concerned to separate the ritual sphere from the positivist or the cosmic from the human. It was too late for thought of the Greek type to develop in China because the Chinese had already naturalized the divine, and thus closed the way to developing any form of transcendental thought.

In short, a historical approach makes it possible to glimpse the quite surprising links between a people's thought and its political institutions. Chinese rationality that was, in its own way, just as much the fruit of original human experience, may be different from Greek rationality, but does that necessarily mean that it represents an inferior stage in the evolution of the human mind? To make such a claim would be to set up as a norm one specific type of thought and to condemn as misguided and derisory any attempts to uncover a universal rationality that falls outside the particular methods adopted by the Western world.

JACQUES GERNET

II. *In Greece*

The undertaking of a comparison between Greece and China in parallel studies depends on two necessary conditions. First, the authors must approach the subject from a similar point of view. Like Jacques Gernet, I shall therefore consider the evolution of ideas from the point of view of its relation to social history. I shall attempt to define the historical factors that were most influential in directing Greek thought into the channels it adopted. However, such a comparison also implies that the juxtaposition is provoked by certain analogies between the two types of civilization.

In point of fact, the resemblances between Greece and China have seemed to some scholars sufficiently striking to point to a kind of convergence in their historical development and in the changes of mentality each underwent. Chronology itself suggests such a comparison. The upheavals in their social life that led to their setting up new forms of state occurred at roughly the same period. In both cases the transition was from an archaic stage in which power essentially rested upon religious privileges and was exercised through procedures of a ritualistic type, to more positivist types of state organization and a mentality that can be described as more modern. Vassal relationships and links of personal dependence are destroyed, the importance of the world of the peasant increases, and towns develop: The same facts appear to recur in China and in Greece. In both cases these social changes appear to be linked to technical innovations of great importance: iron metallurgy, and the use of the metal not only for "noble" objects but also for utilitarian products for general use. There are changes on the military level as well: The peasantry becomes more important as the infantryman takes the place of chariots and horses on the battlefield. Finally, it is during the same period, between the seventh and the third centuries B.C., that the characteristic features of both the Chinese and the Greek cultures emerge. Schools that produce works which deeply affect the humanist studies flourish. The range covers the philosophy of nature, moral and political thought, sciences such as mathematics and medicine, and dialectic and logic. It is therefore easy to understand the desire to assimilate the Chinese and Greek data and assume that these two peoples underwent analogous historical transformations, any differences between them being accounted for by the fact that _.ᴗᴄce developed both faster and further. If that were the case, the purpose of any comparison would be to determine what obstacles were encountered by the Chinese that prevented them from progressing so fast or so far along the same path — as if there was only one path for human evolution to take, and that was the one taken by the West, which today, through technology and science, affects the whole of the rest of the world. Jacques Gernet's study has shown us that to pose the problem in terms such as these is to make it insoluble at the outset. Greek civilization is no more the measure of the Chinese than the reverse. It is not that the

88

Chinese did not get so far as the Greeks; they simply advanced in a different direction. The divergences in their social evolutions and in the orientation of their thought are to be valued, for they help us to seize upon what is original in each of the two cultures. They set in a new perspective and make sense of certain features of the Greek civilization that are so familiar to us that we take them for granted. What I should like to do, in this study, is consider the nature, scope, and origin of these divergences.

There are striking differences even within the similarities that have appeared most noticeable to us. We have mentioned iron metallurgy. But in fact we are dealing here with two very different techniques. China was producing cast iron, a technique that the West did not discover until the dawn of modern times. Such metallurgical work requires more complicated methods and investment on a larger scale than anything in Greece. For this reason it was always more or less in the hands or under the control of the state, which made it an instrument of its power. In Greece the blacksmith was a small independent producer, operating in his workshop to satisfy the needs of the public by selling directly to the customer.

In China the changes in the status of the peasantry result at the same time from a sweeping transformation of the human environment, and from the setting up of vast centralized states. Land-clearance leads to the sole cultivation of cereals over extensive areas. The progress made in this type of agriculture is tied to the development of a central administration capable of controlling it and setting up large-scale schemes using the power of water.

In Greece, peasant life combines the raising in particular of sheep and goats but also of cattle and horses with agriculture of an increasingly diversified kind. Tree cultivation, which is more lucrative and aimed at overseas trade, develops alongside the production of cereals. Here, agricultural production, organized outside the control of a centralized state, has two purposes: to ensure the subsistence of the family, the *oikos*, and to sell any surplus on the open market.

So we can see how it was that the advancement of the peasantry followed different courses in China and in Greece. In China it was fostered by the ruler, who saw the peasant masses as the source of his economic power and military strength, provided he controlled and organized them in their village life as he did when they were recruited for the army. In Greece, the advancement of the peasantry was a liberation not only from the ancient forms of servitude, but from any kind of servitude at all. It was brought about by the peasants in the rural demes opposing the landowning aristocracy who lived in the town and controlled the state. It came about through social antagonisms, conflicts, and confrontations, which were much more violent than in China, where the power of the new states transformed the old social relationships by gradually absorbing them. Through their own efforts the Greek farmers, small peasant owners of a parcel of land, were to confiscate all the ancient privileges of the aristocracy to their advantage, making them "common property": These included access to legal and political magistracies, the administration of public affairs, control of the army and even of the culture, with its particular modes of thought and feeling and its particular system of values. This widening and democratization of the aristocratic culture is one of the features that characterizes the Greek civilization. It explains the persistence of a certain ideal of man, and of certain attitudes: the agonistic spirit, the desire always and everywhere to prove oneself the best; the scorn for utilitarian and commercial values; the ethic of generosity, exalting the concept of largesse and the gracious giving of gifts; disinterestedness; and, finally and above all, a desire for autonomy and non-servitude, coupled with a concept that the human quality of a man depends upon his relation to other men. We should note straightaway that it is only within such a society, in which the concept of the autonomous individual, free from all servitude, has emerged and been confirmed, that the legal concept of the slave can, by contrast, be clearly defined as an individual deprived of all the rights that make a man into a citizen. Greece at one stroke invented both the free citizen and the slave, the status of each being defined in relation to the other. Without free citizens there would be no slaves, but instead a hierarchy of degrees of dependence stretching from the top to the bottom of the social scale, a general state of servitude from which even the king, in his relations with the gods or the divine order, is not exempt.

Nothing better illustrates the importance of this aristocratic ideal of autonomy implying an *isokratia* (in which power is shared equally by all) than the intellectual significance of the urban phenomenon in Greece.

The town, which always constitutes a favorable setting for the flowering of a new mentality, has a particular significance in Greece insofar as it is connected with the institutions of the *polis*. Mycenaean Greece no doubt produced a kind of palace-city; and archaic Greece had its towns that were inhabited by the nobility, as opposed to the countryside that was populated by "villeins" who were responsible for feeding the *kaloi kagathoi*. But, unlike in China, the classical Greek town did not become the royal administrative center for a vast rural territory, populated by civil servants, priests, and political councillors in the direct service of the sovereign, together with a number of merchants and industrial contractors. In Greece the urban establishment is not opposed to the countryside, because the city encompasses both the rural territory and the urban complex without making any specific political distinction between the two. Peasants and town-dwellers enjoy the same rights and assume the same responsibilities; they sit in the same assembly and on the same tribunals, and together elect the same magistrates. So what is the role of the town as such in the system of the city-state? It provides a center for and makes a community of the whole territory, or rather, of the human group established there that cultivates it. Essentially, the urban complex is comprised of those buildings connected with public life, that is to say, everything that, being common rather than private property, concerns the individuals insofar as they are all, equally, citizens; the temples, the buildings set aside for the magistracies, the

91

tribunals, the assemblies, the agora, the theater, and the gymnasiums. Thus, the town is conceived as the center that gives the social space of the Greeks its uniformity: In relation to this common center all the citizens occupy positions that are, in a way, symmetrical and reversible. In a city inspired by the ideal of *isonomia*, power and authority are, as the Greeks put it, placed at the center (*en mesoi*), and are not the prerogative of one individual such as the king or of a privileged minority of citizens.

There is a close connection between this political system of the city-state and the new spiritual world of the Greeks of the sixth century. Of course, their ideas were bound to change, but so long as the city remained alive they were the ideas of men who saw themselves as autonomous and free within the framework of small, independent communities. Just as, in the city, power belongs to everyone, is placed *en mesoi* (an expression that is significantly reminiscent of a military aristocracy's way of conducting its wars and dividing up the spoils), so too does culture belong to all; it is placed at the center, no longer the privilege of a few families or, as in China, of a class of educated men. This democratization is, of course, only made possible by alphabetic writing, which is no longer the speciality of a class of scribes, and which enables all the citizens to learn to read and write. For the rest, by participating in the festivals and going to the theater, the whole city has access to artistic and literary productions of the highest quality.

This common participation in the culture, paralleled by the common sharing of political authority, has decisive consequences for the evolution of ideas. Henceforward, all the knowledge and intellectual techniques that were hitherto the more or less jealously guarded secrets of certain privileged families, are fully and publicly revealed. The rules of political life — that it should take place in public, conducted via free discussion and reasoned debate — also become the rule in intellectual life. Truth is no longer derived from mysterious revelation. Doctrines are made public, submitted to criticism and controversy, and subjected to a form of reasoned argument. Sacred tales of *hieroi logoi* now give way to secular demonstration.

We must now consider from a social and intellectual point of view the historical factors that made such a phenomenon possible, namely the small size of the groups in which men lived, and the dispersed and fragmented character of the population. The demographic scale is of fundamental significance when we compare China and Greece. Because the Greek social unit is so relatively small, two conditions are fulfilled: First, rapid and widespread dissemination of information and communication throughout the entire social body is possible, and this favors a system of direct democracy. It is possible to come to political decisions following public debate since each citizen can rapidly be informed of all that is going on. The world of the city had to be small enough for everyone – or almost everyone – to know each other and be able to enter into discussion with everyone else. And what applies to politics also goes for ideas – witness Socrates finding his interlocutors in the agora.

Second, the state does not have to direct what we today would call the economy; it does not have to administer the details of agricultural and industrial production or the exchange and circulation of goods. All this is left to individual "houses." Indeed, this is the true meaning of the Greek word *oikonomia*. The state only becomes involved when it needs money or materials for the particular ends that are its concern. Its true domain is politics, that is to say the interplay of relations of ruling and submitting to rule between citizens, and the links of domination and submission between different states. Politics, for the city, consist essentially in organizing the methods of exercising power. They revolve entirely around the concept of "power." Within the city how can power be balanced so that all the citizens exercise it in common? And, in its relations with the outside world, how can the city strengthen its power so as to remain always sovereign mistress of itself and affirm its own supremacy over its rivals?

Power is perhaps one of the key concepts in our understanding of Greek thought. André G. Haudricourt once contrasted the mentality of peoples composed of herdsmen and sailors, like the Greeks, with that of "gardening" peoples such as the Chinese. He suggested that the domestication of animals led the herding peoples to conceive the action of a man upon his fellows — in particular the power of a king over his subjects — on the model of the relationship of the shepherd to his flocks, that is to say, as a form of direct and compelling intervention. In contrast, gardening peoples take "indirect and negative action" as their model for human relations. For them, the best authority — that is, that which conforms most closely with the natural order — is that which, being immanent in all things, never needs to intervene. It is, at all events, noticeable that, when not drawing on images taken from the field of navigation, Greek political terminology draws on the experience of the herdsman. The power of the leader over those whom he directs is represented as a constraining action in which the inferior is bent beneath the yoke of the stronger and forced to submit to being guided and trained, just as the shepherd trains and guides his flock with his crook, by virtue of his superior power of "domination." This image of the leader, seen as an agent intervening directly from without to impose compulsion upon his subjects, is deeply rooted in religion. The Greek gods form, as it were, a society of Powers who are both competitive and at the same time mutually supporting. The gods are agents possessed of a superior strength to which men must submit. Among these gods Zeus proves himself to be, on his own, stronger than all the others put together. *Kratos* and *Bia*, brutal domination and compelling violence, who flank Zeus' throne, never leave the side of the sovereign of the gods.

One must bear in mind this concept of might seen as a power of coercion, as violence done to others, or the deployment of a superior force of constraint, if one is to understand how it was that Greece could produce a social system in which power, the *kratos*, should be made common to all, placed *en mesoi* so that it should no longer belong to any one person. In such a situation commanding and obeying cease to appear antithetical and form, rather, the two terms of a single reversible relationship. The same men in turn obey and command, following a temporal order that is numerically determined because it revolves around the common center where the power of command is henceforth deposited. Domination by brute force is replaced by the abstract order of an egalitarian distribution of responsibilities.

This political ideal of *isonomia* takes shape gradually as moral ideas develop between the seventh and the fifth centuries. During a period of social crisis and religious upheaval Greece develops an ethic of wisdom, *sophrosunē*, which puts one in mind of China. It involves the rejection of luxury and the condemnation of riches, excess, and violence, and the exaltation of moderation, self-control, and the just measure. This moral idea impinges, through legislation, upon social realities, leaving its mark upon them. The aim is to produce a balanced, harmonious, united human group and to rationalize social relations, to achieve a balance between them and set up a geometrical model for them. In this way moral thought, while frequently retaining its religious character, leads to the instituting of Law and essentially positivist political reforms such as those introduced by Cleisthenes, although it never becomes a Machiavellian type of *realpolitik* aimed at strengthening the power of the prince through any possible means, as it does among the legalists in China. Nor does Greek moral philosophy lead, as it does for the Confucianists, to an attempt to bring human society into harmony with the ancient ritual order. The *nomoi*, the body of rules introduced by the legislators, are presented as human solutions aimed at obtaining specific results: social harmony and equality between citizens. However, these *nomoi* are only considered valid if they conform to a model of equilibrium and geometric harmony of more than human significance, which represents an aspect of divine *Dikē*. The link between *Dikē* and the human *nomoi* is never quite broken. True, there are some sophists who claim that there is no absolute *Dikē* or that, if there is, it cannot be known. But theirs is a

95

"paradoxical" opinion and is felt to be such. For the great majority of Greeks the *nomoi* are human, subject to discussion and even revision; yet they are not radically separate from divine *Dikē*. With Socrates and the beginnings of moral thought, in the strictly philosophical sense, this dual aspect of ethics, which is an autonomous human discipline and at the same time demands an absolute basis, acquires its full significance. Socrates takes concrete behavior and the virtues practiced by every individual in the diverse circumstances of life as his starting point, but he does not stop there. He desires to put the actions of his fellow citizens face-to-face with criteria that are permanent and self-justifying: Piety, Courage, and Justice themselves. These absolute criteria are not religious, and moral behavior is, in a sense, the opposite to ritual obedience. Such values imply that they have been arrived at through critical evaluation; they are the fruit of rational analysis, discovered through debate, dialectical argument, and a quest for definitions. Ethics thus constitutes a system of transcendental values considered as universally applicable truths from which it should be possible to deduce the various courses of behavior suited to particular circumstances.

Alongside this moral thought, a philosophy of nature starts to develop at the beginning of the sixth century in the Greek cities of Asia Minor. The theories of these first "physicists" of Ionia have been hailed as the beginning of rational thought as it is understood in the West.

In a recent study we have attempted to show that the physical thought of the Greeks of the sixth century is intimately linked with their political thought. In their conception of nature the physicists of Miletos make use of conceptual equipment and a terminology which had been developed in social practice. They interpret the physical universe in accordance with a model of equilibrium between opposed powers that is in keeping with the ideal of *isonomia* that governs their organization of the human world.

Certain aspects of the new view of the world presented by the Milesians may seem close to the concepts of the Chinese. The gods are no longer seen as being outside nature and the human world; instead, the natural order itself is, in a way, considered as divine. And yet there are considerable differences. The Greek image of the world is fundamentally geometrical in character. The cosmos is imagined in spatial terms. The order that governs it is egalitarian rather than hierarchical. It assumes a balanced distribution between contrary powers so that no one of these can come to dominate the others. Finally, the Milesian philosophers, far more than the Chinese thinkers, had to break with traditional religious beliefs, and on many points they deliberately take up a contradictory position to them. For this reason the opposition between this emerging philosophy, on the one hand, and religion or myth on the other is, in certain respects, extremely marked.

Nevertheless, Greek religion is more of a practice, a manner of behavior and an internal attitude, than a system of beliefs and dogmas. So, on this level, philosophy fills a gap; in its attempt to construct a coherent world system, philosophy has no cause to come into direct conflict with religion.

Besides, philosophy does not reject the concept of the divine; rather, from the very first it uses and transforms it. For the Ionian physicists the divine is present within the world that they seek to explain. The universe can be explained not by the activities of the traditional gods but by the interaction of the powers that form the basis for the *phusis*, and represent the principles or *archai* at work in it. These principles still carry a religious charge. In what senses can the Milesians call these physical elemental principles "divine"? Like the gods, these principles are contrasted with natural phenomena in that they are invisible; they belong to the domain of what is *adela*, not of what is *phanera*. They are eternal and indestructible, not mortal and perishable; immutable, not changeable and ephemeral; pure, not mixed. In short, like the gods, they are powers that are superior to all others and that, between them, govern the world.

So the physical thought of the Milesians develops within the framework of the great oppositions established by Greek religious thought between a whole series of polar terms: men–gods; the invisible–the visible; what is eternal–what is mortal; the permanent–the changing; the powerful–the powerless; the pure–the mixed; the certain–the uncertain.

Thus, both in its fundamental features and in the way it develops, Greek philosophy appears to take over from Greek religion. Philosophical enquiry takes place within the very framework religion had provided. But now, instead of belonging to the domain of mysterious and secret revelation, the divine becomes the subject of an enquiry pursued in the full light of day. It is no longer manifested in a more or less ineffable vision; now it must be expressed and formulated articulately. Its permanence and unity make it possible to define it unequivocally. Thus the divine, seen as an immutable principle and essence appears in the guise of the intelligible. It can be perceived by a particular way of knowing and expressed in a rigorous language that is a far cry from vulgar speech. Thus, for Parmenides, the *Logos* belongs to the level of the immutable being that he identifies with Truth. This *Logos* is something quite different from the mere words, *epea*, used in their inconsistent talk by those whom Parmenides dubs "two-headed mortals" because they can hold two opinions on a single subject. In this way the opposition between the world of the divine and the human world is transposed in Parmenides' philosophy into two contrary Ways, two contrasting domains: on the one hand Being, and the true word that expresses it in its perfect self-identity; and, on the other, Non-Being that is subject to generation, change, and destruction and that is the object not of true knowledge but only of uncertain and ambiguous opinion. With Parmenides, Greek philosophy finds its true vocation. It is at the same time and inseparably a philosophy of Being, an ontology, and a philosophy of knowledge, a logic. The quest for Being as such is inseparable from a logic of identity involving a refusal of all that is ambiguous, changeable, and relative, and postulating a radical separation between the intelligible and the sensible.

We are familiar with how Greek philosophy develops after

Parmenides, and to a large extent in response to him, down to the moment when Aristotle provides a precise definition of the principle of non-contradiction. But one point should be emphasized. It is that this whole development took place within the framework of a logic of identity, of the exclusion of contraries. Linguists can explain how much the ontology and logic owed to the particular state of the Greek language, and the ease with which it could be made to express the concept of Being and all its different dimensions. But other factors, too, appear to have played their part. Through its analyses of the commonplaces of language, methods of reasoning, and demonstration and types of argument, sophistry prepared the way for the work of Plato and Aristotle. Now the techniques of the orators and sophists cannot be dissociated from the practices of the tribunals and the political contests in the Assembly. The method of the *Dissoi Logoi*, the double speeches that put forward two contrary theses on every question considered, is a first attempt to formulate mutually exclusive arguments. But this method, in its turn, is connected with an important social factor: in the human affairs that were debated at the tribunals and in the Assembly — affairs that could be solved only on the basis of what was probable or likely, not of what was evident or certain — there are always two conflicting viewpoints, two opposed sides between which a choice must be made in order to come to a judicial or political decision.

There can be no question of reaching definite conclusions as a result of the present inquiry. In recalling one or two themes, our purpose is to present them, rather, as problems. As compared with China, in Greece social development and the evolution of thought seem to have a more violent and dialectical character. A greater role is played by oppositions, conflicts, and contradictions and, in corresponding fashion, thought tends to develop on the plane of the immutable and the identical while modes of reasoning aim at the radical exclusion of contrary propositions.

In this inquiry into the ideas of the Greeks we have noted a number of factors: antagonism and conflict in their social history; a dualism in their philosophy between the intelligible and the sensible, between Being and Coming-to-be, and between Truth and Opinion; a logic of non-contradiction; an ethic based upon man's power of choice, of free decision; and judiciary and political practices that imply a confrontation between two opposed causes, the clash of hostile speeches. To what extent are all these features interrelated?

If it is true that tragedy expresses a "torn consciousness," a feeling for the contradictions that divide a man against himself, perhaps this comparison with China can help us to understand why it was the Greeks who invented tragedy.

CHAPTER V

The Society of The Gods[1]

In writing of the Greek gods — and especially of their birth — the gaps in the information we possess, and our ignorance concerning their origins, certainly constitute major obstacles. However, the little knowledge that I may lay claim to on this subject does not make the task any easier. How can such a vast and complex problem be tackled in the space of a few pages without much simplification and a certain measure of distortion? Perhaps I may rather be permitted to discount from consideration a number of interpretations that today seem too outdated, too dubious, or too premature to be of any help in understanding the religious facts.

First, what is the position as regards the problem of origins or, to put the question in the terms in which it has been addressed to me, what do we know of the birth of the Greek gods? An inquiry into origins is always difficult. In the case of the Greeks we are completely in the dark. However far back we may go into the past (that is to say, since the decipherment of Linear B, as far as the Mycenaean period), we are confronted with a religious system that has already undergone many transformations and borrowed much, and in which it is very difficult to distinguish what is Indo-European, Mediterranean, Aegean, or Asiatic. Any attempt at a global explanation, such as the suggestion that the great male gods have an Indo-European origin and the great female deities a Mediterranean one must be open to question.

Furthermore, what is true for a linguistic system is also true for a religious one. In the study of a language, etymology offers possibilities and is sometimes rewarding. In the history of religions etymology is much more obscure, but even in the case of a language etymology cannot enlighten us as regards the use of a term at a particular period, since the native speakers, when they use it, are unaware of its etymology. Thus a word's meaning depends not so much on its linguistic past but rather on the place the word occupies in relation to the general system of the language at the period in question. Similarly, a Greek of the fifth century may well have known less about the origins of Hermes than a specialist does today, but that did not stop him from believing in Hermes and from sensing the presence of the god in certain circumstances. And what we are trying to understand is precisely what Hermes represented in the religious thought and life of the Greeks – the place that this god held in men's existence.

Let us consider one of the examples most favorable to an inquiry into origins, that of Zeus, the greatest god in the pantheon. It so happens that the name of this god is informative. Behind the name of Zeus we can detect the Indo-European root that we find in the Sanscrit *dyau'h*, meaning "to shine." We can consequently connect the Greek *Zeus pater* with the Latin Jupiter and the Indian *Dyaus pita*. But the Greek Zeus is not only an Indo-European god; he has come into contact with other male deities, in particular a Cretan cave god with whom he merged. This Cretan god differs in many respects from the Indo-European Zeus: He is a child god, *Zeus kouros*; he is also a god who dies and is reborn. His tomb used to be pointed out in Crete. The Greek Zeus is the result of these fusions and transformations. What we are seeking to understand is this complex figure, rather more than his affiliation with the ancient Indo-European god.

There is another danger in etymology. We detect in the word *Zeus* the root meaning "to shine." So we conclude that Zeus represents the luminous sky, the shining light of day. We are then tempted to assume that all the great gods of the pantheon can be similarly equated to other natural forces. Thus Zeus is linked with

102

shining sky, Poseidon with water, Hephaestos with fire, Hera with air, Hermes with wind, Dionysos with vines, Demeter with wheat, and so on. Such an interpretation assumes that the universe in our modern conception can be compared term for term with the Greeks' image of it, expressed through their religion. This would be to suggest that their religious thought had the same structure and same type of organization, and used the same conceptual categories as our own scientific thought, the only difference being that in Greek religion natural forces are animated and personified.

The study of religions today is sufficiently advanced for no specialist still to be convinced by such simple naturalistic explanations. So, in attacking them, I perhaps appear to be pushing at doors that are already wide open. But, after all, the only way to open doors is to push them, and I am hoping that our attack will carry us rather further than just over the threshold.

Zeus is the shining sky but also, in a way, the night sky. He is the master of light and reveals himself in and through light, but he also has the power to blot it out. And, as we shall see, Zeus is many other things besides. He is a god in the strict sense of the word, a *theos*, precisely because he is so many things at the same time — things connected with what, to our eyes, are completely distinct or even opposed domains: the world of nature, the social world, the human world, and the supernatural world.

It is I who am distinguishing between these different spheres because they do appear separate to us today, but the religious thought of the Greeks made no such clear-cut distinctions between man and his internal world, the social world and its hierarchy, the physical universe and the supernatural world or society of the Beyond made up of the gods, the daemons, the heroes, and the dead. This is not to say that the Greeks confused everything together and that theirs was a kind of primitive mentality where everything participated in everything else. The Greeks made distinctions in their religious thought, but not the same ones as we make. They distinguished in the cosmos between different types of powers — multiple forms of power that could take action on every level of reality, not just in one of the domains we have mentioned, making interventions within man himself as well as in society, in nature, and in the Beyond.

Thus their religion and their pantheon can be seen to be a system of classification, a particular way of ordering and conceptualizing the universe, distinguishing between multiple types of force and power operating within it. So in this sense I would suggest that a pantheon, as an organized system implying definite relations between the various gods, is a kind of language, a particular way of apprehending reality and expressing it in symbolic terms. I am even inclined to believe that, in those ancient times, there existed between language and religion a sort of co-naturality. When one considers religion as a type of thought it appears to date back as far as language itself. What characterizes the human level as opposed to that of other creatures on the animal scale is the presence of these vast mediatory systems — language, tools, and religion.

However, man is not aware of having invented this language of religion. He feels that it is the world itself that speaks this language or, to be more precise, that reality itself is fundamentally language. The universe appears to him as the expression of sacred powers that, in their own particular different forms, constitute the true texture of reality, the being behind appearances, the meaning that lies behind the symbols that manifest it.

Let us focus our inquiry a little more closely. For the ancient Greek, the luminous sky above seemed to establish a connection between him and Zeus. That is not to say that he believed that the sky was Zeus, but rather that certain features of the sky, the influence that it exerted over human life, constituted, as it were, the ways through which the power of Zeus was made manifest to man. Zeus is made manifest by the sky, but he is at the same time hidden by it: A power can only be seen by men through whatever it is that manifests it, but at the same time that power is always greater than its manifestations: It cannot be identified with any single one of them.

So it is not so much that Zeus is the luminous sky, rather that, for a certain form of power, the luminous sky is simply a way both of being visible and concealing itself. What kind of a power is it? In the case of Zeus, perhaps the least incorrect definition would be to say that what is concerned is the power of sovereignty. One of Zeus' essential features is that, both for the gods and for men, he is enthroned at the summit of the hierarchy, he holds the supreme command and possesses a superior strength that allows him absolute dominion over all others.

Those who are submitted to this sovereign power of Zeus feel the effects of its double and contradictory character. On the one hand this power embodied by the sky, with its regular movements and the periodic cycle of days and seasons, represents a just and ordered sovereignty. At the same time, it also comprises an element of opaqueness and unpredictability. The Greeks make a distinction in the sky between what they call *aither*, the sky that is constantly luminous, the brilliance of an incorruptible zone, and what they call *aer*, that is to say the zone of atmospheric phenomena whose unpredictable violence is of the first importance in the life of men since it is the source of the winds, clouds, and beneficial rain, and also of destructive storms. Zeus' power is a compound of regularity and constancy and, at the same time, unpredictability; it combines aspects of beneficence and of terror. Seen as the sky, then, Zeus already appears in a complex and ambiguous form; he belongs both to the day and to the night and is both auspicious and at the same time inauspicious. But in a way Zeus is also present in everything that evokes sovereign dominion. He is present on the mountain tops – on Mount Pelion where he was worshipped under the name of Zeus akraios, at the summit of Olympos, the mountain that is so high that it links heaven and earth together, and whose rugged peak calls to mind the fortress at Mycenae from which King Agamemnon would survey the flat countryside over which he reigned. Zeus is present in certain trees that are taller than the rest, reaching up through the *aer* as far as the *aither*. This is Zeus Endendros. He is present in the lightning as Zeus Bronten, Keraunios or Kataibates; in the rain as

Ombrios or Huetios, especially in the fertile rains of autumn that herald the season for sowing and thus bring about what can be seen as the divine marriage between the sky and the earth, and here he is known as Zeus Gonaios, Genethlios, Georgos, Maimachtes. Zeus is present in the depths of the earth in the form of the riches which his fertility produces there: Zeus Chthonios, Katachthonios, Plousios, Meilichios. Zeus is present in gold, the metal that is as unchanging as the sky, condensed from the light of the sun whose dazzling beams evoke the brilliance of sovereignty: Here he is Zeus Chrusaor.

However, the power of Zeus is not restricted to these natural forms. It is also at work in human activities and social relations. Zeus is present in the person of the king as Zeus Basileus. There is even a Zeus known as Agamemnon. In particular he is present in the scepter of the king, enabling his decisions to be put into force. In the house of a priest a royal scepter can, by its mere presence, be the focus of the cult addressed to Zeus. Zeus is present at the king's side in all the circumstances in which the human sovereign is exercising a power that comes to him from the gods and that can only be effective through the intermediary of divine powers. Thus, when the king leads his army out to battle he is flanked by Zeus Agetor, Promachos; when he mediates in his council, turning over some plan in his mind, it is Zeus Boulaios; in critical situations, when the people no longer know to which power to address their prayers and come to beg their king to find a way of salvation, he is Zeus Soter. Above all, Zeus is present when the king metes out justice: Just as the sovereignty of Zeus in the sky makes the earth rich and fertile, similarly the justice of the king brings prosperity to the entire territory dependent upon him. If the king is unjust his land produces no wheat, the herds do not multiply, and the women produce deformed children. But if the king respects justice and embodies the sovereign power of Zeus, his whole kingdom flourishes in endless prosperity. This same dominion that Zeus has over the universe and the king over his subjects is also exercised by the head of each family in his own house. So the cult of Zeus also celebrates a number of aspects of him as a domestic deity. When a suppliant who has been ejected from his own home and cut off from his social roots seeks shelter at the hearth of the master of the house, begging for his protection, Zeus Hikesios and Zeus Xenios enter the dwelling with him. Zeus Gamelios presides over legitimate marriage, the essential purpose of which is to place a woman under the domination of her husband and to give her children who will owe respect and obedience to their father. Zeus Herkeios, the Zeus of the enclosure or of the barrier, encompasses the territory over which the head of the family exercises his power, while Zeus Klarios, the apportioner, marks out and protects the boundaries between properties belonging to different masters. Finally, Zeus Ktesios is enthroned in the cellar of the house, in the shape of a jar, as he watches over the riches of the father of the house.

This wide range of epithets given to a god such as Zeus can perhaps help us to glimpse one of the essential functions of the supernatural powers. They make it possible to integrate the human individual into various social groups, each with its own ordered way of functioning and its own hierarchy; and to integrate these social groups, in their turn, into the order of nature which is then made a part of the divine order. So one of the functions of the gods is to impose social order. Emanating as it does from Zeus, the power of the king is truly endowed with efficacy, always provided that it is exercised according to certain rules and in conformity with an established order. The king and his subjects are implicitly agreed upon what might be termed the rules of the game of sovereignty. If the king exceeds his rights it is not simply a matter of an individual being wronged or the social hierarchy being distorted. The whole sacred order of the universe is brought into question by this distortion of just sovereignty. The compromised order has to be reestablished at the expense of the guilty party. Such a reversal of the situation may be seen either as vengeance wreaked by Zeus, who is the guarantor of sovereign power, or equally well as a quasiautomatic way of reintroducing order by restoring the balance between cosmic forces that have been upset. The two interpretations — the one referring to the vengeance of Zeus and the other to the fatality of destiny (Nemesis or Moira) are not contradictory, for there is a Zeus known as Moiragetes.

In this way the power of Zeus establishes the connections between various types of human activities, social relations, and natural phenomena. It links them together but does not confuse them. The Greeks knew perfectly well that a king was not a force of nature and that a force of nature was not the same as a deity. Nevertheless, they saw them as linked, interdependent, as different aspects of a single divine power.

The expression "divine power" is designed to emphasize the point that the Greek gods are not individuals each with a particular single characteristic form and spiritual life. The Greek gods are powers, not persons. It has been correctly noted that, when referring to the gods, the Greeks make no clear distinction between the use of the singular and that of the plural. The same divine power is sometimes conceived in the singular, for example *charis*, and sometimes in the plural, the *charites*. In the words of Rohde: "The Greek is incapable of imagining a god as a single deity but rather envisages a divine power which can be apprehended now in its unity and now in its diversity."

The representations of gods in myth and literary works particularly emphasize their unity. Homer presents us with a Zeus who, as a figure, possesses a relative unity. When a god is worshipped, however, it is rather the aspect of plurality that is stressed. The living religion of the Greeks knows Zeus not in one single form but rather as many different Zeuses, each with its own epithet peculiar to the cult that links it with its own particular area of activity. In worship, the important thing is to address oneself to the Zeus that is suitable in a particular situation. Thus even while he is protected by Zeus Soter and Zeus Basileus, Xenophon is dogged by the anger of Zeus Meilichios to whom he omitted to offer a sacrifice on the occasion of the festival of the *Diasia*. And he sees nothing strange in being favored by two Zeuses while at loggerheads with a third. Zeus' unity is not that of a single and unique person but of a power whose various aspects may be manifested in different ways.

If these remarks are correct they must lead us to eliminate another method of analyzing the religious data. Any study that attempted to define the Greek gods independently from one another, as if they were separate and isolated figures, would be in danger of missing an essential point about them. Much erudition has been brought to studies of this kind and they provide us with much highly valued information. However, it is no longer possible today to be satisfied with such an approach. The work of a historian of religion such as Georges Dumézil has clearly shown that, as with a linguistic system, it is impossible to understand a religious system without making a study of how the various gods relate to each other.

Instead of simply drawing up a list of the different deities we must analyze the structure of the pantheon and show how the various powers are grouped, associated together, and opposed to and distinguished from each other. Only in this way can the pertinent features of each god or each group of gods emerge — that is to say, those that are significant from the point of view of religious thought. The study of a god such as Hermes, who is a very complex figure, must first define his relation to Zeus in order to pick out what in particular it is that Hermes contributes to the wielding of sovereign power, and then compare him with Apollo, Hestia, Dionysus, and Aphrodite. Hermes has affinities with all of these gods but is distinguished from each of them by certain modes of action that are peculiar to him.

In the third place, it would be equally mistaken to study the religious data as if it constituted an independent world, quite separate from the material and social life of the Greeks. I believe that, to understand a religion, it is necessary to connect it with the men who lived by it, to seek to understand how these men related to nature through the intermediary of their tools, and to each other through the intermediary of their institutions. For a historian of religion it is the men who explain the gods, not the reverse. Meanwhile, it must be pointed out that hitherto the history of Greek religion has been concerned to study religious representations and rituals more than to discover the sociology of religious man, the sociology of the believer and of the various types of believer. It is a difficult task that scholars have already undertaken where the great contemporary religions are concerned, but that still remains to be attempted for the religions of the past. Clearly, the task is made the more problematic by the need to consult documentary evidence and the impossibility of pursuing any direct inquiry. But apart from this there is also a preliminary obstacle to be cleared away, namely the existence of certain preconceptions.

The fact is that we approach the study of religions burdened with all the experience contemporary man has inevitably acquired, and with firmly entrenched ideas about the place of religion in man's life and its role in society. Now it is impossible to know *a priori* whether the role played by Greek religion in relation to the men and society of antiquity was the same as that played by contemporary religions in relation to the men and societies of today. We may well wonder whether the function of religion can have been the same in archaic societies, where it dominated social life as a whole, as in modern societies in which the life of the community has been almost completely secularized. Is it not to be expected that, like other important factors in civilization, the religious phenomena too should have their own history reflecting the transformations and changes in meaning that took place? We must therefore ask ourselves to what extent our own religious categories of thought, our own conception of the divine and its relation to men and our concepts of what is sacred and supernatural are applicable to the Greek reality.

For us, the divine is basically external to the world. God transcends the world, as the theologians and philosophers put it. This transcendent deity is the creator of the world and of mankind. It is related to the universe as a craftsman is related to his own creation. The creation does, in a way, bear the imprint of the creator. However, the creator is beyond his production and moves in a world apart from the world he has produced – and produced from nothing.

This god who is foreign to our own world is present within us. Where else could we find him, since he is outside nature, if not within ourselves? So this is an interior god: The point of contact between the deity and man is within the soul of each individual and takes the form of personal communion between the two. This individual relationship is at the same time universal: The link between each separate individual and God is an expression of the fundamental relationship of man and his creator. I am related to God as a human being and as an individual, not as a Frenchman, or as the member of a particular profession, a particular family, or a particular social group.

Finally, in the life of a contemporary man, the religious sphere is in general fairly closely defined. We consider most of our social, economic, cultural, and political activities, our work, our leisure, our reading, our entertainment, and our family relations to be outside the strictly religious sphere and as constituting the secular domain. Religion is thus restricted to one definite sphere of human existence; the religious life of each individual belongs to one particular area of his life with its own objectives.

When I turn to consider Greek religion and the Greek gods I do not find the features that I have just described in simplified form. The Greek gods are not external to the world. They are an integral part of the cosmos. Zeus and the other Olympians created neither the physical universe nor living creatures nor mankind. They were themselves created by primordial powers that continue to exist, providing a framework and substratum for the universe. These are Chaos, Gaia, Eros, Nux, Ouranos, and Okeanos. Thus the gods whom the Greeks worship only emerged at a given point in time; they had not always existed. In relation to the original powers they are "late-comers" who seized power for themselves. Zeus established at the same time his own sovereignty and a world order never again to be brought into question. He holds the scepter and is master and king of the universe, but he did not secure this position without difficulty or without a fight. Zeus is aware of what he owes to the allies who supported him, and what he has to fear from the enemies whom he has put into chains but who are not all totally disarmed; he knows which are the powers that he must treat with circumspection and the prerogatives that he is obliged to respect. Homer shows us Zeus backing down before the ancient *Nux*, Night, seized with reverential and religious awe.

So the gods are not eternal, merely immortal. Their immortality defines them in contrast to the poor life of men, the "ephemeral" beings who appear only to disappear, like shadows or wisps of smoke. The gods are much more consistent. Their *aion*, or inexhaustible vitality, will endure, permanently youthful, throughout time. Meanwhile, there are certain intermediate levels between gods and men. First, in between the immortals and the mortals, there are the *makrobioi* or *makraiones* whose existence covers many myriads of years, such as the *Numphai* whose destiny is linked with the cycle of life of the trees in which these deities dwell. Then, certain gods may experience a waning of their power and vitality, as did Ares, who was on the point of perishing in the jar in which two of his brothers had managed to confine him. And finally, certain men, in particular conditions, may accede to the status of the gods, and in their company live a blessed existence until the end of time.

The gods are no more all-powerful or omniscient than they are eternal. When Hades carries off her daughter into the Underworld, even as great a goddess as Demeter has to wander the world over, searching for her, begging to be told where her child has been hidden. In the end Helios, the sun, does so. It is not, strictly speaking, that Helios is omniscient, but his round eye, which is always open up there in the sky, makes him an infallible witness; his gaze of light misses nothing whatever that takes place on the surface of the earth or waters. On the other hand, Helios knows nothing of what the darkness of the future holds. Only deities of another type, the oracular gods such as Apollo, can know the future. The power of Helios, like his knowledge, is related to the type of activity peculiar to this star. The function of the god sets a limit upon it. When he is angered all Helios can do is threaten to stop illuminating the world. If he attempted to alter the route taken by his chariot, the Erinyes would waste no time in bringing him back to the correct path.

What we find then is neither omniscience nor omnipotence but specific forms of knowledge and power between which certain oppositions may arise. The divine powers have natures sufficiently dissimilar for rivalry and conflict to exist between them. In Homer, Olympos is loud with the quarrels of the gods, in particular the arguments between Zeus and Hera. Of course, the Greeks were amused by such accounts but they knew very well that, over and above the anecdotal level, they expressed a serious truth: They saw the divine cosmos torn by tensions, contradictions, and conflicts over prerogatives and power. At the same time they were also conscious of the unity of the divine world, for all these turbulent and diverse gods are held in check by Zeus and his universal law. However, just as in the physical universe order depends upon a balance between opposed forces – the cold, the hot, the dry, and the wet – and as, in the city, peace results from agreement reached between contemporary groups, so the unity of the divine cosmos consists in a harmony between contrary powers. Although these divine powers may come into conflict and fight each other, man has no right to scorn any one of them, for each represents an authentic aspect of being, expresses one part of reality, stands for a particular type of value without which the universe would, as it were, be mutilated. Thus, when the pure Hippolytos devotes himself totally to Artemis, the virgin goddess, refusing to pay homage to Aphrodite, he is rejecting an entire aspect of the human condition. Aphrodite takes her revenge and Hippolytos meets his doom because he has refused to recognize that there is a part in each one of us that belongs to Aphrodite.

The gods are a part even of the contradictions and conflicts in the world, and they intervene in human affairs. The Greek feels their presence within him in the form of sudden impulses, in the plans and ideas that come into his head, in the panic or frenzy that grips the warrior, in a surge of love or a feeling of shame. This presence of the gods in the entire universe, in social life and even in men's psychological life, does not mean that there are no barriers between the divine and the mortal creatures; indeed, the barriers not only exist but are, in a sense, insurmountable. The gods are a part of the same universe as men, but it is a universe with a hierarchy, a world of different levels where it is impossible to pass from one to another. To this extent the society formed by the powers of the Beyond is an extension of the hierarchical organization of human society as it appears in Homer. The gods are as close to and as separate from men as the king is in relation to his subjects. Perhaps the comparison between the society of the gods and that of men can be taken even further. When the king is the mouthpiece of justice he is not obliged to obey a written law fixed in advance. Justice is actually established by his word and action and executed through his *themis*. Does this mean that the sovereign may do as he pleases? Not at all. His royal power rests on respect for the *timai*, the prerogatives, ranks, and traditional honors that make up the hierarchical order that is inseparable from his sovereignty. Of course, the king can ignore the *time* of others, ride roughshod over the rights of the next man, overreach his *moira*, exceeding the role that is properly his. But if he does so he unleashes forces that, by upsetting the order, recoil against him and threaten his sovereignty. He calls forth a dangerous curse from the man whose *time* he has not respected, a curse that will eventually bear poisonous fruit. In the council and among the people he arouses hostility, slander, and derision — in sum, popular "jealousy" that eventually destroys royal power just as the praise and admiration of his subjects reinforce its prestige and authority. The fact is that words of blame, defiance, and scornful mockery have the effect of diminishing the king, cutting him down to size, just as glorification by his people and by the poets increases the luster of his name and person.

One can see that faults on the part of the king bring into being powers that are, at one and the same time, religious, social, and psychological forces. Zeus' situation is very much the same as that of the king. Greek scholars have often pondered the problem of Zeus' relation to destiny as portrayed by Homer. At times Zeus appears to control destiny and it is he who decides it; at others he seems quite powerless before it and has no choice but to submit to it. This has been seen as a contradiction. But perhaps the problem has not been posed in the correct terms. The fact is that Homer does not conceive destiny as fixed once and for all, quite separate from and above Zeus and the gods as a whole; on the other hand, no more does he imagine that the gods are all-powerful, free always and everywhere to act as they please. Zeus' power is exercised subject to the same conditions as that of a king whose status is higher than that of his peers but whose rule is inseparable from a whole complex of prerogatives and honors. Thus, in the *Iliad* (XVI, 433 ff.), Zeus would like to save his son Sarpedon, who is destined, like all mortal men, to die, and is about to fall under the onslaught of the enemy. He is hesitating as to whether to intervene and alter the course of events when Hera gives him a warning. She tells him he may do as he pleases but she and the rest of the gods will not agree to support him.... If he carries Sarpedon off alive in defiance of the *moira* of human beings he should beware lest another god, in his turn, take it upon himself to do the same for his own children. Zeus heeds the warning and decides to submit rather than to spark a conflict of forces that would eventually threaten to topple not only the order of the universe but also his own supremacy.

Other expressions of this truth are extremely illuminating. In the *Iliad* (XVI, 849 ff.), a warrior on the point of giving up the ghost pronounces the following words, indicating where lies the responsibility for his death: "It is sinister destiny [$\mu o \hat{\imath} \rho' \, \delta \lambda o \acute{\eta}$] that has overcome me; it is the son of Leto [i.e., Apollo]; and, among men, it is Euphorbos." To our way of thinking this may seem like an over-abundance of explanations where one would have sufficed. But the Greek is more demanding. He knows very well that he is dying because his body has been pierced by the spear of his enemy. But after all it could have happened the other way about; the victory might have been his. The reason why it is not so is that he has had bad luck: He slipped during the fight, was blinded by the sun, or else his blow missed its mark. Such things can only be explained by the intervention of some god: Apollo must have intervened on the battlefield to settle an old score; he must have wished to avenge wrongs previously done him. But at the same time Apollo's resentment is in conformity with the law of destiny that insists that every wrong done to the gods shall be paid for and is the cause for men having been made mortal. Thus different explanations can be found for a single event according to which level of reality one has in mind. The various explanations are not mutually exclusive precisely because they do not refer to the same level.

So we can see how it is that the same religion can comprehend a deep feeling of the divine presence in almost everything that happens in human life and, at the same time, the equally strong conviction that man must manage on his own, that it is always first and foremost up to him to save himself. Like any other Greek, Odysseus believes that warrior frenzy and panic on the battlefield are directly inspired in men by the gods, but he also knows that the morale of a band of men is higher when they are fighting on a full stomach. So, against the advice of Achilles, he recommends that the soldiers should be fed and refreshed before returning to battle. There is no denying that the outcome of the war lies entirely in the hands of the gods, but the leaders should nevertheless keep a close eye on the running of it.

At the heart of Greek thought one can perhaps even discern a similar ambiguity with regard to the relationship between men and gods. Poets such as Homer and Pindar are constantly declaring that gods and men belong to two entirely separate races and that man should not seek to become the equal of the gods. "Recognize your limitations," "Be satisfied to be a man," "Know yourself": These are the maxims that express Greek wisdom. And yet, in certain circles — religious sects or schools of philosophy — we can detect a very different line of thought. Here, man is advised to develop the part of himself that is divine, to make himself as much like the gods as possible, to attempt, through purification, to accede to the immortality of the blessed, to become a god.

Two trends are also apparent in the kinds of classification of the powers of the Beyond, in the hierarchy of the society of the gods. The official religion makes clear distinctions between the various categories of supernatural powers. First, there are the *theoi*, the gods in the strictest sense of the term, with whom the *daimones* may be grouped and who occupy the dominant position in the divine world. Second, and below these, come beings who are connected with different rituals; they are known as heroes and are conceived as men who lived in former times on earth but who are now worshipped by the whole city. Finally there are those who are sometimes called the "blessed" or the "strong," that is to say the ordinary dead; they are anonymous powers who are the object of family piety in every home. Thus between the *theoi* at the top of the hierarchy and living men at the bottom of the scale there are the successive grades of the heroes and the dead. The grades remain quite separate, however; there is no communication between them. It is normally impossible for men to escape from their mortal condition. Among the philosophers, however, we find a different system of classification. For one thing the distance between men and gods is increased. The philosophers reject any anthropomorphic image of the divine. They have a purer and more rigorous conception of the divine essence. To this extent, with the philosophers the world of the gods is set further apart from men. But at the same time the *daimones* and the heroes, who have drawn closer together, constitute a class of intermediary beings whose function is precisely to mediate between the *theoi* and men, and to make it possible for the mortals to span the increased distance that separates them from the gods, allowing them to accede, step by step, to the status of hero, then of *daimon*, and then of god.

117

Thus, within the religious thought of the Greeks, there is as it were a tension between two poles. Sometimes it postulates a divine world that is relatively close to men, the gods making direct interventions in human affairs and existing alongside the mortals, while at the same time it conceives it to be impossible to span the gradations between man and the gods, impossible for man to escape his human condition. At other times it imagines a more clear-cut divide and a greater gap between gods and men, but on the other hand introduces the idea that men may rise to accede to the world of the gods.

Finally, this polarity is present in religion itself. On the one hand we find a civic and political religion whose essential function is to integrate the individual who accomplishes the religious rites into the social groups to which he belongs, defining him as a magistrate, a citizen, the father of a family, a host or a guest, and so on, and not to pluck him out from his social framework in order to elevate him to a higher sphere. In this religious context, piety, *eusebeia*, applies not only to the relations between men and the gods but also to all the social relations that an individual can have with his fellow citizens – his relatives, living or dead, his children, his wife, his hosts or guests, strangers, and enemies. In contrast is a religion whose function is, to some extent, the opposite, and that can be seen as complementing the state religion. This cult is addressed to gods who are not political, who have few or no temples, who lead their devotees away from the towns, into nature in the wild, and whose role is to tear individuals away from their ordinary social relationships and their usual occupations, alienating them from their own lives and from their very selves. Because women are less well integrated into the city than men and are specifically excluded from political life, this type of religion is especially associated with them. Since, as women, they are socially disqualified from participating in public affairs on an equal footing with men, from a religious point of view they are in a position to take part in cults that are, in a way, the opposite of the official religion. This "mystic" sense of religion, which differs so much from the communally shared Greek piety in its desire for escape, its cult of madness, *mania*, and its quest for individual salvation, manifests itself in social groups that are themselves peripheral to the city and its normal institutions. *Thiasoi*, brotherhoods, and mysteries are the basis for types of grouping that lie outside the family, tribal, and civic organization. Thus, through a kind of paradox, the powers of the Beyond that men created in particular social circumstances in turn have an effect on those very social conditions and cause new types of groups and new institutions to develop.

How should we conclude an inquiry that is both so long and at the same time so summary? I hope that, in conclusion, I may simply be allowed to stress once more the complexity of a religion such as that of the Greeks. The system itself is complex, as are the relations between it and social life; and at the very heart of the religious experience there is a polarity and tension, an awareness of the contradictions that exist in man, in the universe, and in the divine world. There is no doubt that this religious concept of a world that is at once harmonious and rent by conflict should be connected with the fact that it is the Greeks who are the inventors of tragedy.

Their's is a tragic vision because the divine is ambiguous and opaque, yet at the same time it is optimistic, for man has his own tasks that he can accomplish. I believe that today we are witnessing a kind of rebirth of this sense of the tragic in life; each of us is aware of the ambiguity of the human condition. Perhaps that is why these Greek gods who, as I earlier suggested, seem to form a kind of language, continue, when we listen to them, to mean something to us.

CHAPTER VI

The Pure and The Impure[1]

In his study on the ideas of the pure and the impure in Greek thought, Louis Moulinier was anxious not to impose any predetermined system on them, taking care not to interpret them in the light of our own concepts or of those attested among other peoples.[2] According to him, if we restrict ourselves to the Greek data alone, we cannot help but acknowledge the presence of such diversity as to discourage the formulation of any overall theory. In his study he seeks not so much to unify and explain the facts as to trace the hesitant development of a complex, diverse, and even sometimes apparently contradictory thought through the texts, rituals, and terminology of Greek thought, and even through the philosophy of Plato.

Moulinier's is a historical study ranging from the origins of Greek thought down to the end of the fourth century. He tells us that, so far as the origins are concerned, the testimony of Homer and Hesiod is all we have to go on. Neither archaeology nor linguistics can throw any light on the place of defilement and purification in the most ancient forms of religion among the Cretans and the Indo-European groups that settled in Greece during the second millennium. In particular, there is nothing to be learnt from the etymology of the word *agos*; and according to him there was in fact no real doublet *agos-hagos* that, underlining the link between the pure and the sacred, might have seemed to suggest a strictly religious origin for the concept of defilement. So we must limit ourselves to an examination of the texts and interpret them without any preconceived ideas on the possible nature of primitive Greek religion. Now, in Homer, he suggests, defilement has a purely material character. It is something dirty, a concrete stain of blood, mud, filth, or sweat. It is washed away with water. Man is pure when he is clean. Dirt is the only form of defilement. But physical cleanliness affects more than simply the body. The stain that makes it dirty blemishes the individual and makes him ugly; it affects his inner being, his social and moral personality. It also debars him from any contact with the gods; before taking part in any religious ritual, a man must wash himself. However, Moulinier appears to see this religious obligation as no more than a mark of courtesy shown to the divine powers. At the same time he notes that Homer makes a distinction between two kinds of washing, one of which is ritual, performed with lustral water, *chernips*, and has the purpose — according to one scholium — of "making a man resemble the god as much as possible."[3] Could it not be that physical cleanliness is, from the outset, seen as a religious value? The author does not appear to think so. In his view, all efforts directed toward cleanliness essentially reflect a desire for hygiene.[4] As he sees it, Hesiod's testimony supports that of Homer. He believes that the same positivist spirit imbues the long list, in the *Works*,[5] of the many ritual prohibitions so close, in their quaintness, to popular religion. Before approaching the divine, man must shed any physical dirt by washing and cleansing himself. The only difference is that, in Hesiod, this religious cleanliness takes on a more explicitly moral quality as it is the sign of man's obedience to the will of the gods.

Having considered the origins, Moulinier examines the state of ideas in the archaic period. He poses the problem in a familiar way: Does a new conception of defilement develop during the seventh and sixth centuries? This is, in fact, the period in which we find testimony for the ideas of the defilement of the murderer and the impurity of death, both apparently absent in Homer's day. Moulinier draws up a list of the innovations of this period. First, there are the cathartic rituals: the purificatory sacrifices — especially for murderers, the ritual of the *pharmakos*, the expulsion from sanctuaries of corpses and of perpetrators of sacrilege; then, figures such as Epimenides who were purifiers; new words such as *euageōs, agēs, enagēs, amiantos*; and, finally, the extension of old terms to cover a more moral meaning and apply to more abstract subjects, for example a city can now be described as "defiled." Should we conclude from this body of new practices and ideas that, as Glotz believed, the religious concept of defilement only appeared at this stage, in response to a desire for justice that was not satisfied in this period of crisis? In all honesty Moulinier finds that he cannot accept such a thesis, though it supports his original position. He points out that in the fifth century the Greeks traced the idea of all types of defilement, including that of the murderer, back to the earliest times. He emphasizes, quite correctly, that in the classical period, just as in the time of Homer, defilement continued to be thought of in a very concrete way. It is always a stain that is washed away by the purificatory sacrifice. It is simply that the matter in question has now become more subtle and can henceforth extend to more beings — to corpses, for instance. Besides, the fact that it is not mentioned by Homer cannot be considered as conclusive, for the defilement of the murderer may have taken a long time to be reflected in literature.

From the fifth century onward our information regarding ritual becomes more precise. Moulinier examines the various circumstances in which religious purifications were considered necessary: when a child was born, after a woman had given birth, before a sacrifice to the gods, at a death, and even, in certain cases, when the anniversary of the death came round, and, finally and above all, when murder had been committed. Defilement could affect men, families, cities, holy places, and even the gods themselves. The many types of defilement are matched by many different forms of ritual. There is not just one form of sacrifice but many different cathartic sacrifices. Lustrations employ water but also fire, sulphur, and plants such as the squill bulb or the fig, as well as incantations, the blood of the victim, and so on. Games and dances may have a purificatory value. Does this multiplicity of ritual forms indicate that the religious sensibility of the Greeks was obsessed with the idea of defilement? Some have thought so but Moulinier disagrees. In the official religion the quest for purity plays only a minor role: It is a means of preparation but never an end in itself. Apart from certain superstitious practices, religion was bent rather on obtaining release from defilement. It did so by imposing none too severe conditions, in some cases a time limit and in others statutory rituals and acts of reparation. Furthermore, defilement does not affect all spheres of life. Woman is never seen as an impure being, not even — according to Moulinier, who is perhaps over-emphatic here — when she is pregnant or at the time of her period. When legitimate, the sexual act is never impure. In sum, it could be said that the multiplicity of rituals reflects a general spirit of reserve and moderation. It is in the case of death, especially violent death and in particular homicide, that the community feels threatened by defilement and manifests a deep fear of contagion. By continuing to have contact with the murderer and by not refusing him access to the sanctuaries, public places, and city territory, each member of the community assumes the defilement of the murder and so the whole country eventually becomes affected and corrupted. In this instance defilement is indeed a *miasma*, a power of contagion that demands that the city should remain anxiously on its guard.

As well as the rituals, a study of the words used and intentions expressed in them should enable us to define the nature of this dangerous *miasma* more closely. But here again Moulinier alerts us to the existence of a disconcerting diversity. Defilement connected with murder remains, as in the past, associated with the image of the blood that spurts forth from the wound, staining the arms of the murderer and making him "the man with impure hands." This is not the only relevant image, however. The stain reaches the mind, *tas phrenas*, as well as the hands and body, and can even be indistinguishable from the personality of the murderer. Orestes declares, not that he has wiped out the stains of defilement in the course of his voyages, but that he has worn himself away in his contact with so many houses and paths.[6] The *miasma*, can always be purified by washing, but it can be "consumed" as well, it can be "lulled" and "dispersed." It is described as a stain but also as a "thing that flies," a "weight," a "sickness," a "trouble," a "wound," a "suffering." Nor is this all. Hitherto, all the many forms taken by the symbolism have related to the state of the murderer. Now, we know that in the fifth century his defilement left him at the frontier of his homeland. As soon as he ceased to tread the soil of his own city, the murderer could consider himself pure once more, as if he were leaving his defilement behind him in the place haunted by his victim. So the defilement no longer appears to be a part of the personality of the murderer, but is associated rather with the dead man and his anger and dangerous thirst for vengeance. It would seem that in order to purify the impurity it was necessary, not to wash away the stain from the guilty party, but rather to appease the rancor of the deceased. And indeed, when the victim, before dying, pardons the murderer, forswearing vengeance, the murderer is "undefiled" by the murder.

There is yet another problem. Whether the defilement is associated with the blood on the hands of the murderer or with the desire for vengeance on the part of the dead man, there is nothing to indicate that it had anything to do with the criminal intention. And yet it has. Quite apart from the distinction made between "voluntary" and "involuntary" murder, in some cases murder does not appear to have involved any impurity at all. Demosthenes tells us that the man who kills in certain conditions remains pure, *katharos* — if he kills by accident in the course of the games, at war when he has mistaken a friend for an enemy, when a man strikes down a traitor, a would-be tyrant or a man who had violated his wife, his mother, his sister, and so on. How is it that, despite the violent death and the bloodshed, there is no defilement in such cases? Demosthenes tells us that it is because the intention, *dianoia*, was not an evil one and the action conformed with the law. Moulinier even thinks that murders which were committed by pure chance, those that were *atuchēmata*, must also have been considered exempt from any stain of defilement. The only murders that had to be purified were those which appeared to imply wrongful intention. Thus pure "bad luck" in a case of homicide could be invoked in favor of the accused to free him from the stain of defilement from the bloodshed. Antiphon's chorus leader says that the important thing is to have one's own conscience clear, to have committed no fault and, if misfortune befalls, for it to be the result of chance, *tuchē*, not of injustice, *adikia*.[7]

But here we are faced with a new paradox. This same bad luck will at other times be interpreted as a proof of defilement; it will be taken to indicate criminal impurity in the individual afflicted with bad luck. Indeed defilement, bad luck, and misfortune can all be seen as aspects of the same thing. The impurity of the murderer becomes confused with the misfortune that it calls down upon him and everything around him. Thus, to prove his innocence, an accused may argue that nothing untoward has ever happened to the ship on which he has been voyaging.[8] From this point of view, fatality now condemns him (whereas in the previous instances it had exonerated the murderer from responsibility and from the stain of defilement); it is interpreted as the stain of defilement itself, pursuing the guilty man and dogging his steps.

Thus, a simple and unequivocal concept of defilement is no more conveyed by the terms used than by the rites. It appears as a material stain but also as something invisible. It is both objective and subjective, both external and internal to man. It is also both a cause and consequence; it unleashes a scourge and at the same time is the very scourge that it provokes. It is a part of the murderer, indeed *is* the murderer; yet it is just as much a part of the victim, it is his vengeful spirit. How is such contradictory thought to be understood? Moulinier does not believe that we should assume that the structures of Greek thought differed from our own. The human mind is always the same. The answer is simply that one must beware of seeking a logical unity in these representations, which are first and foremost expressions of an obsessive anxiety: Defilement is seen as anything that arouses this anxiety. Nevertheless, Moulinier does go on to make a remark that seems to us to touch on the essential point, although he lays no emphasis on it and does not seize upon its implications. He notes that while defilement is invariably connected with material objects it nevertheless has a "supernatural existence." But if it thus relates to two different levels, representing in the visible world the presence of a "power of the Beyond," should we not recognize in it the character of a religious force? However, not only has Moulinier from the start been anxious to reduce it to the − in our view, narrow − idea of physical dirtiness, but his book as a whole is aimed against any theories that attempt to restore the concept of the defiled, with all its contradictory aspects, within the context of religious thought.

This trend can be clearly seen in his chapter devoted to the relation of defilement to the gods and to what is holy. First, Moulinier criticizes the idea (often repeated since Rohde) that the Greeks regarded all types of defilement as religious powers of the nature of *daimones*, harmful spirits that, through motives of revenge, give rise to impurity and propagate it. Purifying defilement would, if this were the case, be a matter of appeasing their anger or of enlisting the help of the gods to combat them. Moulinier declares that, although one comes across belief in figures of this kind in tragedy, in the shape of the *alastopes* or *alitērioi* mentioned by Antiphon in the *Tetralogies*, this idea is strictly limited to drama. There is no evidence for it in the historians, the comic writers, or the orators. It does not reflect the thought of the people but is rather the view of poets or theorists promoting a new doctrine. On the contrary, the Greeks regarded defilement as inseparable from real material objects such as blood and dirt, or from concrete beings such as the murderer and the corpse. Similarly, purification is effected through physical operations involving washing or burning, not through action directed against spirits.

Moulinier then considers the theory according to which whatever is defiled is, in certain aspects, close to the sacred. And here again his thesis is altogether negative. In his view, the concepts of the sacred and the defiled are quite separate. Against the view of Eugen Fehrle,[9] Moulinier suggests that there is no connection between the two roots *ag-* and *hag-*. Thus, he distinguishes two quite distinct groups of terms; on the one hand, the terms *enagēs* and *enagizein* are connected with *agos* and the idea of defilement, on the other, the terms *hagizein, kathagizein,* and *exagizein* are connected with *hagnos* and *hagios* and the concept of the divine, seen as something pure, clean, and holy. He claims that no contact, shift in meaning, or interference exists between the two series of terms any more than there is any semantic connection between *agos*, meaning "defilement," and *hagnos–hagios*, denoting the quality of what is divine or what can enter into contact with the divine. He concludes that we are faced with "no ambiguity, not even a primitive one, between the sacred and the impure but, on the contrary, a profound connection linking the sacred, the pure and the moral."[10]

But this raises a problem. During the classical period defilement appears to be connected, *par excellence*, with death, and death manifestly has a sacred character. The dead man is both impure and at the same time consecrated. So, as well as the essentially pure sacred there exists a sacred that is "radically impure." Moulinier reveals himself to be aware of the fact which nevertheless, given the standpoint he has adopted, remains impossible to explain. It is not the case that there are two kinds of gods, one devoted to the sacred that is pure, the other to the sacred that is impure — that is to say, on the one hand the Olympians, the object of prayers and sacrifices, and on the other, the chthonic powers, the gods of punishment and misfortune, the objects of apotropaic rites. Depending on the time, the circumstances, and the place, the very same gods either preside over defilement or else delight in purity alone. What can all this mean? Moulinier sees it simply as evidence of a contradiction between the ideal and reality where things sacred and the gods are concerned. The Greek ideal – as revealed by any study of the terms used to denote purity – is that purity is inseparable from justice and from what is sacred. The reality, however, is that the gods, who are related to what is pure but who are "all too human," are themselves fallible. They too may err, hate, and defile themselves, as men do. It does not seem a very pertinent solution, for it is not the case that the gods simply defile themselves as men do; they control defilement, it is they who send it to men. One and the same god, Apollo, is both a healer and cause of sickness, he can both purify and taint. Admittedly, at certain times this double aspect may be seen as a contradiction between the ideal and reality, as for instance when the author of the *Sacred Disease* takes issue with the idea that defilement is sent by the gods; at other times or in other milieux, however, it indicates the presence in the divine of two opposed qualities that are felt to be complementary. At the conclusion of Moulinier's study the problem of the relation between defilement and the gods and the "relatedness" of the impure and the sacred seems to us as unresolved as ever.

Moulinier is certainly to be congratulated on having tried to analyze the pure and the impure respecting the complexity of the data and without yielding to the temptation of theoretical oversimplification. Perhaps, however, he himself has oversimplified in a different way. First, let us consider the question of origins. It would have been interesting to show how a physical state such as cleanliness can assume a religious significance. Furthermore, some indication should have been given of the different levels on which the concepts of dirt and cleanliness, which for us are essentially positivist,[11] come into play, and their religious implications should have been underlined. Even in Homer the "dirtiness" of blood is not simply a matter of a material stain; even when it has been washed away with water it is still necessary to purify the taint, *kaka*, with sulphur.[12] Equally, if it is no more than dirt besmirching the hands of the murderer, why does it call down misfortune upon him and upon those around him? Why does it strike the inhabitants of any house whose threshold he crosses with stupefaction, *thambos*?[13] And, if the term *apolumainesthai* in line 314 of Book I of the *Iliad* simply means the washing of a physical stain of dirt, and carries no overtones of religious defilement, why did the Greeks, having completed their ablutions, have to throw the *lumata*, that is, the polluted water, into the sea? It makes no sense if there is no more to it than dirty water. It makes more sense, however, if we remember that, after Agamemnon has sworn an oath calling down divine vengeance if perjury is committed, the body of the sacrificed boar, which is charged with a fearful religious power, is likewise cast into the sea.[14] Admittedly, in general Homer demonstrates a very positivist attitude toward defilement. We must even recognize that here, as in other domains, there is evidence that he adopts a deliberately positivist attitude determined to ignore certain aspects of religious thought. This means that the examples that do convey the religious implications of defilement acquire even greater significance. Equally, the rules listed in Hesiod's *Works* appear to us incomprehensible if we restrict ourselves to a narrow interpretation of the meaning of dirt. Material defilement is not there a function of a desire for hygiene but is to be seen in relation to a religious vision of the world. He tells us that at a feast of the gods one should not detach with black metal what is dry from what is green on the stem with five branches: In other words, one should not cut one's nails. But why should the nails be any dirtier than other parts of the body? Can they too not be washed? Hesiod also says that near the hearth one should not reveal parts of the body spattered with semen. This seems to indicate that semen is dirty. But Moulinier does not think that women's periods are considered to be dirty.[15] And elsewhere he refers, quite correctly, to Empedocles and Aristotle, according to whom this same semen, *gonē*, is composed of whatever is most pure, in man and in the world.[16] So the problem is not such a simple matter after all. According to Hesiod, it is also forbidden to wash in water in which a woman has bathed. Because it is dirty? Moulinier's explanation does not even satisfactorily account for the examples that seem most in his favor. For instance, it is forbidden to urinate at the source of rivers and where they meet the sea because, according to Moulinier, urine is dirty. But then it is equally forbidden to bathe there.

Dirt, as understood by Moulinier, does not explain to us what the Greeks called defilement. This is not a simple concept, sufficient unto itself and self-explanatory. Moulinier argues as if dirtiness were a property of certain things, as if it were an absolute quality, evident no matter what the circumstances. He suggests that blood is dirty and dust is dirty. But this is not always so. The blood that circulates in a man's body is not dirty. It is the very life in him. Yet when shed upon the ground or on the hands of the murderer or the corpse of the victim, it dirties and defiles them. Why is this? Is it because, from an entirely positivist point of view, it makes a mark there, covering up the surface? But then a cosmetic, a cream, or even a garment may also cover up the body yet they do not dirty it. And again, when shed on the altar, the blood of a sacrificed animal does not defile but, on the contrary, consecrates it. When blood is seen as something dirty and as a defilement it is because, when shed in certain conditions (especially if it is mingled with dust, *to luthron*), it represents murder, death, and thus belongs to a domain of reality that is the opposite of life and a threat to the living. Dust and mud on the human body are indeed considered as *lumata* that must be washed off before addressing the gods, for earth is made to cover up the dead, and when a relative of the dead spreads dust on his head it is a mark of his making contact with the world of death. In contrast to this, the Selli, the priests of Dodona, whose official duties demand that they be in constant contact with the powers of the earth, are ritually forbidden to wash their feet.[17]

Thus "physical" dirt, in the sense understood by Homer and Hesiod, can itself only be understood within the framework of religious thought. A "besmirchment" seems to indicate some contact that is contrary to a certain order of the world in that it establishes communication between things that ought to remain quite distinct from each other. Such a contact is the more dangerous the more powerful the objects concerned. Seen from this angle, Hesiod's text acquires its full significance. Nails should not be cut at the feast of the gods because the nail, detached from the body where the green and the dry meet, is a dead part of the man and, as such, it defiles the divine. The "dirtiness" of the nail consists in its impurity in relation to the gods. Semen is not dirty in itself; however, it defiles the fire of the hearth because Hestia, the virginal goddess, must — like Artemis or Athena — keep away from all contact with sex.[18] Woman, as such, is not unclean, but for a man it can be dangerous to bathe in the same water as her. Finally, the source and mouth of a river, the points where it emerges from the earth and enters the sea, are particularly dangerous, so man should avoid contact with them. He should treat them with respect, taking care not to urinate in them just as he does not urinate during the night, which is the time of the gods. He does not bathe in them either. In all these examples the physical disgust for whatever is felt to be unclean also reflects the religious fear of any contact that is forbidden.

Moulinier's position also seems to us open to objection from another point of view. In the course of his criticism of Rohde he declares that stains of defilement are not invisible *daimones* but, on the contrary, very concrete things, just as purifications are entirely material operations. But is the matter really so simple? Even if defilement seems generally — although not invariably — to be inseparable from visible objects, it transcends the concrete beings through which it is manifested. There is a supernatural side to it. And the purification aims, through the material operation, to bring about some result on a plane beyond that of its observable effects. When an individual pours lustral water over his hands before taking part in an act of worship he does indeed desire to cleanse himself, but in a wider sense than simply washing his body. In short, these are objects and operations with symbolic significance. Moulinier gives them a narrow interpretation that only considers the concrete beings who embody them as signs, and ignores the meaning they derive, on other levels of thought, from their relation to religious forces as a whole.

Moulinier's argument against the daemonic concept of defilement is, in our opinion, falsified by his failure to recognize its symbolic character. Taking certain remarks of Rohde quite literally,[19] he imagines the *daimōn* as a kind of individualized genius quite distinct from the concrete objects that confront man in his experience of the impure. Now, in religious thought, the salient characteristic of this type of supernatural power referred to by the term *daimōn* (with the indefinite plural *daimones* and the neuter form *daimonion*) is that, in contrast to the divine figures that are conceived as being external to our world, the *daimones* are not very clearly delineated; they operate in a diffuse and faceless manner on the lives of men. When portrayed stylistically in tragedy the *daimōn* can, as we have seen, acquire a more independent form and life of its own, and in other contexts it is more directly connected with the great personal gods and seen as the agent of divine chastisement. However, in general, as Louis Gernet points out, the *daimōn* is no more than "a situation in human experience in which religious thought finds a *numen* at work."[20] So it is indeed quite true that defilements are visibly embodied in concrete objects such as a particular blood-stain, criminal, or corpse; but what the concept of a *daimōn* conveys is the presence of a dangerous supernatural power in all these things insofar as they defile. Besides, we should note that even the personal gods who are conceived as external to the world have to manifest themselves through concrete objects and, in order to enter into contact with men, they too often make use of material things and operations. But even though the Greeks may parade, wash, and clothe a statue and may, when performing rituals, handle objects considered sacred, and even though they may call the thunder Zeus and fire Hephaistos, does this mean that, in these instances, the god is no longer distinguished from material things? Whether concentrated or diffuse, transcendent or immanent, the divine is only ever apprehended through its manifestations. Nor, to be sure, is it ever totally identified with whatever manifests its presence. The divine is in it yet always remains some distance beyond it. It is simply that the distance may be greater or less.

We are anxious to stress the symbolic nature of defilement because this makes it easier to understand how, despite the diversity of forms it assumes, it nevertheless retains a unity, never being fully identified with any one of them. Also, when seen as a religious force, it becomes more closely comparable to other forces of the same type which reflect a similar pattern of thought. To cite Louis Gernet, *hubris* and *atē* are at the same time powers of misfortune both external to man and within him, and the misfortune itself, the crime, the origin of crime, its consequences, and its retribution.[21] To say that all these aspects of syncretism can be explained in terms of a logic of participation would perhaps be too general a remark to be useful. However, we should like to point out that, in the religious thought of the Greeks, the category of action seems to be defined differently from in our own. Certain actions that run counter to the religious order of the world contain an unpropitious power that quite overwhelms the human agent. The man who commits such deeds is himself caught up in the force that he has unleashed. The action does not so much emanate from the agent as if he were its origin; rather, it overwhelms and envelops him, engulfing him in a power that affects not only him but a whole sequence of actions of greater or less duration that are influenced by him. The effects of the defilement thus cover a field of action in which the constituent parts and moments are all connected. In the case of murder, for example, the *miasma* is embodied in all the beings or objects that are involved in the crime: the murderer, the weapon, the blood, and the victim. If the crime is of a directly sacrilegious nature, the uncleanliness, in the form of a *loimos*, may even embrace an entire territory, causing the land to be infertile, the herds to be barren, and the children to be born deformed. The objects on which the power of the *daimōn* works comprise a whole more or less extensive system of human, social, and cosmic relations the order of which has been upset by the sacrilegious disruption. Basically, it is this disorder that the defilement makes manifest through all the various concrete forms it adopts. There is one last point on which we feel obliged to take issue with Moulinier's thesis. He is quite right to point out that there is no such thing as "the sacred" in general, but rather many different forms of the sacred, whether they be pure or impure, which vary according to whether they are linked with the gods, with the city or with the dead. But is he not oversimplifying here too when he denies that there was any ambiguity for the Greeks between what is sacred and what is defiled?

Since the publication of Moulinier's book, an article by Pierre Chantraine and Olivier Masson has examined the problem from a philological point of view and has come to conclusions quite different from those of Moulinier.[22] Against Moulinier, who does not believe in the existence of an ancient *hagos*, the doublet of *agos*, these scholars show that the compound words in -*agēs* cannot be related to *agos*, meaning defilement. Semantically they must be related to *hagios*: They express a relation to the awesome domain of the divine. This is evident in the case of *euagēs*, which clearly has nothing to do with defilement and means that one is in a good state as regards the *agos*. The same goes for *enagēs* which has the opposite meaning. The term does not refer to the state of those who are defiled, but to those who are caught up in the *agos*, who are in the power of the *agos*. The construction of *enagēs* plus the genitive of deity does not mean defilement of the deity, but rather, in the power of the deity. In *Oedipus Rex* (656-7), it is clear that *enagēs* is the equivalent of *enorkos*, and to be *enorkos* is to find one-self in the grip of the power that is immanent in the object by which the oath has been sworn. Similarly, through the curse that he pronounces against himself, Creon gives himself over to a fearful power: From that time on he belongs to it but, by the same token, he is protected against all profane attacks. Finally, in the *Supplices* (122), the adjective is given its favorable meaning and signifies the offerings consecrated to the god. The verb *enagizein* does not mean, as Moulinier supposes, to behave as an *enagēs*, that is to say as a man defiled by the death of a close relative. The word does, it is true, refer to the chthonic sacrifice for the dead and the heroes, but with the meaning indicated by Stengel of *tabu facere*. It is a matter of liquid libations or blood directly offered to the gods of the under world, "poured out into the sacred world." Finally *agos* itself cannot be fully understood unless its meaning of defilement is connected with the wider concept of the sacred that is forbidden, a domain that is dangerous for man. In the words of the oath sworn by the Greeks before Plataea: "Let there be an *agos* for those who perjure themselves." The word denotes the dangerous power that the perjuror must fear. As well as its meaning of sacrilege, the term retains a reflection of its connection with *hagios*: In the *Choephori* (155) and in *Antigone* (775), it refers not to a sacrilegious defilement nor, as Moulinier would have it, to the impurity inseparable from the victim of an expiatory sacrifice, but to an action performed in accord with the world of the gods. Hesychius explains the term as follows: *agos, hagnisma, thusia.*[23] More generally, the ambivalence of *agos*, which was appreciated by the ancient Greeks, is attested in the article *agos* of the *Sunagōgē* and in Photius' lexicon, and most notably in *Et. Magnum* (12, 26) and Eustathius, *ad Iliad* (13, 56, 55-60).[24]

If we may now pass on to the terms in the second group, we again find that some of them, in particular *hagizein*, support the argument in favor of the existence of an ancient *hagos* and that, overall, they cannot be isolated from the terms in the first group. The connection between *kathagizein* and *enagizein* is evident: Both denote total consecration, through fire in the case of the former, through libations in the case of the latter. *Exagizein* does not mean to exclude from the sacred, but to deliver up entirely to the sacred, *ek* (ex) indicating that the action is completed. Thus Eustathius can connect *exagistos* with *enagēs* meaning defiled, accursed, wholly in the power of the *agos*. However, the same term can also take on the opposite meaning of very holy, very sacred, as in the case of the *exagista* mentioned in *Oedipus at Colonus* (1526). Here again we find an ambivalence. Finally, the meanings of *hagnos* and *hagios* are not fundamentally different from that of *agos*. They refer to what is forbidden, prohibited in the sacred. This is the same idea as that conveyed by *agos* but there is one difference: *Hagnos* and *hagios* suggest a distance, the barrier that must not be crossed, the mystery that must be respected; *agos* refers to the same religious power when it takes hold of men and delivers them up to the deity. The first two terms are related rather to that which makes the divine, as such, untouchable; the latter to the power that possesses man when he is in contact with the sacred. So it would appear that there are not two independent series of terms after all, but rather one semantic group embracing polar notions that in general can be expressed in the opposition *agos–hagnos*, but each of which can also be detected to a greater or lesser degree in each series; and the etymology of this semantic whole is connected with *hazonai*: the respectful fear that the sacred inspires.

According to this interpretation, the concept of defilement is connected with one of the aspects of the sacred, namely its awful nature. It now becomes easier to understand how it is that some supernatural beings are seen both as defilements and as forms of the sacred. From one point of view in religious thought the "purity" of a divine power is in effect gauged by the number and strictness of the interdictions that protect it. Even as these reinforce the purity they multiply the possibilities of sacrilegious defilement in the god's relations with men. But if this progression is carried to its ultimate conclusion the two opposed poles of the pure and the defiled meet and become one. Ultimately, what is pure is that which is totally forbidden, that is to say, whatever living men must never come into contact with. Thus the sacred that is perfectly pure may be altogether abominable to men, since any contact with it becomes a defilement that delivers him up to the power of its *agos*. The powers of death are certainly of this type. For man, they represent the defilement *par excellence*; in themselves they are the "χθόνιοι δαίμονες ἁγνοί" mentioned by

Aeschylus,[25] or the "ἁγνή" Persephone. To enter into direct contact with death is to be so completely overtaken by defilement that, by this very token, one is at the same time liberated – one is still a source of defilement for other living men but, because definitively excluded from the profane life, one is, in fact, "consecrated." The living are defiled by the dead but consecrated by Death. When the defilement is so total that it takes over one's whole being, nothing escaping it, it is no longer defilement but sacredness. In certain cases the logic behind sacrilege is not very different. When Tiresias sees what men are forbidden to see, that is, Pallas naked in her bath, death overtakes his eyes; but this defilement on his face is none other than the religious power that qualifies him to be a diviner: Because he is blind to the light he can see what is invisible. Thus sometimes defilement can be seen as the reverse side to a positive religious quality, the effect of a supernatural power on one whose religious standing is inadequate to receive it. We can now see how it is that defilement may carry a religious force, that the very blood and dust that defile may also consecrate, the cloths stained with menstrual blood and the garments of women who have died in child-birth may be consecrated to the *hagnē* Artemis, and the bones of the dead or of a criminal, of a sacrilegious being, an abominable creature such as Oedipus or the *pharmakos*, may also be the source of blessings for a whole country. What must be done is to find ways to channel the religious power in the direction of what is good.[26]

This idea of making use of the sacred by means of a system of rites and rules that govern its intervention in the human world reflects another need in religious thought. If these extreme cases in which man loses himself in the divine represented the only means of entering into contact with it, the religious organization of earthly life would be impossible. This other concept of the sacred as something usable and used appears to be what the term *hieros* denotes, just as *agos* refers to the idea of the sacred possessing a man, and *hagnos* (originally at least) referred to the concept of the sacred that is doubly forbidden, being, on the one hand, dangerous to man and, on the other, itself pure from every profane contact.

Moulinier would no doubt counter this interpretation with the objection that he has already made to Williger's thesis: If *agos* refers to the religious fear inspired by the divine, how can it also mean exactly the opposite, namely that with which man can come into contact without danger — in other words, no longer that which is forbidden but that which is permitted?[27] We should note that the word *hosios* undergoes the same semantic evolution: When applied to the mysteries it retains its stronger meaning, but it can also come to mean the profane interests of the city as opposed to those things that are *hiera*. The fact is that, in the Olympian religion, where emphasis is laid essentially upon the regular organization of relations between man and the divine, the concept of what is sacred comes to be, as it were, "extenuated and intellectualized" (*exténuée et intellectualisée*).[28] However, the very way that religious thought operates, and the ambiguity of ideas that it exploits, suggest a number of internal reasons for the way it has evolved. A comparison of the same episode as it appears on the one hand in the *Supplices* and, on the other, in *Oedipus at Colonus* shows how the Greek mind inclines in opposite directions depending upon whether it conceives the *hagneia* in relation to that which is divine and consecrated or in relation to that which is not. At the beginning of the former tragedy the Danaids, having sought sanctuary on a holy hill in front of the communal altar of Argos, consecrate themselves as suppliants to the gods of the city. Seated here, ἐν ἁγνῷ, they are separated and protected from the world more effectively than if they were surrounded by a wall. But when Oedipus and Antigone take a rest, sitting in the grove consecrated to the Eumenides, overlooking Athens, the holy place (which they are, incidentally, urged to leave) is called χῶρος οὐχ ἁγνὸς πατεῖν. The *hagneia* gave protection to the consecrated suppliants but it repulses Oedipus and threatens him with defilement. Thus the same holy place may be *hagnos* in relation to itself or to consecrated beings, and *ouch hagnos* in relation to the actions of one who is profane. If we now turn to consider the matter from the standpoint of the other term in the relationship, namely the *hagneia* in man, the same interplay of relative ideas shows us how it comes to take on a significance that is the opposite of its original meaning of forbidden. For the suppliants, the *hagneia* is a positive quality conferred upon them by the holiness of the place, and it makes them "untouchable" too. But, for Oedipus, the *hagneia* seems, on the contrary, to refer to a quite negative quality of abstention: respect shown for a prohibition. Because he oversteps the bounds his sacrilegious defilement sets him apart from other men, just as the purity of the Danaids does: So he too becomes "untouchable." The Coryphaeos refuses to approach him until he has purified his defilement. Consecration and sacrilege are two positive qualities which produce similar effects although their significances are opposite. In contrast, "purity," for Oedipus, would not confer any kind of consecration upon him but would simply make it permissible for him to have dealings with other men: He would be *hagnos* in relation to them in the sense that there would be no danger of him defiling them. Here the word takes on the meaning of a permitted contact. It is this purely negative quality of *hagnos* that is dominant in the use of the verb *hagneuein*, which does not generally have the meaning of "to purify" or "to consecrate," but merely "to hold oneself at a distance from defilement." Characteristically, the expression can be used equally well to convey two opposite emphases, to refer to the sacred that holds itself apart from the defiled and also to the defiled that holds itself apart from the sacred; so that, provided that they respect the ritual prohibitions connected with their particular form of defilement, it can be said of both the murderer and the woman giving birth that each *hagneuei*.

Moulinier's objection, then, appears not to be decisive. From the point of view we have indicated it does perhaps become possible to understand how it is that, depending upon the context and level of meaning, the relation between the defiled and the sacred may assume very different aspects. Moulinier's study is valuable as a historical analysis of the many different concrete forms the pure and the impure may take. We believe, nevertheless, that it was necessary to relocate such a historical perspective within the framework of religious thought. Moulinier does not appear to us to have fully understood that a body of religious thought constitutes a system in which the various concepts are defined and are modified in relation to each other. It is a system of symbols the logic of which may not take exactly the same form as our own.

CHAPTER VII

Between the Beasts and the Gods[1]

From the Gardens of Adonis to the

Mythology of Spices

Marcel Detienne's quest for the gardens of Adonis leads him to take us by the long way round. This is the same route Plato mentions when he advises those seeking the truth to follow patiently along every bend in its winding way. We have to leave the well-trodden paths of mythology and, as we do so, the mirage of the conventional view of the East, transplanted to Greek soil, melts away – the mirage to which we have become accustomed and that the historians of religion at the turn of the century explored exhaustively (as they believed) without ever encountering there any other forms or species than those they had already classified and listed. They found, for instance, a god who disappears in the full flower of youth, vegetation that dies and is revived each year, and the spring reawakening of the forces of nature that slumber through the cold winter or are consumed under the burning summer sun. In this book we discover new horizons, a landscape full of perfumes, extraordinary plants and marvellous beasts, an unknown land retaining all the appeal of a fairy tale country yet whose features are delineated with all the rigorous austerity and sober logic of a scale diagram. There are Herodotus' fabulous stories to fascinate us, telling of the harvesting of spices in the Land of the Sun. Starting with myrrh and ending with lettuce, we see displayed before us the full range of plants in whose context Adonis' story is set. The whole scale of the animal kingdom rises before us, stretching from the beasts that fly to those that grovel:

At the top is perched the eagle, then come the vulture, the bat, and the winged snake; at the very bottom lurk the snakes of both water and land. But with the rising of the fabled phoenix the two ends of the scale are brought together. The phoenix belongs far above the eagle, close to the sun, yet it is in the form of a larva, a worm born of corruption, that it must be reborn from its own ashes and thus, all of a sudden, we behold it placed lower than the snake and even closer to the earth and waters. We see how the sad stories of Adonis and his mother Myrrha are interwoven with those of Mintha or Mint, Phaon the ferryman, Iunx the wry-neck bird and sorceress, and Ixion the ungrateful, the father of the Centaurs. We are truly once again in the land of fairy tales, but the pleasure we once felt there as children is now supplemented by the scholarly interpretation of a code, or rather, of many interlocking codes that offer us the keys to a whole mental universe different from ours, not easy to penetrate, even disconcerting, yet in some ways familiar. It is as if the Greeks had used these fantastic and marvellous tales to transmit as clearly as possible the code to statements in which they express their own distinctive view of the world. It is this code that Detienne helps us to decipher.

Such is this book that simultaneously affords us both delight and instruction. As for the former, we can do no more than express the pleasure we have experienced in reading it — and above all, in rereading it. As for the latter, no book can have less need of an introduction. It is self-sufficient and speaks for itself. So rather than write a preface to it, I should prefer to accompany the author on his way to raise and discuss certain questions about some of the guiding themes in his inquiry.

My first question is this: How should we interpret a myth such as that of Adonis? The Frazerian type of classical interpretation saw Adonis as an example of the "spirit of vegetation." Detienne rejects this from the outset, but he also challenges the over-facile global comparisons that attempt to assimilate one myth to another without taking any account of the particularities of different cultural systems. The attempt to decipher the story of Adonis by tracking down, here and there, gods and heroes that appear analogous to him implies three interdependent assumptions that are bound to affect the entire view of the myth. In the first place, it is assumed that every mythical figure can be defined as a separate entity in and by himself and that he possesses some sort of essence; second, that this essence corresponds to some reality which, in the last analysis, must be considered to be a part of the natural world since it is found to be represented by one god or another in the most widely differing civilizations. The third assumption is that the relationship between the mythical figure and the reality it represents is a "symbolical" one, in other words, that it rests upon metaphor or analogy: Thus, Adonis is born of the myrrh tree, therefore he embodies a spirit of vegetation; he spends a third of his life in the underworld and the remainder with Aphrodite in the light of the sun, therefore he embodies the spirit of wheat in the same way as Persephone does. This threefold hypothesis has already been completely demolished by the work of Georges Dumézil and Claude Lévi-Strauss. A god has no more one particular essence than a single detail of a myth is significant on its own. Every god is defined by the network of relations that links him with and opposes him to the other deities included within a particular pantheon; and similarly, a single detail in a myth is only significant by virtue of its place within the ordered system to which the myth itself belongs. So the Greek scholar must start again from scratch. It is not that he totally rejects the comparative method; on the contrary, he has constant recourse to it, but he applies it from a different standpoint, giving it a different meaning. Now the comparisons are made within the context of the particular civilization to be studied, by making systematic cross-references between cycles of legends that seem, at first sight, to revolve around figures having nothing to do with each other. The partitions separating the purely mythological tradition from evidence from other areas of the material, social, and spiritual life of the Greeks are done away with. The aim is to define, as one proceeds, as exhaustively as possible, the framework within which the myth must be set so that every detail in its structure and episodes may take on a precise meaning that can, in every case, be confirmed or refuted by reference to other parts of the body of data as a whole. The comparison is only valid insofar as it is carried out within a definite field of inquiry that can adequately ensure, on the one hand, comprehensiveness and, on the other, internal coherence. With an aim such as this the nature of the work of comparison becomes infinitely more demanding. The study takes just as much account of differences as of similarities, or – to be more precise – it does not attempt to establish analogies between figures or legends of different types but rather to establish the relative positions of various elements within a single complex. Thus it distinguishes separations, distances, intervals, and inversions as well as points of symmetry, with the final aim of establishing an ordered system. Instead of postulating as if it were self-evident that Adonis is equivalent to vegetation and so connecting this Greek god at times with deities of the *dema* (tubercules) type, and at others with the Oriental gods who die and are reborn in accordance with the cycle of plant life, the study tries to identify accurately the position occupied by myrrh, considered as a species of spice, within the hierarchical classification of plants which the Greeks elaborated. This method gives rise to a number of consequences that affect questions of procedure as well as problems of content. The field of inquiry must inevitably embrace all the evidence concerning the Greeks' view of the relation of the spices to other plants. This evidence includes the writings of botanists, doctors, and philosophers, the use of incense in religious ritual and of perfumed ointments in daily life. Thus, as the investigation widens it involves the progressive deciphering of a botanical code whose components range from the myrrh from which Adonis was born to the lettuce that became his deathbed. The structure of this code appears to be strictly based upon a vertical axis passing from the "solar" plants that are hot, dry – even

146

scorched — incorruptible, and perfumed, to the plants from below that are cold, wet, and raw, and are closely connected with death and foul smells. In between these two extremes, occupying an intermediate position at what one might call the "right" distance, are those plants that in the Greek view correspond to the normal life of civilized men, in other words the cereals, cultivated plants in which the dry and the wet are balanced and that constitute a specifically human type of food. Far from embodying the spirit of wheat, Adonis' position is sometimes above and at other times below the cereals; never does he belong to the same sphere as they. His destiny leads him directly from myrrh to the lettuce and this is, in a sense, an indication that he bypasses the cereals which lie quite outside his path. It thus illustrates the temptations and dangers of a way of life that would seek to elude normality.

To indicate the differences between the traditional form of interpretation and the type of study that Detienne, following Lévi-Strauss, proposes, we could say that a shift has taken place from a naturalistic symbolism of a global and universal kind to a system of complex, differentiated social coding characteristic of one culture in particular. We use such terms as "system" and "social" advisedly. For the botanical code does not and could not stand in isolation. It is interlocked with a number of other codes which constitute so many different levels of approach, each one complementing the others. In the first place there is the zoological code for which the evidence is, first, the stories in Herodotus, which introduce certain categories of animals to act as the necessary mediators between man and the spices; and, second, the myths about the Phoenix, the spice bird. Then there is the dietary code, in which the vegetable kingdom is subdivided into the three categories of food reserved for the gods, food for the humans, and pasture for the wild animals. Finally, there is the astronomical code, in which the spices are placed under the sign of Sirius, the Dog Star, whose appearance marks the moment when earth and sun, normally distant from each other, are in the closest proximity: It is a period both of extreme danger and also of the wildest exaltation.

In this way we discover that the decoding of the body of evidence is based upon a series of oppositions linked with one another: below–above, earth–heaven, wet–dry, raw–cooked, corruptible–incorruptible, stench–perfume, mortal–immortal; these terms, which are at times united and brought together through intermediaries and at others set apart and mutually exclusive, are organized into a coherent system. The validity of this interpretation – or, to use a term from linguistics, its pertinence – is confirmed by the fact that these same pairs of antinomies, arranged in the same order, reappear each time the Greeks are concerned with the power and functions of myrrh or spices, whether in their "scientific" writings or in the most diverse myths and religious rituals. Seen as a whole, this system appears to have a fundamental social significance: It expresses how a group of people in particular historical circumstances sees itself, how it defines its condition of life and its relationship to nature and the supernatural.

We are thus led to pose a second category of problems, this time not merely concerning the methodological question of how a myth should be read, but of a more fundamental kind: What, in the final analysis, does this myth mean, and in what sense does it have a meaning? In order to understand how the story of Adonis is linked to the ritual of the Adonia, Detienne distinguishes two central themes around which the whole body of relevant evidence is organized and that form, as it were, the keystones in the structure of the various codes that he shows to be strictly economical.

The first theme concerns foodstuffs and eating practices. It is most fully expressed in the structure of the sacrificial meal, in which spices have a definite and significant role. Sacrifice separates the man from the beast despite their common nature. Both are mortal animals; both, to survive, need to keep up their strength each day by taking in food that itself is perishable. However, man's food consists of plants that have first been cultivated, such as cereals, or of the cooked meat from domesticated animals such as the beasts that are reserved for sacrifice — in other words, food that is, in every sense of the term, "cooked." Animals, on the other hand, feed upon wild plants and raw flesh, that is to say food left in its original "raw" state. Sacrifice also separates men from the gods, marking the opposition between them with the very action whose purpose is to unite them. In the religion of the city-state the sacrificial ritual is the normal channel of communication between earth and heaven. However, through its very form, this contact emphasizes the radical disparity in status between the mortals who inhabit the sublunary world and the immortals who, forever young, are enthroned in the luminous heights of the ether. Man's share of the sacrificed animal is the dead, corruptible meat; the gods' share is the smoke from the charred bones, the smell of perfumes, and incorruptible spices. The ritual that brings men and gods together at the same time sanctifies the fact that it is impossible for man to have any direct access to the divine and to establish with it a true commensality. Thus in the context of blood sacrifice, the cornerstone of the state religion, spices and myrrh represent the portion allotted to the gods alone, the portion that men could never assimilate and that remains outside their nature and alien to it, despite the place they assign to it in their dietary rituals. Within the context of sacrifice, which is a model for normal human eating habits, myrrh does indeed appear as an instrument of mediation, the link between opposites, the path connecting earth to heaven. At the same time, however, its status and position in the hierarchy of plants gives it the further significance of maintaining the distance and establishing the separation between these two opposites. It represents the inaccessible character of the divine, the fact that men must renounce the far-off heavenly Beyond.

The second theme is marriage. Here myrrh and the spices again have a role to play. This time they do not take the form of fragrant incense rising up to the gods, inviting them to associate themselves with the meal of the mortals, but of perfumes whose aphrodisiac powers provoke feelings of desire and thus bring the

two sexes together. Here the mediation does not operate verti-
cally between the world below, given over to death, stench, and
corruption, and the world above, forever unchanging in the shining purity of the sun, but horizontally, at ground level, through
the attraction that draws men and women irresistibly toward each
other. The allure of erotic seduction is a part of marriage just as
the spices are a part of sacrifice; but it is neither its basis nor a
constituent element in it. On the contrary, it remains, in principle, alien to the tie of marriage. Although its presence is necessary – since on their wedding day young couples are crowned with
myrtle and sprinkle each other with perfumes – it presents both
an internal and an external threat to marriage. There is an internal threat because if the wife abandons herself to the call of desire
she rejects her status of matron and assumes that of the courtesan, thus deflecting marriage from its normal end and turning it
into an instrument for sensual enjoyment. Pleasure is not the
object of marriage. Its function is quite different: to unite two
family groups within the same city, so that a man can have legitimate children who "resemble their father" despite being the issue
of their mother's womb, and who will thus be able, on the social
and religious level, to continue the line of their father's house to
which they belong. The danger from this threat from within is
greatest during the canicular period which is not only the time
when the earth, being close to the sun, gives off all its perfumes,
when the spices that have reached maturity must be gathered if
they are to prove efficacious, but also when women, however
chaste and pure, are in danger of abandoning themselves to the
lasciviousness which totally overwhelms them at this period, and
of changing, under the influence of the summer sun, from model
wives into shameless debauchees. The seduction of desire also
presents an external threat to marriage. One of the striking features of the Greek civilization in the classical period is that true
relationships of love, whether heterosexual or homosexual, occur
outside the home. The pseudo-Demosthenes puts it as if it were
an incontrovertible fact: "We have courtesans for pleasure...and

wives in order to have a legitimate posterity and a faithful guard-
ian of the hearth" (*Contra Neera*, 162).

It is not difficult to see then that the vegetable, astronomical, and dietary codes do not apply to the sacrificial meal alone.
They do indeed provide a logical framework for this meal, within
which it assumes its allotted place: in an intermediary position
half-way between the raw and the burned, the rotten and incorruptible, the bestial and the divine. Its position confers upon it
a status that exactly corresponds to that of the cereals, which,
positioned as they are in between the plants that are cold and wet
and the spices that are hot and dry, stand for the truly civilized
life, the type of existence led by men who are tied to the earth
they must cultivate by farming in order to live. Their position is
half-way between, on the one hand, the bloody bestiality of the
wild beasts that devour each other raw, and, on the other, the pure
felicity of the Immortals who need do nothing to enjoy every kind
of good, as used to be case for men in that bygone Golden Age
before Prometheus' crime occasioned the institution of sacrifice –
which is the sign of the human race's definitive separation from
the race of the gods.

However, these codes also concern marriage, whose position,
within the same system, is strictly equivalent to that of sacrifice.
Monogamous marriage is a solemn public contract placed under
the religious patronage of Zeus and Hera, which unites two families through the union of a man and a woman. In the eyes of the
Greeks it thus raises the relationship between the sexes to the
level of "civilized" life. You could say that marriage is to sexual
consummation what sacrifice is to the consumption of meat: Both
assure continuity of existence to mankind, sacrifice by making
it possible for the individual to subsist throughout his life and marriage by affording him the means of perpetuating himself after
death through his child. The "wild" state involves first and foremost, to be sure, cannibalism and the eating of raw meat: Wild
beasts all devour each other, and raw to boot. But it also involves
generalized sexual promiscuity: They have sexual relations with

each other, crudely, in broad daylight, as chance dictates. The off-spring born of these unregulated wild unions have admittedly a mother to whom they are linked by the natural, animal bond of childbirth; but they have no father. Without marriage there can be no paternal filiation, no male line of descent, no family — all of which presuppose a link which is not natural, but social and religious. Within the system the Golden Age represents the oppo-site pole to the wild state, its exact counterpart, since, instead of living like beasts, men then still lived as gods. During this age men put no living creature to death nor ate any meat. They knew neither sexual union nor the eating of meat, and since the race of women was not yet created men did not need to be either con-ceived or engendered but were born directly from the earth.

So the human condition is exactly like that of the cereal plants. During the Golden Age, before the institution of sacrifice, fruits and corn germinated spontaneously in the soil. It was as unnec-essary to plough the land and plant it with seed in order to reap the harvest as it was to labor with women and fill their wombs with seed in order to obtain children from them. The sacrificial meal, instituted by Prometheus, has two effects. It introduces a diet in which the consumption of cooked meat from domesti-cated animals goes along with agricultural labor and the harvest-ing of cereals. Its other immediate consequence is, as Hesiod tells us, the appearance of the first woman and the establishment of marriage. The fact is that for the Greeks marriage is a form of ploughing, with the woman as the furrow and the husband as the laborer. If the wife does not, in and through marriage, become cultivated, cereal-producing land, she will not be able to produce valuable and welcome fruits — that is, legitimate children in whom the father can recognize the seed that he himself sowed as he ploughed the furrow. Demeter, who is the goddess of agriculture, is also the patroness of marriage. When a young girl enters into marriage she enters the domain that belongs to the deity of cere-als. To enter this domain and remain there she must rid herself of all the wild character inherent in the female sex. This wildness can take two, opposed forms. It might make the woman veer toward Artemis, falling short of marriage and refusing any sexual union, or, on the other hand, it might propel her in the opposite direction, beyond marriage, toward Aphrodite and into unbridled erotic excess. The position of the *gunē enguētē*, the legitimate wife, is in between that of the *korē*, the young girl defined by her virginal status, and that of the *hetaira*, the courtesan entirely devoted to love. Shunning contact with males, living far from men and the life of the city, the *korē*, like Artemis, the virgin huntress, mistress over wild animals and uncultivated land, shares in the life in the wild that is symbolized, in the marriage rites, by the crown of thorny plants and acorns. The civilized life of a wife, the "milled wheat" life as it was called, was symbolized in the marriage ceremony by winnowing basket, pestle, and bread, and opposed to life in the wild as good is to evil. To accede to this life the virgin had to renounce the wildness that hitherto held her at a distance from man. The yoke of marriage domesticated her, in the strongest sense of the term. By belonging henceforth to one of the family hearths of which the city was composed she became integrated, so far as any woman could be, into the civic community.

Like that of the *korē*, the position of the courtesan is also outside marriage, but toward the opposite extreme. Her wildness consists not in a hatred and intractable rejection of the male but in an excessive seductiveness and unbridled license. As she gives herself to the passing embraces of whoever comes along she fosters in each of her men the dangerous, seductive illusion of a life all perfume and spices, which, in relation to the life of milled wheat, occupies the opposite pole to the life of acorns. Under the beguiling mask of sweet Aphrodite, the *hetaira* reintroduces into the very heart of the civilized world the very same general sexual promiscuity that used to reign in the wild times before civilization.

Positioned as it is between, on the one hand, a radical rejection of physical union and, on the other, exaltation of the pleasures of love to the exclusion of all else, lying between sexual impotence and an excess of sexual potency, both of them equally infertile, marriage like the cereals stands for the "right distance": This alone can guarantee that the labor of marriage will bring forth an abundant harvest of legitimate fruits of good stock.

Marriage brings us a stage further on from sacrifice in our decoding of the myth. The analysis of sacrifice was necessary to interpret every level of the code implicit in the story of Adonis and the network of oppositions on which it rests. However, that analysis did not produce an interpretation capable of revealing how the story conveys a unified message, having a general significance as such, within the context of Greek culture. Marriage on the other hand leads us straight to this interpretation. Although on the face of it the myth does not appear to be any more concerned with marriage than with sacrifice, its silence on these themes is not comparable in the two cases. The fate of Adonis is not directly related to sacrifice, although we find the same system of codes at work in both. On the other hand it does involve the status of marriage directly. You could say that the silence of the myth on this point makes it a story about non-marriage. Implicitly it speaks of erotic seduction in its pure, fundamentally extra-marital state. Every detail in the myth acquires its significance when related to the state of marriage – which, to the Greeks, represented the correct norm, and which for this reason does not need to be explicitly mentioned to remain the constant point of reference and essential theme of the entire story. The author's demonstration of this point seems to be conclusive. I shall not here repeat or summarize it, but only emphasize some of its important features.

We have already pointed out that in passing directly from myrrh, from which he originates, to lettuce, which becomes his deathbed, Adonis cuts the cereals out of the vegetable code on whose axis they held a central position. But put in this way, this remark does nothing to further our search for the meaning of the myth. Adonis in fact has nothing to do with the consumption of particular foods. He is the irresistible seducer whose erotic powers of attraction are capable of bringing together the most opposite of terms, terms that would normally remain widely separated

154

from each other. Adonis is a human being, yet hardly is he born than he arouses the love of goddesses. He brings gods and men together, inspiring an equally passionate love for him in both Persephone of the Underworld and the heavenly Aphrodite. As he moves between the two of them he links heaven and earth together. He is himself the product of a union between a man and a woman who are, sexually speaking, set poles apart and should never have been united: a father and his daughter. The circumstances of his birth encapsulate all the themes which are to be illustrated in the adventures of his brilliant but brief career. His mother is initially a young untamed virgin. Like the Danaids and like Hippolytos, she scorns Aphrodite and rejects all the normal marriages proposed for her. Seeking revenge, the goddess inflicts upon her a passionate love that is not only outside marriage but also destroys its very foundations from within. The incestuous union takes place on the occasion when the married women celebrate the festival of Ceres-Demeter, during the days when separation between the two sexes is a ritual obligation for married couples and when, in consequence, the daughter is most closely associated with the wife who, having the status of a legally married woman, appears as a mother accompanied by her child. The very movement that brings the daughter closer to her mother separates her as much as possible from her father who, as a male, represents the other sex in the family, the sex with which erotic union, which is possible in nature, is now strictly forbidden.

First Myrrha scorns all the men who could possibly marry her; then she is fired with passionate love for the only being who cannot become her husband. Because she wanted to stop short of marriage she finds herself placed at the furthest forbidden point beyond it. The gods effect her metamorphosis into a myrrh tree. From the seed that she received when she managed to seduce her father despite the barriers between them, Myrrha gives birth to Adonis whose destiny follows, but in the opposite direction, a path that corresponds to that of his mother's. At an age when other little girls and boys, devoted to chaste Artemis, know only the games

155

of innocence, the aromatic child who is endowed with an irresistible seductiveness is totally devoted to the joys of erotic pleasure. But when he has to cross the threshold of adolescence, which, for the young man, marks the moment of his integration into society as a warrior and future husband, his career as a lover is brutally curtailed. He fails the test which normally gives a boy access to full manhood. The son of myrrh is discovered in the lettuce bed where he has either been killed or placed. Having flourished during the period that is normally innocent of amorous relationships, his excess of sexual potency disappears as soon as he reaches the age for marriage. It is arrested where marriage begins, and so represents, as it were, its converse. Now we can solve the problem of the by-passing of the cereals. It is a reference not to any anomaly in food consumption but to the perversion of Adonis' sexual consummation that, because it takes place outside marriage, projects him straight from a premature excess of potency into a precocious impotence. The erotic significance of spices is balanced, at the end of our hero's career, by the lettuce that is not only a cold, wet plant but also (as so many authorities stress) one that possesses anti-aphrodisiac qualities and represents sexual impotence. And whether Adonis' powers of erotic seduction are exercised beyond marriage or fall short of it, they invariably fail to produce any fruit; whether spices or lettuce be concerned, Adonis' seed remains equally infertile.

Our interpretation of the myth of Adonis is substantiated and enriched when we take into account further types of evidence. The first consists of a body of legends that, despite their different episodes and figures, are also intended to express the theme of erotic seduction and to throw light on its nature, role, and effects. The second type of evidence is what we can reconstruct from both written and pictorial evidence of the ritual of the Adonia in fifth- and fourth-century Athens. Phaon, the ferryman, is presented — as is Adonis — as an irresistible seducer. Through the favor of Aphrodite, who has presented him with a perfume with erotic properties, he acquires the power to inspire all women with love for him so passionate as to ignore the duties and prohibitions of marriage. There is another side to this limitless power of seduction. Phaon dies the victim of the jealousy of a deceived husband, or — as other, highly significant, versions have it — he disappears, like Adonis, hidden in a lettuce bed. Like Myrrha, Mintha (or mint) is a fragrant plant. As Hades' concubine she shares his bed in the Underworld. When the time comes for the god to pass on to a legitimate marriage with Persephone, Mintha boasts that she, with her beauty and seductive charm, will supplant the legitimate wife within her husband's house. Demeter is angered and punishes the over-forward rival of her own child by changing her by metamorphosis into a plant that has equivocal properties; it is an aphrodisiac, for sure, and yet it procures abortions; it is perfumed but "insignificant" and sterile. The wheat-mother, associated with her daughter in her capacity as the patroness of legitimate marriage, turns Mintha into a plant that is *akarpos*, a term which means incapable both of bearing fruit and of having children.

The theme of the stories revolving around Iunx, whose name Mintha once bore — according to one Alexandrian source — is again one of vanity in conjunction with the powers of an entirely self-centered erotic seduction. Iunx denotes in the first place a bird, the wryneck; this bird's ability to twist its head right round, the constant motion of its tail, and the piercing sound of its cry make it a creature of strange and disconcerting mobility. Just as light and shadows whirling together in an illusionary manner perplex and make one dizzy, the wryneck projects a dangerous and uncontrollable fascination. Pindar calls it the "bird of delirium." The second meaning of Iunx is an instrument of erotic magic which is made to whirl and whistle like a wryneck by women wishing to attract men, even against their will, to their beds. Thirdly, Iunx is a sorceress nymph, the daughter of *Peitho*, the persuasion of amorous desire or — in other versions — of *Echo*, the will-o'-the-wisp, the ghost of a sound that, being nothing in reality, can imitate all voices with equal success. The nymph attempts to cast her love spells against the couple formed by Zeus and Hera, trying to separate them by making Zeus either desire to possess her, Iunx, or to be united with Io. Iunx is changed by Hera into a wryneck; and her male equivalent is Ixion, whom Zeus punishes by fixing him, spread-eagled, to a wheel whirling in the sky.

Ixion's mythical adventures present him, systematically, as negating marriage as a social institution. Whether marrying Dia, the daughter of Hesioneus, or coveting Hera and attempting to take her by force or seduce her by guile, in every instance his behavior manifests the same scorn for marriage as a contract, as an accepted exchange based on mutual agreement. Hesioneus gives his daughter to Ixion but Ixion refuses to reciprocate by giving him the *hedna*. This was the price paid for a wife that in the archaic time in which the legend takes place, constituted the basis and visible sign of marriage because it publicly set the seal upon an alliance effected through marriage between two family groups. By so doing it made the daughter not just an ordinary companion for the bed but a true wife given to the husband to provide him with a legitimate line of descent. By first undertaking to pay the *hedna* and then refusing to honor his pledge, Ixion makes a pretense of entering into marriage in order the better to destroy it from within. He does away with the distinction between the *damar*, or legitimate wife, and the *pallakē* or concubine. He reduces Dia, whom he has received from her father's hands to be his wife, to the level of a companion in sexual activity, like a slave captured by force in battle or carried off during a pirate raid, or like any woman installed in the house without ceremony to do her master's pleasure. However, Ixion does not simply deny Dia the status of wife, within the context of marriage. He also destroys the alliance with his father-in-law, changing it into its opposite, a relationship of hostility. When his son-in-law invites him to a feast to celebrate their reconciliation, Hesioneus goes trustingly to attend it and perishes in the trap treacherously set for him. In return for the gift of Hesioneus' daughter Ixion offers only vain and misleading words and then repays the friendly trust of the father with trickery, duplicity, and murder. He negates all the forms of exchange and mutual generosity called for by marriage and, in place of the mutual exchange of gifts or — to express it in Greek terms — the *charis*, which is the basis for the marital bond, he substitutes the mere use of constraint in the form now of deceitful persuasion, or *Peitho*, and now of brutal violence, or *Bia*. Although *Peitho* may, in many contexts, be opposed to *Bia* where marriage is concerned they have this in common, that they both act in the exclusive interest of one party without the agreement of the other. *Peitho*, the persuasive power of the deceitful word or of beguiling appearances, can be said, like *Bia*, to force submission upon one of the two partners instead of bringing them into agreement, as does *charis*.

The second stage of myth throws further light on this collusion between *Peitho* and *Bia* who, by moving in on either side of *charis* and together blocking the circuit of exchanges over which it presides, unite to destroy the institution of marriage. Ixion, the first human being to shed the blood of a relative, is obliged to flee the earth. Zeus receives him in heaven and Ixion, characteristically, repays his host's kindness with ingratitude and the negation of *charis*. He covets the wife of his host within his very house. In order to gain access to the marriage bed of the divine couple who are the patrons and protectors of *hymen* he uses any means possible, resorting to violence as well as the artifices of seduction. He imagines he has already won the day once he holds Hera in his arms, apparently thereby celebrating a mockery of hierogamy, consummating with the patroness of weddings a marriage that becomes an anti-marriage since Zeus had been usurped. However, this man of misleading words, this deceitful seducer, can experience only the phantom of a true loving relationship, only the illusion of *hymen*, a marriage that is hollow because "devoid of *charis*." In reality Ixion caresses and embraces not the true Hera but a false ghost, a vain illusion, an empty cloud, *Nephele*. Such a mockery of the union between man and woman can produce only the mockery of a child and *Nephele* duly gives birth to a monstrous offspring, a being without race, family or lineage with which to identify, which remains alien to all that exists either on earth or in heaven: the ancestor to the Centaurs. Neither gods nor men will recognize it, although it is not, strictly speaking, a true beast. Ixion fathers an illusory son, a creature that is, as it were, the bastard of the universe, a pure *nothos* for whom there can be no place within an order of filiation. The apostle of brute seduction is condemned to whirl forever in the sky where Zeus has, for the edification of mankind, transformed him into an *iunx*, there to celebrate day after unending day the virtues of the very *charis* that he presumed to deny and without which sexual union is nothing but a game of make-believe, incapable of giving rise to any authentic descendants.

Having thus cleared the ground with his analysis of the myths, Detienne is in a position to propose an entirely new interpretation of the ritual of the Adonia, and one which carries conviction. The force of his demonstration does not depend simply on the concordance between myth and ritual that complement and mutually illuminate each other. Every detail in the festival, without exception, is taken into account, and, in the light of the various codes previously identified, each one takes on a precise meaning that gives it its place within an ordered whole. Not a single detail is neglected or dismissed as being of secondary importance, gratuitous, or without significance. First, the question of date is considered: The Adonia are celebrated during the Dog Days, the period when spices are collected, when women experience sensual abandonment, when earth and sun are in the closest proximity, and when erotic seduction in all its aspects is at its height. Next, there is the question of location: The festival takes place in private dwellings, not in the public sanctuaries; and furthermore on the terraces of these private dwellings, on the house tops so that a closer union between the above and the below is effected. Then there is the instrument that characterizes the festival: a ladder set leaning toward the top of the buildings, up which the god's devotees climb in order to place their "gardens" in position. Then there are the participants: These are women, concubines, and courtesans, adorned and perfumed, who feast and dance with their lovers whom they have invited there to join them. Then, there is the religious atmosphere of the festival: noisy, unbridled, improper, to the point of drunkenness and sexual license. Next, its purpose: to carry miniature gardens set in little earthenware pots up to the rooftops where they are exposed to the intense heat of the summer sun. In these imitations of true agriculture, the mere ghosts of real plantations, there are lettuce and fennel (which here assumes the role of substitute for the spices, a gardener's version of myrrh), and also seeds of wheat and barley, which the women treat as garden plants. Exposed directly to the sun as they are, in their pots, the seeds take only a few days to germinate, grow, and become green, and thereupon immediately die, completely dried up. The women then cast the pots and their contents into the cold water of springs or into the barren sea. These pseudo-gardens, which pass in a few days from greenness to desiccation, from vigor to exhaustion, do not merely evoke the young god, born of spices, whose precocious career of seduction ends up in the cold and sterile lettuce bed. They also, at every level, represent an anti-agriculture: a make-believe game rather than a serious and useful occupation, a pastime for women, not the work of men, in which a cycle lasting only eight days takes the place of the eight months that elapse between the normal time for sowing and the harvest; in which the plants are abruptly and forcibly roasted instead of ripening slowing and naturally. The canicular period alone takes the place of a harmonious and balanced collaboration of the different seasons, and ludicrously tiny receptacles replace the vast mother earth. The gardens of Adonis that never come to maturity, that have no roots and bear no fruit, are indeed sterile, infertile "gardens of stone." Their rapid, illusory blooming simply serves to emphasize more strongly the productivity of the ploughed field in which Demeter, having received the seed at the propitious time, in due course makes the cereals on which men live germinate, ripen, and be fruitful.

This first set of oppositions is overlaid by a second. Or rather, the same characteristics which set Adonis' gardening and Demeter's agriculture in diametrical opposition on the astronomical and botanical levels, also set up an opposition, on the social level, between the unbridled license of the Adonia and the solemn gravity of the Greek festival of Demeter. According to myth it was the Latin equivalent which Myrrha's mother was celebrating at the very moment when her daughter was carrying out her guilty attempt at seduction. The Adonia represent more than simply an inverted agriculture. They must also be seen as a counter-Thesmophoria. On the one hand, with the lover of Aphrodite, we have the lascivious heat of summer, courtesans and concubines together with their lovers, in intimacy in their own houses; revelry, carousing, and sexual license; the climb up the ladder to place the gardens on the rooftops; a profusion of perfumes heightening the atmosphere of erotic seduction. On the other, with the mother of Persephone, we have the season of autumn rains when the sky makes the earth fertile, which at the onset of winter at the time of sowing marks the beginning of the period that is propitious for marriage; married women, mothers of families, celebrating as citizens accompanied by their legitimate daughters an official ceremony in which they are, for the time being, separated from their husbands; silence, fasting, and sexual abstinence; they take up an immobile position, crouching down on the ground; they climb down into underground *megara* to collect talismans of fertility to be mixed in with seeds; a slightly nauseous smell prevails, and instead of aromatic plants there are clumps of willow branches, the willow being a plant with anti-aphrodisiac qualities.

At this point, however, we are faced with a difficulty. The parallelism to be seen in the table of strict oppositions appears to raise a problem. By reason of their status or profession, the devotees of Adonis — concubines and courtesans — are relegated to a position outside the family. So how can it be that they celebrate their god, and his power of seduction, with a ritual whose every characteristic constitutes a negative imprint of the model forms of conjugal union created by the very institution from which these women are excluded? How can they glorify sexual attraction, the power of eroticism, and the pleasures of love with a language and within a framework borrowed from a religion that refuses to recognize anything but the procreation of children and the establishment of a legitimate line of descent within marriage? Why do they honor their god with gardens whose significance appears to be purely negative, whose sole *raison d'être* seems to lie in the contrast that they set up with true agriculture and that can only be defined in the negative terms of their deficiencies — as lacking serious purpose, rootless, fruitless, good for nothing but to be thrown away?

We may find part of the answer to the problem in considering the nature of the evidence that portrays this aspect of the Adonia. It comprises texts from the authors of comedy, remarks made by philosophers or scholars, maxims, and proverbs — all of which, on the whole, represent the prevailing views of the city, the official line of thought, the opinion of citizens well integrated into the public life. It is quite possible that the point of view of the devotees of Adonis was very different. Indeed, this seems all the more probable given that there is another aspect to the Adonia, this time an altogether positive one, and, far from having no connection with the ritual creation of the gardens, it forms the necessary counterpart to it. At the same time as they hold their celebration with their friends and grow their short-lived gardens for Adonis, these women carry out on the rooftops what seems to be an imitation of the collection of spices, carrying these down the very ladder which they previously used to carry up the gardens. Frankincense seeds and loaves fashioned from myrrh are then deposited in incense and perfume burners, and serve both to honor the lover of Aphrodite and to promote the power women exert over men through their seductive wiles.

Seen from this point of view the gardens of Adonis appear in a different light. The inverted image of agriculture turns out not to have a purely negative significance after all. On the contrary, it appears as a necessary preliminary condition in order to gain access to spices. One can only enjoy the life of perfumes and taste its precious, short-lived delights at the price of having no earth in which to put down roots, and no fruits as end product. The ritual of the festival does indeed express the incompatibility of Adonis and Demeter, of seduction and marriage, but it does so in order to choose and glorify Adonis and seduction. The Adonia thus have a place within the same system of codes that is at work in the official city religion. But it is a code that can be approached, so to speak, from two different, diametrically opposed points and that can be interpreted in two different ways, depending on which of the two poles one chooses to make the positive one. Although they employ the same language within the framework of the same religious system, the adherents of the official cult and the devotees of Adonis use it to convey truths that are different or even opposed. Once the plants that have been forced too quickly to be fertile have been cast into the spring or the sea, the Adonia, the festival held to grieve for the lover, reaches its culmination with the joy of perfumes, the promise of pleasures to come, and the assurance of seduction. At the end of the Thesmophoria, held to grieve for the daughter, the matrons abandon their silence, mourning, and abstinence and celebrate the joy of reunion. The last day of this festival, which held husband and wife ritually apart from each other, went by the name of *Kalligeneia*, betokening assurance and promise, in this case the assurance of a good harvest and the promise of a fine offspring.

We have been considering the question of the meaning of the Adonis myth. In our view Detienne's analysis resolves this question. His reading of the myth and ritual of this god provides the modern interpreter with a meaning, that is, it reveals a well-defined position for them within the Greek religious system (even if – as we have seen – this is a somewhat marginal position), which determines where erotic seduction stands in relation to the other elements in the system as a whole. However, a third category of problems remains to be tackled, concerning the organization of the system of codes discovered by Detienne, how it is balanced and where there are internal distortions and tensions. The structure of the system would appear at first sight to be startlingly asymmetrical. Sacrifice and marriage appear to occupy the same position at the center of gravity of the system, this being exactly comparable to that of the cereals that, placed between the wet rawness of grasses (the food of animals), on the one hand, and the incorruptible dryness of the aromatic plants (the food of the gods), on the other, represent the midway position, the human norm. So far as the consumption of meats is concerned, sacrifice stands in between cannibalism in general (as in a state of wildness) and the refusal of any food in the form of meat (as during the Golden Age); and with regard to erotic consummation, marriage stands in between general promiscuity (as practiced in a state of wildness) and total abstinence (as during the Golden Age). Sacrifice and marriage are also the two human institutions where spices have a part to play — in sacrifice to bring gods and men together, and in marriage to bring men and women together. But the union does not, in the two cases, have the same meaning and value. In sacrifice the spices have a purely positive quality. They represent the share of the gods, a superfood for which men can only yearn without themselves ever attaining to it. So, in a sense, to have the spices predominate to the exclusion of everything else in sacrifice (as Empedocles does when he replaces the ox to be slaughtered by little figurines fashioned from spices, which the participants divide among themselves instead of each eating his portion of roasted meat) is to destroy the sacrifice by making it reach beyond itself. In contrast, in marriage the role of myrrh and perfumes is dangerous and negative. If they are allowed to predominate in the conjugal union — instead of their effects being first restricted and later totally eradicated (a matron is supposed to eliminate all perfumes both on her own person and on her husband's) — the marriage is destroyed, not by over-reaching itself but by being perverted. Thus, when spices are seen not in the context of sacrifice but in that of marriage, their meaning and value are inverted.

At the beginning of his inquiry Detienne examines the figure of Adonis somewhat indirectly and from a particular angle, since he takes sacrifice as his starting point and this is not a subject with which either the myth or the ritual connected with the god are directly concerned. The full light of his inquiry is brought to bear upon sacrifice since, in order to distinguish its meaningful elements, he considers the subject not from the standpoint of the official religion but from the point of view of a sect, the Pythagoreans, whose attacks on sacrificial practice questioned the very foundations of the public religion. The Pythagoreans either rejected all forms of blood sacrifice, or else they excluded oxen and sheep and allowed the slaughter only of pigs and goats that were to be eaten. What they did depended on whether they saw themselves as a religious sect quite outside the city, or as a brotherhood committed to political life and seeking to transform it from within. In both cases the purpose of the religious challenge to sacrifice, to the murder of domesticated animals and the eating of meat, was to establish a more or less vegetarian diet, which should ideally bridge the gap separating men and gods and thus wipe out the original, insuperable distance between them that sacrifice was supposed to have established, and that, in the official religion, was celebrated, confirmed, and consecrated each time that an animal was ritually slaughtered and subsequently eaten. The Pythagoreans thus sought to outflank sacrifice by going one better than it and to replace it with a way of life and of eating that could restore the community of existence, the total commensality with the gods that used to exist in the olden days before the crime that Prometheus committed against Zeus, currently commemorated by sacrifice. In order to live in the company of the gods they were, as far as possible, to eat like the gods themselves did. They were to consume vegetable plants that were altogether "pure" like the foodstuffs eaten in the Golden Age, and now offered up to the deity on altars that were not bloody, that had never been defiled by the murder of sacrifice. And holy men, such as Pythagoras or Epimenides, would even be able to nourish themselves from nothing at all, to live on fragrant perfumes just as the immortals did.

By the end of his analysis Detienne is thus led to emphasize the positive character of spices. In the context of the consumption of foodstuffs the "life of spices" represents an ideal, an ideal that, according to the official religion, men must necessarily forego and that, according to the Pythagorean sect, they must seek to attain by giving up the portions of meat that in sacrifice are allotted to men as their share. However, when Detienne considers marriage, the institution to the heart of which he is led by the religion of Adonis, he has to characterize the spices as negative. These perfumed and incorruptible essences bring together both earth and heaven, and men and gods. But when they unite men and women too closely they break up a marriage instead of cementing it. In the context of marriage they represent, not the ideal, but the kind of erotic seduction that in itself bodes ill and is evil. How then can one explain, in such a precise and consistent system of codes, the same element taking on opposite values in the contexts of two similar and parallel institutions? For Detienne the problem is all the more crucial in that it is within Pythagoreanism, chosen by him to throw light upon the significance of sacrifice, that the contradiction appears in its most startling form. The sect aligns itself with spices to the point of refusing all forms of blood sacrifice and the eating of meat; yet to defend the institution of marriage it aligns itself with lettuce. When the Pythagoreans condemn all kinds of seduction together with the use of perfumes, harass concubines and courtesans, and forbid illegitimate love affairs, it is not the element of myrrh in their diet that they are celebrating but that of lettuce, whose anti-aphrodisiac qualities they extol. Within the framework of Greek religion they thus occupy a position that is the extreme opposite to that of the devotees of Adonis. It is as if the choice of spices in the one case was incompatible with their choice in the other, as if their being prized in the context of sacrifice and the consumption of meat implied their necessary depreciation in the context of marriage and sexual consummation.

How does Detienne account for this asymmetry? We should first point out that the picture is, in fact, not as simple as we have made out. In both the forms in which we have come across them — as incense bringing men and gods together and as perfumes uniting men and women — spices have ambiguous aspects in their role as mediators, aspects which Detienne quite rightly emphasizes. They are plants "of the sun," dry and incorruptible, and as such are related to the fire above and the divine; yet they grow here below, upon the earth of mortal men. And it is only under particular conditions of time, place, and harvesting that they acquire their fully fiery quality. The role of the spices is to bring opposites together, and it would be impossible for them to fulfill it if they were once and for all totally on the side of one of the terms to the exclusion of the other, in the couple they are supposed to unite. In order to unite earth and heaven they must shuttle between the below and the above; to bring men and gods together they must be in some way connected to the former even while they are close to the latter. This equivocal status of the spices explains the extraordinary stories in Herodotus of the ways in which they are collected. These are really myths, although disguised as accurate accounts, and in various forms they were later echoed throughout Greek literature, from historians and geographers to botanical writers. Spices grow in a land that is both quite real and at the same time utterly mythical, in Arabia, a country that, like any other, can indeed be described and located on a map but that is also (like the homeland of the Ethiopians, known as the Long-Lived, the most just, beautiful, and pious of men) a land of the sun — as it were, an enclave of an age of gold preserved within our own corrupted world. Part of the spice harvest is for men to use, while the rest is placed on the altar of the Sun where it bursts spontaneously into flames. The spice harvesting — one might even call it the spice hunt — is carried out according to two opposed methods which, through their very contrasts, emphasize the ambiguous nature of the quarry and the role as mediator that it plays. Men cannot procure it directly. Intermediaries are necessary in the form of animals, some of which are hostile, others benevolent, some chthonic, others heavenly. In some cases the spices grow "below," in the waters of a lake or in a deep ravine. In order to collect them it is necessary to overcome the animals that guard them — chthonic beasts, monstrous bats or snakes, all related to the realm of the wet, the earthy, the corrupt. To do so the collectors must use the pelts of flayed oxen (that is, the out- ermost, incorruptible, inedible part of the animal) to cover their entire bodies, except their eyes, which are, as it were, the lumi- nous, sunlike element in a man. In other cases the spices are to be found "above," in the nests of birds of the heavens, perched on top of inaccessible rocks. In order to bring them down, these creatures related to the fire from above are lured by pieces of meat that, in contrast to the pelts, represent the internal, corruptible, edible part of the animal. The heavenly birds swoop down and grab the hunks of dead flesh; they carry them up to their nests, which collapse under the weight of the meat, meat that can be said to be doubly out of place, being carried up from below to the heights where it is incongruous and whence it returns to where it should be, bringing down with it as it falls the spices that the hunters are then able to seize. Thus for collecting spices men have at their disposal two methods whose means and modalities are the reverse of each other. In the one case the spices are brought up from the depths, despite the chthonic beasts, thanks to a dried pelt that repulses the attacks of these creatures, which are putrid, albeit sometimes winged. In the other they are made to fall from up above with the help of heavenly animals, thanks this time to the hunks of bloody meat that attract these creatures, which are related to the fire above although they still need foodstuffs that are "wet." In both cases emphasis is laid on this tension between opposite terms, which is the characteristic feature of the status of spices and which causes them to oscillate between the above and the below, the dry and the wet, the incorruptible and the putrid. This constant shuttling to and fro is most strikingly expressed in the myth of the phoenix, the spice bird that, oscil-

lating suddenly from the fiery to the corrupt, and thence returning to its original incandescent nature, simultaneously and, as it
were, with the same movement, emphasizes both the antinomy
that exists between two mutually exclusive orders of reality and
also their necessary conjunction in the earthly world. The phoenix occupies in the hierarchy of animal life a position equivalent
to that of spices in the hierarchy of plants. It is a creature of the
Sun, belonging to the highest sphere. Each day it accompanies
the fiery star in its course, regenerating its strength from this contact and being fed by its purest rays, and it thus escapes the mortal condition while yet not acceding to the immortality of the
gods. It is perpetually reborn from its own ashes. The power of
celestial fire that is pure, incorruptible, and spontaneous is forever sufficient unto itself; it perpetuates itself in a constant, imper-
ishable youth. Human fire, stolen by Prometheus and given to
mortals in the form of a "seed of fire," a fire that must be generated for the purpose of cooking the meat from the sacrifice, is a
hungry fire: It must be constantly fed or else, like man himself,
it will die for lack of sustenance. The phoenix's incandescent life
follows a circular course, waxing and waning, being born, dying,
and being reborn. This cycle carries the spice bird, which is closer
to the sun than an eagle of the heavens, to the state of a worm,
which is putrid, a creature even more chthonic than the snake
or the bat. From the ashes of the bird that is consumed at the
end of its long existence in a nest of fire made from spices a tiny
grub is born, nourished on dampness and eventually, in its turn,
becomes a phoenix.

This myth makes it quite clear that if they are to bring together
the above and the below and fulfill their role as mediators between
the gods and men, spices must occupy an intermediary position
between the two opposed terms. The gods enjoy an eternal form
of existence outside time, in the permanence of an unchanging
youth. Men live within a limited time, always facing in the same
direction, namely toward death; they are born, grow old, and disappear forever. To perpetuate themselves they must unite with a

creature of the opposite sex and produce a child that is a continuation of themselves in a new being, different from themselves. The phoenix lives in boundless, cyclical time, alternately facing in opposite directions. It perpetuates itself without being physically united to anything, without producing another creature that is not itself but by being born from its own ashes. So it can be said that, according to the logic of the myth that expresses in the most condensed form the mediatory role of spices, these perfumed essences have the power to bring together earth and heaven, and men and gods, to the extent that they represent in the botanical and zoological codes a form of life that is self-renewing, which has no need of a union of opposite sexes, no need consequently of marriage and the procreation of children. In a way the phoenix's mode of existence recalls that of men in the Golden Age before the introduction of sacrifice, before the use of corruptible and generated fire, before agricultural labor, before the creation of women and marriage, when mankind — exclusively male — still led a pure life, a life incomparably longer than nowadays, knowing neither old age nor death in the strict sense of these terms, being born spontaneously from the earth just as the phoenix is from its own ashes.

These remarks will perhaps enable us to supplement Detienne's explanation concerning the mismatch that we have noted between the positive function of spices used as incense and their negative role when used as perfumes.

Detienne makes the point that, in the eyes of the Greeks, there is a good way of using spices — namely in sacrifice — and a bad one — namely in erotic relationships. This is because once perfumes are principally used for erotic ends they are "diverted" from their proper religious and ritual purposes. They are "withdrawn from their correct role which is to return to the gods the substances with which these have particular affinities." But where and why does this diversion occur? There are two possible answers. One is simply that in using perfumes for erotic seduction there is none left for sacrifice, that one neglects to sacrifice, one fails to do so at the very moment when one indulges in any sexual enjoyment. But this is obviously untrue. In a matter of sacrifice lovers, voluptuaries, and sensualists are neither more nor less scrupulous than those who are chaste or prudish. Besides, as the Adonia show well enough, even spices used for erotic purposes have a ritualistic and religious role to play. Alternatively, there is a more complex explanation: Because the aim and significance of spices are reversed in the two cases of sacrifice and seduction one cannot give unqualified support to them in both cases at once. A Pythagorean celebrating the Adonia is as unthinkable as a devotee of Adonis being converted to the Pythagorean way of life and vegetarianism. And of course this opposition, which takes the form of a radical incompatibility at the two extreme poles of the religious system, is also expressed at its center, in official ceremonies, by a tension between the spices that are an integral part of sacrifice and the perfumes that are an integral part of marriage. According to the method that, with Detienne, we have followed, the solution should, first and foremost, be a structural one. It should account for the disparity in terms of the overall structure of the system. The phoenix myth gives us our first clue: The spice bird is the embodiment of a form of existence that corresponds, in Greek philosophical terms, to a moving image of eternity, and in terms of Greek mythology to the life of the men of the Golden Age. In the context of a sacrifice the role of the spices is positive since they point toward this Golden Age. It is true that sacrifice commemorates the passing of this happy state of former years, but within its context spices represent the share that, even now, is truly divine. To give them a heightened or even exclusive role is to promote a religious experience that stands for a return to the Golden Age; it is to make oneself aromatic in order to find once more that original condition in which one used to live and eat in company with the gods. In marriage, however, spices point in the opposite direction. They preside over sexual attraction, without which marriage cannot be physically consummated and thus, at the very center of this institution, they consecrate the break with the Golden Age, the duality of the sexes, the need for a sexual union, for birth through generation and, correspondingly, also for old age and death. Sacrifice and marriage occupy analogous positions on the same level. But in sacrifice spices are connected with what, in myth, preceded the need for meat as food. In marriage they are connected with what, in myth, led man to sexual consummation. The greater the part played by spices in sacrifice, the greater the apparent power of spices to unite gods and men. The more limited the role of perfume and seduction in the union between man and woman, the more their marriage is legitimately established. From a religious point of view the justification for sacrifice is the offering of spices that are thus enabled to return to the deity. The religious justification for marriage lies in the very definite restrictions it imposes upon the sexual attraction that is stimulated by the use of perfumes. If it were possible, indeed, marriage would do without perfumes altogether, but the human condition that resulted from man's separation from the gods forced it to make, as it were, a virtue of necessity.

This does not solve our problem but it enables us to rephrase it in the following manner: Given the role that they play in sacrifice, why is it that spices also preside over erotic seduction? Hesiod provides us with the answer in the two versions he gives of the myth about the introduction by Prometheus of blood sacrifice. Originally men and gods live in the closest proximity, feasting together. When the moment comes to establish their respective shares Prometheus kills and cuts up a huge ox, dividing it into two parts. The men receive the meat and all that can be eaten while the gods are left with the bones and a little fat, the very portions still assigned to them, in the form of rising smoke, in the sacrifices made on perfumed altars. Zeus takes his revenge by hiding his fire from men — the heavenly, pure, inexhaustible, ungenerated fire which men had presumably enjoyed hitherto. So it is now impossible to cook the meat. Prometheus steals the seed of fire, hidden in the hollow stalk of a fennel plant, and presents it as a gift to men. So the flame of sacrifice burns on earth, where men are now able to sustain their failing strength by eating the cooked meat. Zeus, cheated, counter-attacks. He hides the seed of wheat from men and buries it in the depths of the earth: It will henceforth be necessary to labor in the fields in order to harvest grain and eat bread. At the same time he creates the first woman, with whom it will be necessary to labor in order to produce children. Hephaistos models her out of clay moistened with water. She is a chthonic creature, damp and earthy, and not only is her condition mortal but also close to bestial by reason both of her insatiable appetite for food and also of her sexual appetite unleashed during the Dog Days when, being better protected against the burning heat of the sun than her husband, whose constitution is hotter and dryer than hers, she literally roasts her man; "without any torch she dries him up," delivering him over, even while still green and raw, to the desiccation of a premature old age. Pandora is, through her excessive animal sensuality, a fire to make men pay for the fire that Prometheus hid and stole from the gods. But she is more than this. She is herself a hidden trap, a double being whose appearance disguises and masks the reality. Hephaistos makes her out of clay and water but he fashions her in the images of the immortal goddesses, and the beauty that shines forth from her body as if she were divine strikes not only men but gods too with wonder. The cunning of Zeus' vengeance lies in his having endowed with erotic seduction, that is, a divine appearance, a being whose soul is that of a bitch and who hides her gross bestiality beneath the winning gentleness of her smile and the deceitful flattery of her lips. Pandora is an evil, but an evil so beautiful that men cannot, in the depths of their hearts, prevent themselves from loving and desiring her. The seductive attraction of her physical appearance is further enhanced by the grace with which Aphrodite endows her whole body, and the clothes, flowers and jewels with which Athena and Hephaistos adorn her. Pandora emerges from the hands of the gods as a young bride, leaving the women who have prepared her for her wedding, anointed with perfumes, crowned with myrrh, and clothed in the wedding tunic and veil; and she makes straight for Epimetheus, the Thoughtless One, who despite the warning of his brother Prometheus, the Foreseeing One, receives her into his house as his spouse. An irresistible enchantment emanates from her and illuminates her whole being; yet her first action is to lift the lid of the jar and release all the evils men had hitherto not known: hard labor, sickness, painful old age, and death.

In the world of men erotic seduction is embodied in the equivocal figure of Pandora, the poisonous gift sent from Zeus as a counterpart to fire, as the opposite of the good thing that Prometheus fraudulently presented to them. And seduction – like Pandora – is a dual and ambiguous thing. In virtue of what it imitates it is divine. All beauty comes from the gods and the grace of a human body can only be reflection and emanation of theirs. The perfumes are divine too. The gods smell fragrant; their presence is made manifest not only by intensely bright beams of light but also by a marvellous smell. So the attraction exercised by beauty and stimulated by perfumes has in itself a fully positive significance; it is an impulsion toward something divine. However, in erotic seduction it is a perverted impulsion toward a false semblance of the divine, toward the deceptive appearance of beauty disguising something in reality quite different: female bestiality. Just like Ixion, who embraces the ghost of a goddess in the form of *Nephele* who has the appearance of Hera, the man who yields to the call of desire falls into the trap Zeus laid in the person of Pandora; because he is clasping at an illusion, his prey eludes him, and he is left empty-handed. Because he has desired to taste the divine life of the spices in the illusory guise of erotic seduction he forfeits, in the union of the sexes, man's rightful share, which allows beings now become mortal to perpetuate themselves through marriage in a line of descent, and which makes of woman – who is divine in virtue of her seductively beguiling appearance and a beast in her true appetites – the companion, if not the equal, of her husband. Together they form a couple whose condition of life is neither that of the gods nor that of the beast, neither the Golden Age nor state of wildness but something between the two: the life of man as it has been defined ever since the separation of mortals and immortals through sacrifice, agriculture, and marriage.

In finding a solution to the difficulties that arise from the presence of spices in both sacrifice and marriage where their roles are parallel but inverted, one is paradoxically led to formulate a new, and final, category of problems. We have tried in our consideration of Detienne's work to emphasize the analogy between the two institutions and to distinguish as accurately as possible the implications and consequences of this symmetry. However, when the two institutions are replaced within the total system to which they belong, a radical difference between them becomes apparent that affects the entire harmony of Greek religion and culture. Sacrifice is the cornerstone of the religion of the city. Yet it is attacked from both sides, both where it establishes a gap between men and gods and where it separates men and beasts. In both cases the attack is prompted by a desire to use different approaches (which, while being opposed to each other, may nevertheless be common to the same sect) in order to attain a religious experience that is unlike that offered by the official religion and that confers upon the devotee the privilege of a more direct contact, a closer union with the divine. We have seen how the Pythagoreans outflank sacrifice by going one better than it, by giving up eating meat, in an attempt to bridge even during life the gap separating gods from men. They are not alone in making such an attempt. A whole current of religion and philosophy follows the same trend, from those who were known as the Orphic sect to the greatest thinkers in classical Greece, Plato and Aristotle. For them, the object of the philosophical life is to make man like a god to the greatest extent possible, as opposed to the teaching of the official religion, which can be expressed in the Delphic maxim, "Know yourself," or, in other words, "Recognize your limitations, know that you are not one of the gods, and do not seek to equal them."

176

But sacrifice can also be outflanked on the other side. There were groups of the devotees of the Dionysiac religion that practiced a form of worship in which the central rite was *ōmophagy*, the devouring of the absolutely raw flesh of an animal not led ritually to the altar to be slaughtered, cut up, roasted, and boiled according to the rules, but captured as it ran wild, cut up, torn apart while still alive, and consumed while life was still warm in it. Here the frontier that is wiped out is that separating man and nature in the wild, the aim being to abolish the barrier between humanity and bestiality. Instead of feeding on pure foods and, ideally, aromatic smells like the gods, these people eat raw flesh like wild beasts. This retrogression to a state of primitive wildness, which is, as it were, the reverse of the Golden Age, is also expressed in other aspects of the cult. Dionysus is seen as a wild hunter leading to their quarry a group of women who have themselves become wild, who have abandoned their homes, their domestic duties, and their husbands and children in order to roam the wild, uncultivated countryside among woods and mountains far from the towns with their sanctuaries and far from the cultivated fields. The animals which these women track down and then eat alive are presented as being at times wild — lions, tigers, or fawns — and at others domesticated — such as cows or goats — as if the difference between them had disappeared. Yet this difference between the two kinds of animals is recognized and consecrated by the usual form of sacrifice in which, unlike in the hunt, only domesticated animals are killed and — in principle at least — not until they have given some sign to indicate their acquiescence. Cannibalism is added to omophagy. The frontier between men and beasts is abolished. In the myths in which they appear there is nothing left to distinguish Dionysus' frenzied Maenads from the wild animals that they hunt down even in their lairs. They themselves become the very vixen, does, and panthers whose blood they are about to lap up. Or else the reverse is the case: Those whom they in their madness believe to be the wild dwellers of the forest turn out to be, in reality, their own race, their own family, of all living creatures those that are closest to them and most like them — their children, their parents, their brothers. And they tear at them with their teeth without realizing what they are doing — humans devouring other humans as birds eat the flesh of other birds.

This foray into wildness has a positive, religious significance: Once the barriers within which man is enclosed (being confined as well as protected by them) are down, a more direct contact with the supernatural can be established. The Maenads, beyond themselves, overwhelmed by *mania*, the divine delirium, accede to a state that the Greeks call "enthusiasm"; they are taken over by the gods who (in a religious sense) ride and possess them. The Dionysiac religion, in the savage form of possession, and Pythagoreanism, in the intellectual and ascetic form of spiritual purification, both — in opposite ways — bypass sacrifice in order to draw nearer to the gods. The aim they share explains how it is that, despite their mutual opposition, omophagy and vegetarianism are (as there is evidence to show) in certain instances practiced within a single sect: Eating raw flesh and a vegetarian diet reinforce each other, the one serving as necessary condition for the other, the one falling short of and the other going beyond sacrifice. Perhaps it could be said, to use a distinction sometimes used by anthropologists, that where it is a question of falling short of sacrifice, on the side of wildness, of omophagy and maenadism, it is the gods who take charge and draw near to men, descending to their level in order to take possession of their devotees. Beyond sacrifice, on the side of vegetarianism, asceticism, and inner purification, it is men who take the initiative and strive to develop their own spiritual resources in order to be able to rise to the level of the gods, to reach them by an internal effort to pass beyond the normal limitations of human nature. At all events, by taking up a position outside the framework imposed by the practice of sacrifice, both these "mystical" experiences shaped the religious world of the Greeks and had a decisive effect on the orientation of ancient thought.

There is nothing comparable so far as marriage is concerned, and yet, from a structural point of view, the same possibilities existed here. Marriage, like sacrifice, could have been outflanked in two different ways. This could have happened either in the name of total chastity, with a rejection of sexual consummation along with the rejection of the consumption of meat in order to find again the Golden Age in which both were unknown; or, on the contrary, in the name of sexuality and eroticism seen, in their brutish forms, as religious forces that can no more be limited and regulated in man than in wild beasts. Why did the Greeks not exploit this double possibility that appears to us to be implied in the architecture of their religious system? In their quest for a life that is totally pure — alien to anything concerned with death and generation — the Pythagoreans could have adopted toward marriage the same dual attitude as they adopted toward sacrifice. On one level, as a brotherhood integrated within the city and seeking to transform it from within, they could have cut their losses by accepting sexual union only in the form of legitimate marriage, and rejecting concubinage and prostitution in the same way as they accepted sacrifice only for goats and pigs and not for oxen and sheep. On a second level, as a religious sect, they could have taken up a more radical position and refused sexual union in all its forms just as they totally rejected blood sacrifice. Although there is much evidence to show that on the first level such an attitude was adopted, it does not seem that the sect ever defended the second attitude. The Pythagoreans are not religious extremists where marriage is concerned. The need for descendants is never directly questioned, despite the fact that the procreation of even legitimate children fuels the cycle of rebirths which, from a Pythagorean point of view, is to some extent an evil. Nor do they appear to have had the idea that sexual activity is impure; they only considered it to be so if the union was an illegitimate one. The marriage couple remained pure in the carnal act that united them as husband and wife. The ideal of *hosiotēs*, of complete sanctity and the hope of a return to the Golden Age, did away with sacrifice but bypassed the institution of marriage without attacking it, for there was no tendency — not even a sectarian one — to reject this. Marriage does not appear ever to have been challenged from a religious standpoint in Greece. Figures such as Hippolytos who, in tragedy, are the embodiment of a religious insistence on total purity, are presented with such equivocal features, and display a puritanism so ambiguous in its very excesses, that there is a whole side to their characters that tips the scales over toward wildness. Hippolytos whom his father, Theseus, considers as a devotee of Orpheus and as a fervent follower of the vegetarian diet desires and claims at the same time to be as chaste as a virgin. He rejects carnal union with the same intransigent disdain as a vegetarian rejects animal flesh. He is a strange vegetarian, though, for he also appears to be very close to the wild beasts that he devotes his time to hunting and slaughtering and that then, once the hunt is over, he shares as a meal with his male companions — a meal that he enjoys with the best of appetites. While he speaks of marriage only to reject it with indignation and horror, this young man, believed to be all modesty and reserve, has difficulty in masking under the artifice of a sophistic rhetoric the brutish violence of his true temperament. As for the Danaids who flee from marriage like timid doves escaping from the hawk that seeks them as its prey, the first time the king of Argos comes across them he compares them to the Amazons, "the women who devour raw flesh," and the full force of this comparison becomes apparent when one considers the treatment they later mete out to their husbands, actually slaughtering them on their wedding night. For Greek thought in general, as well as for the Pythagoreans in particular, purity consists not in the rejection of marriage but in the rejection, in the name of marriage, of all illegitimate sexual relationships. And to renounce marital life altogether is not to beat a path toward the Golden Age but rather to detain boys and girls in the primitive state of wildness from which marriage can deliver them by introducing them into the very heart of civilized life.

Marriage is equally successful in resisting such attacks as could assail it from the opposite quarter. All that we learn from Detienne about the religion of Adonis indicates clearly that it does not attack marriage head-on. There is nothing in either the myth or the ritual that constitutes a challenge to its legitimacy or denies its religious value. In the religion of Adonis the attitude remains defensive. It goes no further than asserting the rights of erotic seduction, not claiming that it should take the place of marriage but that it should be practiced alongside marriage and apart from it. This happens within the framework of a religious system that revolves around legitimate union, and no attempt is made to deny the wife's recognized and proper privileges, namely her capacity to produce true fruits, to engender a line of descent firmly rooted in the earth, fixed to the very hearth of the house, a line of descent that is, in this way, directly continued and perpetuated with every birth of each new generation. Sacred prostitution, which is commonly practiced in the East, is significantly absent from the Greek world. Even where, as in Corinth, there is evidence that it existed, it is a matter of a phenomenon that is in some way atypical, a reflection of Oriental influences which remains profoundly alien to the Greek mentality. And the Greeks did not consider erotic activity to be a religious experience in itself any more that they consecrated total sexual abstinence. Unlike other civilizations they never made erotic activity a discipline for the body to acquire and develop, a kind of inverted asceticism. It is the fact that they consecrated neither abstinence nor eroticism that assures the undisputed legitimacy of marriage and that establishes it, alongside cereals, at the center of the religious system. There were some sects for whom men were not considered to be those who ate the cooked meat of a sacrificed animal; but nevertheless they remained those who ate bread and practiced a form of marriage without which there could be no civilized life, no *polis*. At the same time, the fact that the Greeks consecrated neither sexual abstinence nor eroticism raises problems. By providing a solution to longstanding disagreements, Detienne's study, like any work that is truly original and marks a turning point in scholarship, alters the entire field of traditional views and suggests new areas of inquiry. To solve these new problems it would no doubt be necessary to enlarge the investigation beyond a mere stuctural analysis of the religious system. We should have to examine, this time from a historical point of view, how marriage became instituted in archaic Greece, how it developed from infinitely more open and free forms, and how, within the institutional framework the city imposed upon it, marriage was transformed as, in part, it became established but also, in part, continued to seek its own identity. As the author indicates in his last pages, one might formulate the hypothesis that religious thought was all the more insistent in consecrating the unique significance of marriage by opposing it systematically to erotic seduction, since, in default of an unequivocal legal definition, the distinction between concubine and legitimate spouse remained in the fifth and fourth centuries somewhat hazy and uncertain. However, that is another story, which we can but hope to see told in its turn one day, following the same lines as those indicated by Detienne. In this way this book, which is full of seductive attractions and which is bound to prove seminal, would have the effect of uniting the two opposite qualities, and of reconciling the hostile figures, of Adonis and Demeter.

CHAPTER VIII

The Myth of Prometheus in Hesiod[1]

Hesiod devotes two long passages to the episode of Prometheus' theft of fire. The first occurs in the *Theogony* (l.535-616), the second in *Works and Days* (l.45-105). The two versions of the story are not just complementary but interlocking, for each contains, in the form of an allusion, an episode that is explicitly described in the other. (The first passage in the story as told in the *Theogony*, concerning Prometheus' trick when he allots the shares of food, is alluded to in l.48 of *Works*; and conversely the last part of the story, as told in *Works*, concerning Epimetheus' acceptance of Zeus' fatal gift to men in the shape of Pandora, is alluded to in the *Theogony* in lines 512-514, as a prologue to the myth of Prometheus.) The two versions thus form a whole and should be analyzed as such.

Let us start by making a formal analysis of the story, considering first in the *Theogony*, and then in *Works*, the agents, actions, and plot. We shall then attempt by comparing the two texts to make out the general logic of the story seen as a whole.

First Level: A Formal Analysis of the Story

A. THE AGENTS
1. In the *Theogony*
In the presence of gods and men,

| on the one hand there is Prometheus, | on the other Zeus and, acting as the executors of his final decisions, Athena and Hephaistos. |

Prometheus is defined by his *metis* (511, 521, 546, 550, 559), that is to say, his guile, his cunning intelligence, and by his *doliē technē* (540, 574, 551, 555, 560), his skill in trickery.

Zeus is defined by his *metis* of a sovereign (520, 550, and 545) and also as god the father (542), master of the thunderbolt and of the sky (558, 568, 602).

2. In *Works*

| There are on the one hand Prometheus and Epimetheus, | On the other, there is Zeus (assisted by Hephaistos, the Charites, Peitho, Aphrodite, Athena, and Hermes), |
| who represent men. | who represents the gods. |

The *metis* of Prometheus, a compound of cunning foresight, guile, and deception, is matched by the lack of *metis* in Epimetheus, who understands nothing until it is too late and who is always fooled by everything. This pair of brothers, who are the complementary opposites of each other, in other words this union of subtle foresight and stupid shortsightedness, is characteristic of the human condition.

B. The Actions (functions or performances)

The whole story concerns a duel in cunning — each party trying to fool the other — between the Titan endowed with *metis* and the Olympian king of the gods, the *metioeis* one.

In the *Theogony*, the duel is played out before gods and men who are as yet still united, and the result of the duel is to determine the allotment of shares and honors between them and fix their respective *timai* (shares) and *moirai* (honors).

In *Works*, gods and men are presented as already separated, and the duel between their respective heroes (Zeus representing the gods, Prometheus/Epimetheus representing men) is to some extent a confrontation between the two sides.

In both texts the actions of Prometheus and Zeus are strictly comparable.

They consist in:

1. preparations (which are carefully premeditated) for the disposing and setting up of certain ploys (*tithemi* and its compound forms; cf., for Prometheus: *Theog.*, 537-9, 541; for Zeus and his assistants: *Theog.*, 577-8, 583, 601; *Works*, 61, 74, 80) aimed at deceiving (*apatan*) the adversary. This deception (*apatē*) or fraud (*dolos*) is expressed in the case of both protagonists by a series of similar operations designed to "hide," "conceal from view" (*kaluptein*, *kruptein*) and, in Prometheus' case, also to steal without being seen (*kleptein*).

2. reciprocal offers of deceptive gifts, trick presents that may be either accepted or refused. The rules governing this interchange conform to the following formal pattern, which provides a summary of the entire logic behind the story:

to give
$\left\{ \begin{array}{l} \text{to take the gift} = \text{to accept it} \\ \text{not to take the gift} = \text{to reject it.} \end{array} \right.$

not to give
$\left\{ \begin{array}{l} \text{not to take what is not given} \\ \text{to take what is not given} = \text{to steal.} \end{array} \right.$

C. THE PLOT

1. In the *Theogony*

This general analysis explains the structure of the story. Each episode is introduced by an expression indicating the temporal sequence which links it to the preceding episode. The consecutive episodes of the narrative can be distinguished as follows:

First episode (535–61)

535–6: καὶ γὰρ ὅτ... τότ ἔπειτα

[When indeed... then, after that]

In the presence of gods and men, and in order to distinguish between them (*ekrinonto*), Prometheus sets out, at the same time hiding them (539: *katethēke kalupsas*, 541: *euthetisas katethēke kalupsas*), the two portions of the ox he has brought before the gods and men (537: *prouthēke*), and then sacrificed and cut into pieces.

He "offers" to Zeus the portion of beef that seems appetizing but is, in reality, inedible. Zeus accepts this share that appears to be the best one and so is tricked (although this trickery is in effect an integral part of the *metis* Zeus has premeditated in order to undo mankind). Zeus is angry.

In this way are determined the shares that fall, in blood sacrifice, to men (the flesh and fatty entrails = the edible parts) and those that fall to the gods (the bare, white bones that are burned on altars perfumed with incense).

Second episode (562–9)

562: ἐκ τούτου δὴ ἔπειτα.... [From that time on....]

Ever mindful of this fraud perpetrated by Prometheus, Zeus refuses to hand over (*ouk edidou*), the celestial fire (the thunderbolt) which men had hitherto been able to use.

Without being seen by Zeus, Prometheus steals (*exapatēsen... klepsas*) the flame of fire. So, in default of celestial fire, this Promethean fire now burns among men (who can use it to cook their food).

Zeus is angry at having been fooled in this manner.

Third episode (570–84)

570: αὐτίκα.... [Forthwith....]

As a counterpart to the fire that he refused to give but which Prometheus has stolen, Zeus sets about making for men something which has not hitherto existed: It is an evil (*kakon*), namely, woman.

Hephaistos and Athena prepare this evil and "set it out" just as, in the first episode, Prometheus "set out" the shares of food.

Fourth episode (585–613).

585: *αὐτὰρ ἐπεὶ δὴ....* [Then when....]

The counterpart to fire, woman, the "beautiful evil," once created is led by Zeus before gods and men just as Prometheus earlier led the ox that was sacrificed before them. Woman, however, is a gift prepared exclusively for men (570 and 589) and she is the visible sign of their wretched condition.

Indeed, the race of women are to men what the drones are to the bees: a hungry stomach (*gastēr*) that swallows up the fruit of others' work (599).

Thus, henceforward men are presented with a choice: either not to marry, and to enjoy a sufficiency of grain (since the female *gastēr* does not take it from them) but not to have any children (since a female *gastēr* is necessary to give birth) — the evil thus counterbalancing the good; or to marry and, even with a good wife, the evil again counterbalances the good (609).

Among human beings, goods and evils are inseparable because Zeus, by the gift of woman, presented men with a *kakon ant' agathoio*, an evil, the counterpart of good.

Conclusion (613–16)

Prometheus may have been successful in stealing (*kleptein*) the fire; but it is not possible to *klepsai noon*, to elude the mind of Zeus. However knowing he may be, the Titan is submitted to the grip of a terrible bond.

We may summarize the structure of the story as follows:

Prometheus offers a *dolos* (a trick present, a fraudulent gift) to Zeus.

—Zeus accepts it.

In anger, Zeus denies (celestial) fire to men.

—Prometheus will not accept this denial: He steals fire and

gives it to men.

Zeus then makes and presents men with woman who is a *dolos*.

A distinction is thus made between gods and men.

Prometheus has given men the flesh of sacrificed animals to eat; and to the gods the bones that are burned.

Prometheus has given men the stolen fire while Zeus has kept celestial fire for the use of the gods alone.

Zeus has given to men – and to men alone – the race of women.

Thus, to the extent that men are differentiated from the gods, the human condition implies (1) sacrifice; (2) "Promethean" fire, together that all this implies, that is, cooked food; (3) marriage.

2. In *Works*
Introduction (42–8)
The gods have hidden (*krupsantes*) men's life, *bion*, from them, that is, food in the form of cereals, that is, grain.

If they had not done this there would have been no need for men to work and labor in the fields; however, Zeus concealed it (*hekrupse*) when Prometheus tricked him (an allusion to the first episode of the *Theogony* story).

First episode (49–59)
49: τοὔνεκ᾽ ἄρ᾽.... [Thenceforward....]
From that time (when he was tricked) on, he planned sad trouble for men and hid fire from them (*krupse de pur*, 50).

Prometheus stole it, provoking the wrath of Zeus.

Zeus declares that, as a counterpart to fire, he will give (*dōsō* 57; cf. in opposition: *ouk edidou*, in line 563 of the *Theogony*) an evil which men will surround with love.

Second episode (59–82)
59: ὡς ἔφατ᾽.... [Thus, he said....]
Preparation of the harmful and beguiling gift by Athena, Hephaistos, the Charites, Peitho, and Aphrodite.

This evil is called Pandora, being "the gift of all the gods" to men who "eat grain" (82; cf. the same expression in *Theogony*, 512).

Third episode (83–9)
> 83: *Αὐτὰρ ἐπεὶ....* [But when....]

Hermes brings the *dōrōn theōn*, the "gift of the gods," from the gods to Epimetheus. Prometheus has forewarned his brother never to accept any gift from Olympian Zeus but instead to refuse it and send it back whence it came. But Epimetheus accepts the gift. By the time he realizes his mistake the damage is done.

Fourth episode (90–104)
> 90: *πρὶν μεν....* [Before that....]

Hitherto, men had known no evils in their life: neither work nor sickness nor old age.

However, Pandora has lifted the lid of the jar and all the evils have been dispersed among men. Now they are ever present but cannot be avoided because they are always unpredictable: They are invisible, unlike woman who is a visible evil but one that beguiles through the deceptive beauty of her appearance. They are also inaudible, again in contrast to woman who has a *phonē* which she uses the better to seduce with her lying words those who are so imprudent as to listen to her.

Thus, the evils which men would attempt to avoid, could they but see them, remain invisible.

And the evil that can be seen and heard deceives and seduces through its misleading appearance of something good.

Conclusion
So it is not possible to elude the mind of Zeus (and this men should not forget).

The structure of this version of the story may be summarized as follows:

The gods have hidden men's livelihood from them.

Zeus, the victim of the *apatē* or trick of Prometheus (who "hid" the shares of the ox) hides the fire.

Prometheus, concealing himself from Zeus, steals this hidden fire and offers it to men.

Zeus makes the "gift of all the gods" and offers it to Epimetheus, who is the counterpart to Prometheus. Instead of refusing it, Epimetheus accepts it.

Human life is therefore full of evils: Some are invisible, hidden; others, which are visible, conceal themselves beneath their misleading appearance which suggests that they are good and desirable.

D. COMPARISON BETWEEN THE TWO VERSIONS: THE LOGIC OF THE STORY

The account in *Works* differs from that in the *Theogony* on several points.

1. The episode of the Promethean *apatē* with the shares of the ox is only alluded to; on the other hand, the episode of Epimetheus' (men's) acceptance of Zeus' gift (Pandora) with all its sorry consequences (the opening of the jar of evils) is fully developed; but it was also present, in the form of an allusion, in *Theogony* 511-12.

2. Extreme emphasis is laid, in *Works*, on Pandora being a gift, a harmful trick of a gift that could have been either accepted or refused (cf. the interpretation given to the word Pandora and lines 57, 82, 85, 86). But this theme of the gift, the offer, was also present in the version in the *Theogony* and dictated the entire logic of the story told there (cf. in particular, *heleu* in line 549; *ouk edidou* in line 563; and the datives indicating the recipients of the offer, *anthrōpoisin*, in lines 570 and 589).

3. The action of "hiding" (*kaluptein, kruptein*) attributed explicitly to Prometheus and implicitly to Zeus in the *Theogony* is explicitly attributed to Zeus in *Works*. This *kruptein* even assumes a general theological significance in respect of the relationship between Zeus (the gods) and men.

4. The episode of the theft of fire is identical in the two versions. The episodes of the preparation of the first woman and/or Pandora match exactly, although the *Works* version is more precise and fuller. In both cases the female creature fashioned by the gods

for the human beings is described as a *parthenos* adorned to celebrate her marriage.

Thus, the two versions can be considered to be complementary, together combining to form a single unit.

This comparison between the two versions makes it possible to distinguish more clearly certain aspects of the logic of the story. We have already picked out two kinds of actions performed by the figures whose roles in the intrigue are those of agents:
(1) Preparatory actions: setting out while concealing;
(2) Actions directed toward others: giving or not giving on the one hand, and accepting or refusing the gift or the absence of the gift on the other.

Now when the two accounts are compared it becomes clear that these two types of action are not simply superimposed on or coordinated with one another: They are seen to be integral parts of one another.

The fact is that "not to give" is exactly the same as "to hide" (cf. *Theogony*, 563: "Zeus no longer gave the fire," and *Works*, 50: "Zeus hid the fire"). For the gods, no longer to give to men something good which the latter had previously freely enjoyed is "to hide" it from them. Seen from this point of view, "to hide their livelihood," that is to say cereals, and "to hide the fire" are two aspects of a single operation. Originally, wheat grew of its own accord, being offered to men through an *aroura automatē* (*Works*, 116-17). They had but to stoop to gather and eat it. Henceforward, since wheat is "hidden," cereals (that is, "cooked" plants as opposed to raw grasses that grow of their own accord) imply agricultural labor (hard *ponos*); the earth must be ploughed and the seed (*sperma*) sown in order to obtain wheat. Similarly, originally celestial fire was freely available to men on the ash trees where Zeus placed it; but henceforward, since fire is hidden, it must be buried deep "in a hollow stem" or one must preserve its seed (*sperma*, cf. *Odyssey*, V, 490; *sperma puros*, associated with *kruptein* and *kaluptein*) by concealing it beneath ashes, and then it must be continually fed, for this fire only lives if it is fueled (cf. Herodotus,

191

III, 16). Finally, in the same way, men used to be born spontaneously from the soil just like the wheat springing from the furrow
or like the fire from the ash trees; henceforward it is necessary
to labor the female belly (which, like the fire, needs to be fed
and, like the earth, needs to be ploughed) in order to plant man's
seed (*sperma*) there.

But if, for the gods, "not to give" to men means "to hide,"
equally "to give" to men means "to hide" for since every gift from
the gods is a *dolos* or trap, an *apatē* or snare, in reality the gift with-
holds what it seems to be offering; beneath its deceptive appearance of a proffered good it hides an invisible evil. In other words,
once good things have been hidden (not given) by the gods, men
can only reach them through the evils in which they have been
placed (*ponos*, woman). Conversely, whatever the gods have given
to men turns out to be an evil camouflaged by its deceptively
desirable appearance.

Thus the opposition which seemed to govern the logic of the
story, namely to give/not to give, can be resolved into two different forms of one and the same action: to hide,
(1) not to give = to hide a good thing so that it can only be
obtained through the evils which envelop it,
(2) to give = to hide an evil under its beguiling appearance of
something desirable.

The logic of the story reflects the ambiguous character of the
human confition in which, as a result of the "hiding" action taken
by the gods, good things and evils, whether given or not given,
always turn out to be indissolubly linked together. At the same
time the story defines the status of man, midway between that
of the beasts and that of the gods: It is characterized by sacrifice, fire for culinary and technical operations, the woman seen
both as a wife and as a bestial stomach, and cereal foods and
agricultural labor.

* * *

Hitherto our analysis has concentrated on the narrative structure
of the text, its syntax and its logic.

Now we must continue it on a different level, undertaking a study of its semantic content, taking into consideration every detail in the structure of each episode and the complex network of relations connecting the different episodes.

We shall then, on yet a third level, be able to make out the cultural context of the story or, to put it more precisely, the organization of the mental space (with its classificatory categories, its way of organizing and codifying reality and its delineation of the different semantic fields) within which these myths were produced and in relation to which the modern interpreter can rediscover their full and complex significance.

Second Level: The Analysis of the Semantic Content

In the interests of brevity we shall present the results of our analysis of the significant terms of each episode in the form of general conclusions. On a whole series of levels we find that there are analogies and correspondences between the shares of the sacrificial animal, the stolen fire, the first woman/Pandora, and the cereal *bios*.

We may describe these relations schematically as follows:

I. Pandora (at the end of the story) corresponds to the shares of the sacrificed ox (at the beginning of the story),
(A) inasmuch as she is a beguiling gift offered by Zeus to men just as Prometheus earlier offered Zeus the more attractive of the two portions of the animal;
(B) inasmuch as she is a *dolos*, a trap, a trick the exterior of which conceals a reality that totally belies the outward appearance. In the case of the ox, the edible parts are hidden under the double covering of the skin (*rhinos*) and stomach (*gastēr*), which looks quite revolting; the inedible parts are camouflaged beneath a coating of appetizing white fat (*Theog.*, 541: *kalupsas argeti dēmoi*). In the case of Pandora, within (cf. *Works*, 67: *en de*; 77 and 79: *en d'ara*...) there is the spirit of a bitch, a thieving nature and a voice (*audē*) designed for lies and deceit (*Works*, 67 and 78), but this internal

"bitchiness" (the *kakon*) is disguised beneath a doubly seductive appearance (the *kalon*): the bodily form of a virgin in every respect like the immortal goddesses, and the garments and jewels which adorn her, in particular the white dress (*Theog.*, 574: *argupheei esthēti*; cf. 541) and the shimmering veil which covers her (*Id.*, *kaluptrēn daidaleēn*). The divine *charis* which illuminates the body and clothing of Pandora turns her into a trap (*dolos*: cf. *Theog.*, 589; *Works*, 83) that disguises her true bestial nature in the same way as the appetizing white fat turned the apparently better share of the ox offered to Zeus into a trap (*dolos*: *Theog.*, 547, 551, 555, 560, 562) disguising the inedible bones;

(C) inasmuch as she is a *gastēr* (*Theog.*, 599), an insatiable belly devouring the *bios* or nourishment that men procure for themselves through their labor (cf. on the appetite of the woman, *Works*, 374 and 704). Now the edible part of the ox which Prometheus kept for men in externally enveloped in the *gastēr* of the animal. As well as its meaning of container, receptacle for cooking food (cf. *Od.*, XVIII, 44-5; Herodotus, IV, 61), the term *gastēr* has another semantic significance: Prometheus' trick of hiding all the edible pieces of the animal inside the *gastēr* condemned the human race to being unable henceforth to live without eating, without filling this "paunch" that has been used to disguise their share of food. Henceforth they are slaves to this *gastēr* (the hateful, accursed, harmful *gastēr* that is, as the *Odyssey* puts it: XV, 344; XVII, 286; XVII, 474; XVIII, 55, the source of all evils and cares), and are in danger of themselves becoming "like bellies" (*Theog.*, 26; cf. also Epimenides, fr. B1, F.V.S.). The figure of Pandora represents this "bitchiness" of the belly which characterizes the human condition once it has been separated from the gods as a consequence of the trick played by Prometheus: "Is there anything more bitchy [κύντερον] than the hateful belly?" Odysseus asks in the *Odyssey* (VII, 216). And Hermes hides within Pandora a *kuneos noos*, the nature of a bitch.

But the appetite of the female belly craves not only food but also sex. During the canicular period (the Dog Days) women, with their erotic hunger, reveal themselves to be lascivious and shameless (*Works*, 586–7; cf. Alcaeus fr. 347,4, Lobel and Page). Pandora's *kuneos noos* implies not only voracity but also lasciviousness, *machlosunē*.

II. Pandora also corresponds to the Promethean fire whose converse or counterpart (*anti puros*: *Theog.*, 570, 585, 602; *Works*, 57) she represents on several levels as well as according to the logic of the story:

(A) Inasmuch as she is a *dolos*. The Promethean fire is, in fact, a trap in exactly the same way as the share of the ox and Pandora herself. It is invisible, concealed inside a stem of fennel the interior of which is not damp but dry, fibrous, and secretly burning. Placed *en koiloi nartheki* (*Theog.*, 567; *Works*, 53) in a hollow stem, the stolen fire is disguised as a green plant carried in the hand. Furthermore, Promethean fire, in contrast to celestial fire, is as it were hungry: When not fed, it dies. It is also a fire that must be created: To light it one needs a "seed" of fire — a seed like that which Prometheus hides inside the fennel just as the laborer hides the seed of wheat in the belly of the earth or the husband buries his seed in the belly of his wife.

(B) Pandora also proves herself to be *anti puros*, the counterpart to fire, in that she is herself a fire that burns her man, desiccating him with fatigue and cares (through her twofold appetite and also through all the evils that she brings him). However vigorous he may be (*euei ater daloio*) she burns him without a brand (*Works*, 705) and even when he is in the prime of life (*ōmos*, raw) she turns him into a desiccated old man. (Cf. Euripides, Fr. 429, Nauck.; *Anth. Pal.*, IX, 165 and 167.) As Palladas of Alexandria writes in a gloss to Hesiod, "As a ransom for fire Zeus made us the gift of another fire, woman.... Fire can at least be extinguished but woman is an inextinguishable fire, full of ardor and ever kindled.... She burns a man up with worries, she consumes him and changes his youth into premature old age."

(C) Finally, Pandora is characterized by her *epiklopon ēthos* (*Works*,

67), her thieving nature — a feature noted in *Works*, 375: "Whoever trusts a woman is trusting himself to a thief." The "stolen" fire that Prometheus' cunning sneaked from Zeus in order to give it to men is matched by its "converse," the "thieving" fire that Zeus, to get his revenge, slips to Epimetheus, who is himself the converse of Prometheus, so that he shall spread the poison to all mankind.

III. Pandora corresponds to *bios*, the cereal food that Zeus "hides" when he also hides his celestial fire, just as Prometheus hid the food in the form of meat in the *gastēr*, and the seed of stolen fire in the hollow stem. The belly of the woman, which man must plough if he wishes to have children, is like the belly of the earth that he must plough if he wishes to have wheat since Zeus has hidden the *bios* in it. As Plato puts it, woman imitates the earth in the way she becomes pregnant and gives birth (*Menexenus*, 238a). Furthermore, Pandora is one of the names given to Earth because, we are told, she offers as a gift all that is necessary for life, which is why she is called fecund, *zeidōros*, and also *Anēsidōra*, she who causes gifts to rise from below (*Sch. to Aristophanes, Birds*, 970; Hesychius and *Et. Magnum* s.v. *Anēsidōra*). Pictorial depictions stress this aspect of proffering gifts that are hidden in the earth, in Pandora/Anēsidōra: Her fertility is no longer the spontaneous generosity of the *zeidōros aroura automatē* (*Works*, 117-18) of the Golden Age, but a fertility that henceforth demands agricultural toil, fatigue (*ponos*), and labors (*erga*). At Phlius it was Demeter, associated with Gē, who bore the title of Anēsidōra (Pausanias, I, 31, 4). Marriage, which is introduced into human life with the coming of Pandora, is itself none other than a ploughing with the woman as the furrow (*aroura*) and the man as the ploughman (*arotēr*). Seen on this level, the woman's belly is associated not only with feeding and sexual activity (all that is consumed or consummated in this belly), but also with the procreation of children and the fertility of cereals, both of which are closely connected with marriage (all that the female belly produces having first hidden it, and that cannot be produced except through this belly which first hides it).

Finally, this analysis that we have limited to cover only the major aspects of the myth shows that the grammar of the story (the logic accounting for the actions) and the semantic content are interlocking. The logic of the story exploits a reversible equation: in the case of the gods, in their relations with men, both to give and also not to give = to hide. This grammar of the story has a semantic significance (for men, desirable things are hidden within evils while evils are sometimes hidden within desirable things and sometimes concealed by their invisibility). All the semantic relationships revolve around the same theme illustrated on a number of different levels and developed in a number of different ways by the network of correspondences. These flesh out the idea that, in every form that it takes and from every point of view, human existence is governed, through the gods' "hiding" operations, by a mixture of goods and evils, by ambiguity and duplicity.

Third Level: The Sociocultural Context

The trick of Prometheus that, through the institution of the sacrificial meal in its normal form, consecrated the separation of men and gods, is attended by a number of inevitable consequences and correlations: (stolen) fire, woman and marriage (implying birth through a process of engendering, and death), and cereal agriculture and work — all these different elements are embedded at the core of the myth in a web of interrelations so dense as to be inextricable.

A number of points may be noted:

1. Throughout pagan Greek thought this network of interrelations provides the framework of reference within which the human condition is defined in its distinctive characteristics insofar as man differs both from the gods and from the beasts.

2. At the level of social institutions, sacrificial procedures, the use of fire, marriage rituals, and agricultural practices appear inter-

connected in a variety of ways. The sacrificial meal involving rit-
ualized cooking implies the use of fire: The god's share is burned
upon the altar while men can only eat the edible parts once these
are roasted or boiled. Sacrifice also appears linked to agriculture.
The domesticated animals (which are sacrificed) stand in the same
relation to wild beasts (which are hunted), from the point of view
of their proximity to man, as the cultivated plants (considered
to be cooked) stand in relation to wild plants (considered to be
raw). The practice of sacrifice stresses this similarity between
sacrificial animals and cultivated plants by incorporating barley
and wine into the ceremonial killing and burning of the ritually
sacrificed animal.

The affinities between marriage and agriculture find expression in the organization of the pantheon, in marriage rituals, in
religious festivals such as the Thesmophoria, and in a whole series
of other myths.

3. Each of the features that are noted in the myth to differentiate
men from the gods is equally relevant to the opposition between
men and beasts. The sacrificial meal is governed by a double set
of rules: Men do not eat all kinds of meat without discrimina-
tion – above all they do not eat human flesh – and whatever meat
they do eat is cooked. This stands in contrast, in Hesiod himself,
to the omophagy and allelophagy of the beasts that devour each
other (*Works*, 277-8). In a whole series of myths (Aeschylus,
Prometheus Vinctus; Plato, *Protagoras*) the fire Prometheus stole and
gave to men does not so much set a distance between heaven and
earth as wrest mankind from its primitive bestiality. It is seen as a
technical fire with which to master the skills accessible to the
industrious mind of man. Marriage also draws a clear-cut line
between man and the beasts that unite at random, crudely, with
the first comer. Finally, if the gods are immortal "because they
do not eat bread or drink wine" (*Iliad*, V, 341-2) such cultivated
food is equally unknown to the beasts that, when not carnivo-
rous, feed on raw vegetation.

In the *Theogony* and *Works*, Hesiod's account makes Prometheus the agent who brings about the split between gods and men, and it emphasizes the distance that separates them. But this distance between men and the gods presupposes that a corresponding gap separates men from the beasts. The subject of this myth about the origin of sacrifice is the definition of the very status of man, midway between the beasts and the gods. To decipher all the levels of meaning in the text and seize upon all its many implications, it is necessary to place it in a wider context, to integrate it into the corpus of evidence afforded by other mythical versions of the story, to extend the field of inquiry to cover various types of institution and to take social practices into account.

It then becomes easier to understand the special place given in the story to Pandora whose double nature is, as it were, the symbol of the ambiguity of human existence. The figure of Pandora combines all the tensions and ambivalences that characterize the status of man, placed midway between the beasts and the gods. Through the charm of her outward appearance, in which she resembles the immortal goddesses, Pandora reflects the brilliance of the divine. Through the bitchiness of her inner spirit and temperament she sinks as low as the bestial. Through the marriage that she represents, and through the articulated word and the strength that Zeus commands her to be endowed with, she is truly human (*Works*, 61–2; "ἐν δ' ἀνθρώπου θέμεν αὐδὴν καὶ σθένος"). But this humanity in which she shares as man's companion and the inevitable counterpart to his male state is not without an element of ambiguity. Because she speaks the same language as man and he can talk to her, she is a part of the human species, but at the same time she founds a *genos gunaikōn*, a race of women that is not exactly the same as the race of men but at the same time is not altogether different from it. And the articulated word that Zeus has conferred upon her as upon men is not used by her to say what really is, to transmit the truth to others, but, instead, to hide the truth beneath falsehood, to give, in the shape of words, substance to what is not, the better to deceive the mind of her male partners (*Works*, 78).

The fundamental ambiguity of Pandora is matched by the ambiguity of *Elpis* (hope) who alone remains in the house with woman (*Works*, 96–7), trapped deep inside the jar (cf. 97: *hupo cheilesin*) when all the evils have been dispersed among men. If, as in the Golden Age, human life held nothing but good things, if all the evils were still far away, shut up inside the jar (*Works*, 115-16), there would be no grounds to hope for anything different from what one has. If life was delivered up entirely and irremediably to evil and misfortune (*Works*, 200–1), there would be no place even for *Elpis*. But since the evils are henceforth inextricably intermingled with the good things (*Theog.*, 603-10; *Works*, 178, to be compared with *Works*, 102) and it is impossible for us to foresee exactly how tomorrow will turn out for us, we are always hoping for the best. If men possessed the infallible foreknowledge of Zeus, they would have no use for *Elpis*. And if their lives were confined to the present with no knowledge or concern at all regarding the future, they would equally know nothing of *Elpis*. However, caught between the lucid forethought of Prometheus and the thoughtless blindness of Epimetheus, oscillating between the two without ever being able to separate them, they know in advance that suffering, sickness, and death is bound to be their lot, and, being ignorant of the form their misfortune will take, they only recognize it too late when it has already struck them.

Whoever is immortal, as the gods are, has no need of *Elpis*. Nor is there any *Elpis* for those who, like the beasts, are ignorant of their mortality. If man who is mortal like the beasts could foresee the whole future as the gods can, if he was altogether like Prometheus, he would no longer have the strength to go on living, for he could not bear to contemplate his own death directly. But, knowing himself to be mortal, though ignorant of when and how he will die, hope, which is a kind of foresight, although a blind one (Aeschylus, *Prometheus*, 250; cf. also Plato, *Gorgias*, 523d ae), and blessed illusion, both a good and a bad thing at one and the same time – hope alone makes it possible for him to live out this ambiguous, two-sided life that is the consequence of the

Promethean deceit that instituted the first sacrificial meal. Henceforward, there is a reverse aspect to everything: Contact can only be made with the gods through sacrifice, which at the same time consecrates the impassable barrier between mortals and immortals; there can be no happiness without unhappiness, no birth without death, no abundance without toil, no Prometheus without Epimetheus — in a word, no Man without Pandora.

CHAPTER IX

The Reason of Myth[1]

The concept of myth that we have inherited from the Greeks belongs, by reason of its origins and history, to a tradition of thought peculiar to Western civilization in which myth is defined in terms of what is not myth, being opposed first to reality (myth is fiction) and, second, to what is rational (myth is absurd). If the development of the study of myth in modern times is to be understood it must be considered in the context of this line of thought and tradition. Seeking for methods of interpretation and techniques of decipherment that will make sense out of what may at first glance appear as no more than a jumble of grotesque tales, scholars have been led to question the concepts of the ancient Greeks and to ponder the true nature of what we call myth. What social and intellectual status does this type of story have? To what extent does it constitute a specific mode of expression, with its own particular language, thought, and logic? What is the position of myth within the general framework of the collective life of a society, and what distinguishes it from religious belief and ritual, from other elements in the oral tradition – stories, proverbs, and folklore – and from strictly literary fictions? In other words, what is its relation to the individual and to the social group as a whole, and what human significance do we discover in it when we examine it from an anthropological point of view?

I. *Muthos and Logos*
The Greek word *muthos* means formulated speech, whether it be a

story, a dialogue, or the enunciation of a plan. So *muthos* belongs to the domain of *legein*, as such compound expressions as *mutholegein* and *muthologia* show, and does not originally stand in contrast to *logoi*, a term that has a closely related semantic significance and that is concerned with the different forms of what is said. Even when, in the form of stories about the gods or heroes, the words transmit a strong religious charge, communicating to a group of initiates secret knowledge forbidden to the common crowd, *muthoi* can equally well be called *hieroi logoi*, sacred speeches. Between the eighth and fourth centuries B.C. a whole series of interrelated conditions caused a multiplicity of differentiations, breaks, and internal tensions within the mental universe of the Greeks that were responsible for distinguishing the domain of myth from other domains: The concept of myth peculiar to classical antiquity thus became clearly defined through the setting up of an opposition between *muthos* and *logos*, henceforth seen as separate and contrasting terms.

A. Speech and Writing

The first point to grasp here is the transition from the oral tradition to various types of written literature. This transformation had so profound an effect on the position of myth in Greece that many contemporary students of myth are doubtful whether the same methods of interpretation are valid for a body of oral accounts, such as those studied by the anthropologists, as for the written texts that are the concern of Greek scholars; it has even been considered doubtful whether the two types of data should be classified within the same category.

Writing was not necessarily introduced in the different areas of Greek creative literature at a uniform pace or as the result of similar kinds of developments, and we are certainly not in a position to establish the various stages of its evolution, the course of which was neither linear nor unambiguous. We should like simply to identify those aspects in the emergence of a written literature that most directly concern myth in its development and transmission and its place in the culture of antiquity.

First, some general remarks. It is well known that written composition is governed by more varied and adaptable rules than oral composition of the formular type. The writing of prose marks a new departure. As Adam Parry saw clearly, there is a strict correlation between the development of abstract language and the stylistic mastery achieved by the first great Greek writers of prose.[2] Prose composition — medical treatises, historical accounts, the speeches of the orators, and the dissertations of the philosophers — represents not only a different mode of expression from that of oral tradition and poetic composition but also a new form of thought. The organization of written discourse goes hand-in-hand with a more rigorous analysis and a stricter ordering of the conceptual material. As early as in an orator such as Gorgias or a historian such as Thucydides, the measured interplay of antitheses in the balanced rhetoric of written discourse functions as a veritable logical tool. By separating, positioning, and opposing the fundamental elements of the situation to be described, term for term, it allows the verbal intelligence to obtain a grip on reality. The elaboration of philosophical language goes further, not only in the degree of the abstraction of concepts and in the use of ontological terminology (for example, of Being, as such, or of the One), but also in its insistence on a new type of rigorous reasoning: The philosopher counters the persuasive techniques of rhetorical argument with the demonstrative procedures of a type of discourse modeled on the deductions of mathematicians working with numbers and geometrical figures. Emile Benveniste is quite right when he notes that when Aristotle seeks to define the logical status of all the predicates that can be asserted of Being, he is simply falling back on the fundamental categories of the language in which he is thinking.[3] The categories Aristotle distinguishes and establishes as valid in the domain of thought can be seen to be a transposition of Greek linguistic categories into that domain. However, perhaps we should add that this type of thought, in which the definition of the modalities of Being and the explicit expression of logical relationships are founded upon the structures of the language itself, was only made possible by the development of the particular forms of writing that emerged in Greece. To be sure, Aristotle's logic is linked to the language in which he thinks; but then, as a philosopher, he thinks in the language used in philosophical writing. It is in and through written literature that this type of discourse becomes established; where it is concerned the *logos* is no longer simply speech but has come to imply demonstrative rationality and, as such, it is set in opposition, both in form and in fundamental significance, to the speech of *muthos*. In form it is opposed to *muthos* in all the ways that argued demonstration differs from the narrative of the mythical story; and in fundamental significance it is also opposed, to the extent that the abstractions of the philosopher differ from the divine powers whose dramatic adventures are the subject of myth.

The differences between the two are just as great if one adopts the point of view not of the writer but of the public who reads his work. Because it is possible, when reading a text, to turn back and analyze it critically, the operation of reading presupposes a quite different attitude of mind – both more detached and at the same time more demanding – from that involved in listening to spoken discourse. The Greeks themselves were fully aware of this; they contrasted on the one hand the charm that speech must deploy to hold its listeners under its spell and, on the other, the somewhat austere but more rigorous gravity of writing, and often gave preference to the latter. They credited the one with the pleasure inherent in speech – a pleasure that, being a part of the oral message, lives and dies with the discourse that gave rise to it. The other, writing, they credited with the usefulness achieved by a text that one can keep on looking at and that continues to contain a lesson of lasting value.[4] This functional difference between speech and writing has a direct bearing on the position of myth. If the tendency of the spoken word is to give pleasure, this is because it affects the listener in the manner of an incantation. Through its metrical form, its rhythm, its consonances, its musi-

cality, and the gestures or the dances that sometimes accompany
it, oral narration stimulates its public to an affective communion
with the dramatic actions recounted in the story. This magic
quality of speech, which Gorgias celebrated and which confers
the same kind of power upon various types of oral pronounce-
ment — poetry, tragedy, rhetoric, and sophistry — is considered
by the Greeks to be one of the specific qualities of *muthos* as
opposed to *logos*. By deliberately foregoing drama and the marvellous, the *logos* acts upon the mind at a different level from an operation involving *mimēsis* or emotional participation (*sumpatheia*) on
the part of the audience. Its purpose is to establish the truth following a scrupulous inquiry and to express it in a manner that
should, by rights at least, appeal to the reader's critical intelligence alone. It is only when it has thus assumed the written form
that a discourse, divested of its mystery and, at the same time,
of its suggestive force, loses the power to impose itself on others
through the illusory but irrepressible constraint of *mimēsis*. Its status is thereby changed: It becomes something "common," in the
sense that this term had in Greek political vocabulary. No longer
is it the exclusive privilege of whoever possesses the gift of elo-
quence; now it belongs equally to all the members of the community. To put a text in writing is to set down one's message *es
meson*, at the center of the community — that is, to place it openly
at the disposal of the group as a whole. By being written down,
the *logos* is brought into the public square; like magistrates who
have just discharged their duties, it must now give an account of
itself before all and sundry and justify itself in the face of the objections and challenges that anyone has the right to bring against it.
Thus, it can be said that the rules of political intercourse, as they
function in a democratic city governed by *isegoria*, an equal right
to speech for all, have also become the rules for intellectual intercourse. The internal organization of written discourse conforms
with a logic that henceforward implies a form of debate in which
each man fights on equal terms, through discussion and counter-
argument. It is no longer a matter of overcoming one's opponent

by spell-binding, or fascinating him with one's own superior power over the spoken word. It is now a matter of convincing him of the truth by gradually inducing his own internal discourse to fall into agreement, according to his own logic and criteria, with the reasons put forward in the text presented to him. Seen in this perspective, everything that had hitherto given speech the power to impress and convince its audience is now reduced to the level of *muthos*, that is to say, the stuff of the fabulous, the marvelous. It is as if discourse could only win in the sphere of truth and intelligibility by simultaneously losing out in the sphere of what is pleasurable, moving, and dramatic.

B. FROM MYTH TO HISTORY AND PHILOSOPHY

There is already evidence of this change in Thucydides' historical account. This does not grapple with that area of the past that cannot be discussed except in the mythical form assigned to it by tradition. With the exception of the passages devoted to "archaeology," it concentrates upon the facts of recent history that are sufficiently close for the writer to have lived through them himself, or for him to have investigated with the required exactitude. Thucydides, whom one is tempted, notwithstanding Herodotus, to call the first true Greek historian, has three outstanding characteristics. He displays a respect for the truth in presenting the facts, an insistence upon clarity in this account of the changes (wars and political revolutions) that take place in the lives of cities, and a knowledge of "human nature" accurate enough to discern, underlying the web of events, the order that enables the intelligence to grasp their significance. And each of these qualities is associated with a disdainful rejection of the fabulous, *to muthodes*, which he considers fit only as an ornament for the circumstantial character of oral discourse but quite out of place in a written text whose contribution should be one of lasting value:

> To a listener the absence of anything marvellous in the facts being reported will no doubt appear to detract from the charm

of the account; however, if one desires to understand the events of the past clearly and also events of the future that, by reason of the human character they betray may present similarities or analogies with them, then so long as one judges the reported facts to be useful that should suffice: They represent a permanent treasure (*klēma es aiei*), rather than something impressive produced for a temporary audience.[5]

The best commentary to Thucydides' text is provided by the criticism that Polybius directed, three centuries later, against Phylarchos, whom he accused of wishing to rouse the reader's pity and emotion by displaying scenes of terror (*ta deina*) before his eyes: "A historical author should not try to thrill his readers by such exaggerated pictures...but simply record what really happened and what really was said, however commonplace"; for the purpose of history is not to "thrill and charm the audience for a moment" but to "instruct and convince serious students for all time, by the truth of the facts and speeches he narrates."[6]

It is significant that this same opposition between on the one hand the *muthodes*, the marvellous, suited to oral expression and the poetic genres (Plato, *Rep.*, 522a 8; *Timaeus*, 26e 5), and on the other the *alethinos logos*, truthful discourse, reappears in the philosophers and arouses the same response to *muthos* which, in its narrative form, is compared to old wives' tales (*muthos graos*: *Gorgias*, 527a 4) such as nurses tell to amuse or frighten children. When Plato, in *The Sophist*, is out to disparage the theses of his Eleatic or Heraclitean predecessors, he criticizes them for having used accounts of dramatic events and unexpected reversals of fortune as demonstrations:

> Every one of them seems to tell us a story, as if we were children. One says there are three principles, that some of them are sometimes waging a sort of war with each other, and sometimes become friends and marry and have children and bring them up.

Childish minds may well be beguiled by the spectacle of feud-
ing, fighting, reconciliation, marriage, and procreation provided
by mythical tales; but it has nothing to offer to anyone who seeks
to understand, in the strict sense of the word, because understanding refers to a form of intelligibility that *muthos* does not encom-
pass and that only explanatory discourse possesses. If, speaking
of Being, one were to recount misfortunes similar to the misfortunes myth attributes to the gods and heroes, it would be impossible for anyone to distinguish truth from legend. Plato notes
ironically that these story-tellers did not "cast their eyes so low"
as the crowd of those who, like him, distinguish the truth from
falsehood by insisting upon discourse that, at every juncture, can
account for itself if challenged. To put it another way, it can explain
itself by making clearly understood what its subject is, how it tack-
les it, and what it says about it.

On this point Aristotle is in full agreement with Plato. Pos-
ing the question, in *Metaphysics*, of whether the principles of corruptible and incorruptible beings are the same or different, he
refers to the tradition of Hesiod and those whom he calls the
"theologians," that is to say, the authors of myths about the gods,
with the purpose of emphasizing that the distance that separates
him from them is not so much temporal as intellectual:

> The school of Hesiod and all the theologians considered only
> what was convincing to themselves and gave no considera-
> tion to us. For they make the first principles Gods or gener-
> ated from Gods and say that whatever did not taste of the
> nectar and ambrosia became mortal — clearly using these
> terms in a sense significant to themselves; but, as regards the
> actual application of these causes, their statements are beyond
> our comprehension.

This apparently modest statement is in reality an outright condemnation of myth. Aristotle goes on to say: "However, it is not
worthwhile to consider seriously the subtleties of mythologists.

Let us turn rather to those who reason by means of demonstration" (III, 1000a 11-20). The fact is that the difficulties raised by
Aristotle in connection with the food of the immortals do not,
in the excessively logical form of a choice in which he expresses
them, make any sense at all once the myths are seen as accounts
that do not set out to pose this type of question and furthermore
do not formulate in these terms the problems that they do tackle.
Aristotle reads the myth as if it were a philosophical text. He
argues that there are two alternatives: Either the gods take these
foods for pure enjoyment, in which case they do not constitute
the causes of their immortal nature; or they really are the causes
for their being and, if this is so and the gods need to take food,
how can they possibly be immortal? For a historian of religion the
interest lies in the misplaced, not to say misguided, character of
Aristotle's remarks where myth is concerned. There is now such
a gap between *muthos* and *logos* that communication between the
two breaks down; dialogue becomes impossible since the break
is complete. Even when they appear to have the same object, to
be directed toward the same end, the two types of discourse
remain mutually impenetrable. From now on to choose one of
the two types of language is in effect to dismiss the other.

C. The Forms and Levels of Myth

The opposition between *muthos* and *logos*, both as forms of expression and as types of thought, is matched by other oppositions that
can be detected by the very heart of religious tradition in the
sphere of myth. As Herodotus noted, it was Homer and Hesiod
who provided the Greeks with a kind of canonical repertory of
stories about the Powers of the Beyond. This traced, through misfortunes of every kind, the story of their births, genealogy, family
relationships, their respective privileges, functions and areas of
influence, their rivalries and affinities, and their interventions in
the world of men. In the case of both poets, these stories are integrated into literary works that, through their metrical form and
the literary genre to which they belong (heroic epic, theogony,

211

wisdom texts) continue a tradition of oral poetry deeply rooted in the past. Here again, the development of writing affects both the composition and the transmission of the stories. When works are written down, even when they continue to be sung or recited at appointed times, the specifically literary features of the text gain emphasis while at the same time the genres of expression become diversified, each with its own public and its own formal rules and aesthetic aims. Elegiac, lyric, and tragic poets all draw on the common stock of mythology; but while creating literature out of mythical themes, they treat these themes with great freedom, adapting them to fit their needs and sometimes even attacking them in the name of some new ethical or religious ideal.

Quite apart from a writer such as Xenophanes, who rejected the anthropomorphism of the common mythology in the sixth century and – if we are to believe Diogenes Laertius – launched an attack in iambics against Homer and Hesiod, we should note the shifts of emphasis introduced in myth even by a poet as keen on the traditional forms of belief as Pindar was. His victory odes follow a schema of composition in which myth holds a place of central importance. Set between an introduction and a conclusion consecrated to the victor – his person, his family, and his city – the part devoted to myth may, as in the first *Olympian*, take up more than two thirds of the text. However, Pindar may interrupt his account to announce that he will say no more, his lips being loath to attribute unworthy actions to the gods, or even to say that he is about to depart from the traditional version and give his own instead, which is different from those of his predecessors.[7] Thus, in a case like that of the feast of Tantalos, this is to avoid describing any god as cannibalistic.[8] This is because, in the framework of an epinician ode, the traditional stories have acquired a new function and meaning. To adapt the expression suggested by André Jolles, it could be said that it has shifted from myth, in the strict sense of the term, toward legend.[9] It is no longer valid for and in itself but only in relation to something else, to exemplify some action or type of behavior for men to emulate. The story of the pious Pelops becomes the prototype for every victory in a chariot race; that of Tantalos, connected with it, provides a warning against the dangers inherent in success. The myth has acquired the significance of a paradigm. It constitutes the framework of reference that allows one to assess, understand, and judge the exploit that the poem is celebrating. It is only by being refracted through the legendary adventures of the heroes or gods that human actions, conceived as imitative, can reveal their meaning and fall into position on the scale of values.

In the tragic poets the shift is even more marked. The themes for their dramas are borrowed from the legends about the heroes in the form in which they appear in the epic cycles and in various local traditions. But the tragedies do not merely alter certain points in the plot so as to make them truly tragic — as, for example, when Aeschylus and Sophocles change Homer's Oedipus, who died on the throne of Thebes, into a man blinded by his own hand, an exile rejected by the world of men. By setting a myth on the stage, the dramatist both brings it closer to the contemporary audience and, at the same time, distances it from them. In the epic the heroes are men, not supernatural powers such as those worshipped in the public religion of the fifth-century city. The exploits the *Iliad* sings of were accomplished during the Trojan War in the course of a military expedition that, even if we may today doubt its historical veracity, was described by the bard and accepted by the public as if it had really happened and was situated in the same continuum of time as the lives of the bard and his audience. In this way, in the Homeric poems, the mythical stories about the gods are associated with the "high deeds" of the great families, celebrating their exploits and justifying the privileges still considered the due of their descendants.

In contrast, tragedy creates a distance between the characters that it depicts upon the stage and the public who are its spectators. The tragic hero belongs to a different world from the world of the city and to a different age from fifth-century Athens. It is only by relegating them to a far-distant past, a legendary, other

213

time outside the present, that the democratic *polis* can integrate into its own culture the dramas that tore apart those royal houses and the misfortunes and ancestral curses that beset them. The effect of the theatrical presentation, the costumes, the special buskins, the masks and, in sum, their larger-than-life characters was to remove these figures to the level of the legendary heroes to whom cults were devoted in the city. Yet, at the same time, by reason of the familiar, almost prosaic way they spoke and the discussions they entered into with the chorus and with each other, they were brought closer to the ordinary man and were made, as it were, the contemporaries of the citizens of Athens who crowded the stepped banks of the theater. Because of this constant tension and opposition between the mythical past and the present of the *polis* that operates within each drama and each protagonist, the hero ceases to be regarded, as he was in Pindar, as a model and becomes instead an object of debate. He is brought before the public as a subject at issue. Through the debate that the drama sets up, it is the very status of man that becomes the problem. The enigma of the human condition is brought into question, not that the inquiry pursued by tragedy, ever started anew and never completed, can find any resolution or definitive answer. Myth, in its original form, provided answers without ever explicitly formulating the problems. When tragedy takes over the mythical traditions, it uses them to pose problems to which there are no solutions.

This literary manipulation of myth is all the more striking because other accounts were at this time being produced with the purpose of collating the various versions that were current in different parts of the oral tradition. In the fifth century, Pherecydes of Athens and Hellanicos present in their chronicles local legends about the founding of cities and the genealogies of gods or heroes that were the object of public or family cults within the framework of these cities. It must be recognized that these collections are in part concerned to present a reinterpretation of the mythical material — an operation that was certainly set in train even earlier by logographers such as Hekataios, Charon of Lampsacus, and Xanthos of Lydia. But at the same time Pherecydes and Hellanicos were certainly preparing the way for the work of collation undertaken by scholars from the Hellenistic period onward and culminating in the composition of veritable mythographical anthologies such as the Pseudo-Apollodorus' *Bibliotheka,* the *Fables* and *Astronomica* of Hygienus, Book IV of Diodorus' *Histories,* the *Metamorphoses* of Antonius Liberalis, and the collection known as the *Mythographi Vaticani.* To this body of work we must add snippets of information and fragments of stories to be gleaned, here and there, from the glosses of the scholiasts and lexicographers. In contrast to the literary transpositions, these texts provide us with evidence on the myths and their variants that, while not being altogether in the original "untouched" state (for, as we shall see, even in the oral traditions of peoples we describe as "primitive" there is no such thing as myth in the untouched state), nevertheless remains unaffected by any reinterpretation inspired by norms that are anachronistic to mythical thought.[10]

D. MYTHS AND MYTHOLOGY

A distinction needs to be drawn between, on the one hand, these collections of stories put together and more or less coordinated through the diligence of the mythographers and, on the other, what constitutes in the case of the Greeks not simply a number of myths but a mythology, that is to say, a unified, narrative corpus of stories. By virtue of its range and internal coherence, this represents an original system of thought as complex and rigorous in its own way as a philosopher's construction may be, in a different mode. The typical example of such a mythology is provided by the work of Hesiod, in particular the *Theogony.* Gone are the days when philologists used entirely arbitrary logical criteria to justify — as they believed — their condemning the composite, even incoherent character of the text. They used to claim to be able to cut it up into different sections, discovering a whole series of successive strata and additions inserted at different dates, which were quite heterogeneous or even incompatible with one another. However, ever since H. Fraenkel's classic study, it has been impossible not to recognize Hesiod as the first Greek thinker to put forward an ordered, general vision of the divine and human universe.[11] (This is not to deny the reservations one may feel about his reading of Hesiod, which understands him retrospectively and interprets him, on the basis of later philosophy, as having put forward an early form of ontology.) If one wishes to avoid thinking of *muthos* in terms more relevant to the *logos* that superseded it, any decoding of the text must first and foremost pay scrupulous attention to every aspect of the narrative organization of the account. In this connection, the analyses carried out by Peter Walcot, and in particular the study by Hans Schwabl are conclusive: On the one hand they show that the text as a whole is an example of "ring composition" that gives the story its cohesion and makes it possible to distinguish its fundamental structure; on the other, they point out Hesiod's repeated use of syntactical parallelisms that, by linking together the various episodes and rigorously correlating all the details, guarantee the general balance of the work and the unity of its structure.[12] However, the mythologist cannot limit his inquiry to the formal framework of the story. The philological study must be accompanied by an analysis of the contents aimed at revealing the semantic relationships, the interplay of corresponding symbols, the many layers of meaning in the text, and the hierarchy of the codes by which its message is conveyed. Clearly, this decoding operation raises all the methodological and other, fundamental problems in the interpretation of myth, and we shall come back to these later. At this point we should simply like to indicate the exceptional character of the evidence that Hesiod's work provides and the interest it must hold for any mythologist: While they still show links with oral poetry, his works are already written compositions. They belong to a living and complex mythological tradition in which a number of Oriental influences have been detected.[13] At the same time, however, this is a new creation, the work of a unique personality whose theory of poetry constitutes a deliberate departure from that of his predecessors and contemporaries. Hesiod declares that, being inspired by the Muses, he will reveal the "Truth" and celebrate "what has been, what is and what will be," unlike other writers whose works are merely fictional lies designed to flatter the vanity of the aristocratic public for whom they were composed. He displays a proud consciousness of being one who, by introducing a new type of poetry, brings the word of truth, playing a prophetic role that places the poet, seen as the mediator between gods and men, in a position comparable to that of kings. It is this that confers upon the long collection of tales that make up the *Theogony* the force of a veritable body of theological teaching and turns the fables, warnings, and moral or practical counsel generously dispensed in the *Works and Days* into the teaching of a Master of Wisdom who has been deemed comparable to the prophets of Israel.[14] Hesiod sifts the mythical material provided for him by tradition. In particular he as it were recasts his varied material into an original integrated construction. The mythical themes, episodes, and figures that he retains, and sometimes touches up, fit together in the course of his account as the combined parts of a unified message whose global significance and rich complexity it is the poet's purpose to transmit. In the work of Hesiod, then, we have to recognize what may be described as a learned mythology richly and subtly elaborated that possesses all the finesse and rigor of a philosophical system while at the same time remaining totally committed to the language and mode of thought peculiar to myth.

Other theogonies also existed in Greece — vast constructions of the same type as Hesiod's, but of which only a few fragments have come down to us. Although they may not have carried the weight and almost canonical authority that the Greeks responded to in Hesiod's work, their authors — such as Pherecydes of Syros, Epimenides, and the Orphic poets — had similar aims and ambitions in writing them. In that they deliberately depart, on certain essential points, from Hesiod's "orthodox" model, these accounts testify to the presence of an element of criticism and disagreement in the field of myth. It does not take the form of explicit objections or discussion but makes itself felt, rather, through significant divergences and differences in both the form and content of the works. These many alternative versions show that, even when the myths of a culture appear to conflict with one another, they are in fact complementary and their very divergences represent different aspects of a single mode of communication; they are all bounded by the same intellectual horizon and can only be deciphered within this general framework, each version acquiring meaning and emphasis from its relationship to all the others. The importance of this dialogue in which mythical thought constantly engages so long as it remains alive should not be underestimated. In the case of Greece two recent discoveries have confirmed the authenticity and antiquity of these mythical compositions that are sufficiently "marginal" for most Greek scholars to have seen fit, on the basis of their unusual or even contradictory character in comparison with the mainstream of tradition, to treat them as oddities composed at a much later date, mere by-products of the Hellenistic imagination. The first of these texts is a papyrus bearing a commentary on a cosmogonic poem composed by Alcman in Sparta during the seventh century; the second is a roll of papyrus discovered in a tomb at Derveni, bearing the text of a commentary on an Orphic Theology, composed in the second half of the fourth century, proving that the sacred Orphic accounts of the genesis of gods and men attested at a later date are in fact the direct continuation of a much more ancient tradition.

E. Myth Between Nonsense and Allegory

This brief summary of the different types of texts that we, following the ancient Greeks themselves, class as myth gives already some indication of the comparatively disparate character of that category: It includes many different fragmentary versions in the form of short tales or even schematic summaries — literary transpositions more or less artificially elaborated, as well as vast, systematic constructions with theological aims. The first common feature that all these texts belonging to very different levels of thought share is that, despite their divergences, they are all connected with the same tradition. They may introduce modifications on certain points but they nevertheless adopt the same general line and, even when they innovate, they accept a number of constraints and observe the rules of a particular network of themes, associations, analogies, and oppositions without which the message would no longer be intelligible within a given culture. Secondly, they are all accounts capable of captivating their audience, who must enjoy listening to them as they do to ordinary stories and fables; at the same time, however, the mythical accounts have to be "serious"; they adopt a fictional, fantastical manner to speak of things that are essential, touching upon the most fundamental truths of existence. Finally, through their narrative form they present "agents" who, in the course of the story, perform such actions as to alter the initial situation so that by the end it is quite different from what it was at the beginning. In myth, those who operate this transformation – in other words, the figures whose actions determine the series of changes that take place between the beginning and the end of the story – are Powers from the Beyond, supernatural agents whose adventures take place in a different time, on a different level, and in accordance with a different mode of being from those of the life of ordinary men.

Instead of distinguishing these general characteristics of myth and examining how they affect the significance and implications of myth and the way it functions, Greek scholars appear to have been more concerned to select one particular type of text, ignoring the rest, in order to base their general conception of myth upon it. Sometimes, when multiple and apparently contradictory versions of a single story have been considered, the conclusion reached has been that they represent the result of the "free play of the imagination," the uncontrolled product of fantasy run wild. Other scholars have concentrated upon the literary aspects of these creations. Considering them as part of a single written culture in conjunction with many other texts, they have applied to them the historico-philological methods of analysis that are valid for quite a different type of writing; in this way they have limited themselves to tracing the recurrences and transformations of a particular theme from one author to another as if, in order to understand a myth, all one had to do was retrace its literary developments exactly, establishing its family tree and making a complete list of its ancestry. Others, finally, have attempted to discover a hidden truth or secret theology under the veil of the narrative. They have tried to penetrate the veil of mystery of the fable and reach the religious wisdom lying beyond it and transmitted by it, disguised in symbolic form.

Here again modern scholars have simply followed in the footsteps of the ancient authors, remaining in a sense a part of the classical tradition that they had set out to study. Restricted within the bounds of this horizon, they examined and saw the myths as the Greeks did. The ancient Greeks themselves did not simply relegate myth, in the name of the *logos*, to the shadows of unreason and the untruths of fiction. They continued to make literary use of it as the common treasure-house on which their culture could draw in order to remain alive and perpetuate itself. Furthermore, as early as the archaic period they recognized its value as a means of teaching, but an obscure and secret one. They considered it to have some function as truth, but this truth could not be formulated directly, and before it could be grasped had to be translated into another language for which the narrative text was only an allegorical expression. As early as the sixth century Theagenes of Rhegium embarked upon a work of allegorical explanation for the myths of Homer that substituted symbolic equivalents for Homer's own terms and thus transposed his account into the terminology of cosmology, physics, moral philosophy, or metaphysics. Myth was thus purged of its absurdities, implausibilities, and immorality, all of which scandalized reason. But this was achieved only at the cost of jettisoning myth's own fundamental character, refusing to take it literally and making it say something

quite different from what it actually told. This type of interpretation was at its most spectacular when undertaken by the Stoics
and the Neo-Platonists,[15] but it is fair to say that throughout Greek
tradition — whenever, that is, it does not simply ignore myth —
the attitude is the same and myth is seen in one of two ways: Either
it expresses in a different, allegorical, or symbolic form the same
truth as the *logos* expresses directly or, alternatively, it conveys
what is not the truth — that which, by its nature, lies outside the
domain of truth and which consequently eludes knowledge and
has nothing to do with speech articulated according to the rules
of demonstration. Plato often appears to reject *muthos* utterly as,
for instance, when in the *Philebus* (14a) he writes of an argument,
logos, which, being undermined by its own internal contradictions, destroys itself as if it were a *muthos*; or when, in the *Phaedo*
(61b), he has Socrates say that *muthos* is not his affair but that of
the poets — those same poets who, in the *Republic*, are exiled, as
liars, from the city. However, this same Plato grants an important
place in his writings to myth, as a means of expressing both those
things that lie beyond and those that fall short of strictly philosophical language. How could one give philosophical expression,
through an ordered network of words, to the concept of the Good,
the supreme value that is not an essence but, being the source of
Being and Knowing, lies beyond essence in both dignity and power
(*Republic*, 509b ff.)? And similarly, how would it be possible to
speak philosophically of Becoming, which, in its constant change,
is subject to the blind causality of necessity? Becoming is too much
a part of the irrational for any rigorous argument to be applied
to it. It cannot be the object of a true knowledge, only of a belief,
pistis, or opinion, *doxa*. Thus, in referring to the gods or the birth
of the world, it is impossible to use *logoi homologoumenoi*, totally
coherent arguments. One must make do with a plausible fable,
eikota muthon (*Timaeus*, 29b and c). When writing of the soul, its
destiny and immortality, Plato resorts to the old myths of rein-
carnation just as, in his theory of reminiscence (*anamnesis*), he
transposes the most ancient myths about memory in which *Mnēmo-*

sunē in the Beyond personifies the source of eternal life reserved for those who have been able to keep their souls pure from every defilement in this earthly life. The closing words of the *Republic* are as follows: "And it is thus, Glaucon, that the *muthos* has been saved from oblivion and has not been lost. If we put our faith in it it may even save us, ourselves."

In a text from the *Metaphysics* (1074b ff.), Aristotle distinguishes from myth all those fables that men have constructed to persuade the masses, for instance, to conceive the Gods as having a human form and human feelings; but he too immediately goes on to add: "If one separates the myth from its initial basis — that is to say, the belief that all the first substances are gods — and considers this basis alone, it will be seen that the tradition is truly a divine one."

Thus, we can see that while Greek philosophy in many ways countered the language of myth, it at the same time continued to use it or transposed it to another level, divesting it of the purely "fabulous" element in it. Philosophy can thus be seen as an attempt to formulate and demythologize that truth that myth, in its own way, was already aware of and transmitted in the form of allegorical stories.

However, there is another side to this reintegration of myth into the world of philosophical reason from which it had appeared to be rejected: Through being granted the rights of citizenship, as it were, it is naturalized with the status of a philosopher and, by winning acceptance, becomes absorbed. From Aristotle's point of view, to recognize an element of divine truth in myth is to accept it as a forerunner of philosophy in the same way as the speech of a child prepares the way for the language of the adult and is only intelligible in relation to the latter. This is to see myth as a preliminary sketch for rational discourse, to suggest that its fables are the vehicle for the first mumblings of the *logos*.

F. Greek Mythology and Western Thought

If, at the end of our analysis, we attempt to pinpoint the image of myth that classical antiquity has bequeathed us, we cannot fail

to be struck by the paradoxical, at first sight almost contradictory character of the status conferred upon it in Greek tradition.
On the one hand, for more than a millennium it constitutes the
common pool for Greek culture, providing a framework of reference for not only religious but also other forms of social and spiritual life; it can be seen as the canvas, as it were, on which are
depicted not only the literature of educated writers but also the
oral compositions in popular circles. On the other hand, within
this same civilization it seems to have no recognized position, character, or function of its own. Myth is either defined negatively
in terms of what it lacks or fails to offer, as non-sense, non-reason,
non-truth, non-reality or — if it is granted any positive mode of
being — it is explained away as something other than itself. It is
as if its existence depended upon it being transposed or translated
into some other language or type of thought. Sometimes, considered in its aspect of a fabulous tale, it is assimilated to poetic
composition and literary fiction and connected with the power
of the imagination that, to be sure, exerts a fascination over us,
but only as "a mistress of error and falsity." In other instances it
is credited with a truthful meaning but this is immediately interpreted as the truth purveyed by philosophical discourse, and in
this case myth is presented as no more than a clumsy gesture
toward the latter or an indirect allusion to it. In every instance
myth is regarded as allegory and its message read as such. It no
more occupies a position in its own right than it speaks with a
language truly its own. In the tradition of thought that has come
down to us from the Greeks, marked as this is with the stamp of
rationalism, myth, despite its place, its impact, and its importance,
finds its own specific aspects and functions effaced when it is not
purely and simply rejected in the name of *logos*. In one way or
another myth, as such, is always exorcised. It was only with the
advent of a thinker such as Schelling, who declared that myth is
not allegorical at all but rather "tauto-gorical," that the perspective on myth was openly and radically changed. If myth is saying
not "something else" but that very thing that it is quite impossi-

ble to say in any other way a new problem arises and the entire scope of the study of mythology is transformed: What then is myth saying and what is the connection between the message it bears and the manner in which it expresses it?

Meanwhile, like any other paradox, the paradox of classical mythology can teach us something. Myth appears both as the soil in which, in the course of centuries, a culture takes root, and at the same time as a part of this culture whose authenticity the latter seems to fail to acknowledge. The reason for this is probably that the fundamental role, function, and meaning of myth are not immediately apparent to those who make use of it; these things do not, essentially, lie at the surface level of the stories. A myth like those of ancient Greece is not a dogma with a form strictly fixed once and for all because it represents the basis for an obligatory belief. As we have pointed out, myth is the canvas upon which both oral narrative and written literature depict their message, each with such freedom that divergences between different traditions and the innovations that certain authors introduce neither scandalize nor are even difficult to accommodate from a religious point of view. If the myths can vary in this way from one version to another without damaging the balance of the general system it must be because what matters is not the way the story is told, which can vary from one account to another, but rather the mental categories conveyed by the stories as a whole and by the intellectual organization that underlies all the various versions. However, this mental architecture and underlying logic that myth deploys as it elaborates the whole gamut of its many different versions are absorbed unconsciously by each child who listens to the stories and repeats them, in just the same way that he learns his maternal tongue; and it is precisely because they seem so natural and so immediate that they are so difficult to apprehend. We must stand outside a culture, at a distance, feeling bewildered by its mythology and disconcerted by the unaccustomed character of a type of fable and imagination that are unfamiliar to us, if we are to perceive clearly the need for a devious, less direct approach.

This must lead us from the surface text to the bases that provide its structural organization, and guide us through the many different variants of the myth to the structural framework that provides the overall key we can use to decipher a veritable system of thought not, at every level, immediately accessible to the habitual working of our minds.

So it would seem that it is not so much the unfamiliarity of the Greek myths that initially constitutes the principal epistemological obstacle to a vigorous analysis of them. Rather, it is the fact that they are too close to the mental universe of the West and seem too "natural" to us. This would explain why the most spectacular progress in contemporary mythological research has been made by the anthropologists and ethnologists rather than by Greek scholars, despite the fact that the latter were working on material that had long been familiar in every detail, classified and commented upon. Perhaps two conditions needed to be satisfied before any new perspective could be adopted on the problem of how to approach myth. First, it was necessary to disentangle our knowledge of classical antiquity from the general learning of commentators so that it should no longer be confused, as it had been, in Europe, from the fifteenth to the eighteenth centuries, with an "erudition" dating from the Hellenistic period. In sum, the ancient data had at last to be viewed from both a historical and a cultural distance.[16] The second and even more important requisite was that the Greek myths should cease to be regarded as the model, the focus of reference, for mythology as a whole. It was necessary to develop a comparative science of religions so as to compare them with the myths of other great, non-classical, civilizations and to use the contributions of ethnographical research to set them alongside the myths of peoples without writing. The main trends of the contemporary inquiry into the world of myth emerged from this twofold movement that involved on the one hand a distancing from antiquity (making it possible to see Greek civilization as a historical moment, one particular spiritual world with its own peculiar characteristics) and, on the other, the comparison of Greek myths with those of other peoples (making it possible to conceive the mythical, in all its many forms, as one level of thought in general).

II. *Toward a Science of Mythology*

Both these tendencies began to make themselves felt toward the end of the eighteenth century. On the one hand, in Germany in particular, historical philology got going as a legitimate study that related history to Greek scholarship, no connection having hitherto been made between them. (Until then, so far as the ancient world was concerned, history was understood to be simply what the ancient historians themselves — Herodotus, Thucydides, and Polybius, *et al.* — had actually written.) At the same time, first Romanticism and then Hegelianism laid considerable emphasis on the ideas of *Volk, Volkgeist,* and *Weltgeist*, which foreshadow our concepts of culture and civilization and which could be applied in particular to the world of the ancient Greeks. On the other hand, as early as 1724, Father J.-F. Lafitau had established a parallel, further developed later by De Brosses, between the legends believed by the Greeks and the superstitions of the Indians of the New World.[17] The similarity they recognized between the mythology of Greece, the Mother of Civilization and Nurse of Reason, and that of the savages of America was, following the failure of the symbolist interpretations of Friedrich Creuzer, to precipitate a scandal. The three great schools of thought whose rivalry dominates the field of mythological studies at the end of the nineteenth century were all to attempt to dissipate it. The problem was this:[18] If we reject over-facile and gratuitous explanations of an allegorical nature, how are we to account for the presence, among the people that reached "the highest point of civilization," of this "nonsensical and incongruous" type of language used to purvey "savage and absurd" stories[19] that attribute to the gods "things that would make even the most savage Redskin shudder":[20] namely, all the abominations of parricide, incest, adultery, sodomy, murder, and cannibalism? How can one justify the presence, alongside the most rarefied reason, of this irrational element of myth reminiscent of the pronouncements "of a mind temporarily demented"?[21] In short, how is it that in myth one can detect a barbarity lying at the very heart of the culture from which all our science and, to a large extent, our religion also directly proceed?

Three very different types of solutions were provided to this problem by, respectively, the school of comparative mythology, the English school of anthropology, and the German school of historical philology. Marcel Detienne devoted a number of seminars at the École Pratique des Hautes Études, during 1972 and 1973, to situating these three streams of thought in the history of mythological research. Rather than attempt to trace the line of argument that he himself demonstrates in detail far better than we could hope to, we will confine ourselves here to recalling some of the conclusions he reached in his article entitled "Mythe et langage: De Max Müller à Claude Lévi-Strauss."

A. Myth and Language:
The School of Comparative Mythology

Max Müller and the school of comparative mythology (in which, among the Greek scholars, one may include Ludwig Preller[22] and Alexander H. Krappe[23] in Germany and Paul Decharme in France,[24] and the influence of which extends far beyond its declared followers) see the absurd and incongruous character of myth as a kind of aberration, a metaphorical perversion that took place in the development of language, an unhealthy excrescence that afflicted it. For them, mythology is essentially a pathological type of discourse grafted onto and feeding on the tree of language, whose roots lie in the original experience of great cosmic phenomena such as the regular cycle of the sun or the unleashing of storms.[25] The task of the comparative mythologist is thus considered to be to explore the tangle of etymologies, morphological developments, and semantic connections in order to discover the original values which, before their meaning was lost, translated man's contact with nature into the "roots" of language. In this way a naturalistic explanation took over from or even supplanted the analysis of the language of myth, and Paul Decharme went so far as to declare: "You can tell a good mythologist from his feeling for nature rather than from his linguistic reliability."[26]

B. Myth and Social Evolution:
The English School of Anthropology

For Edward B. Tylor and Andrew Lang's English School of Anthropology[27] (which can be said to include James G. Frazer[28] and, among the pure Greek specialists, Jane E. Harrison, Gilbert Murray, Francis M. Cornford, and Arthur B. Cook) the savagery of myth in the great historical cultures cannot be attributed to a degeneration from a previous, better founded and more reasonable state of linguistic consciousness. On the contrary, it testifies to the survival, in advanced civilizations, of the primitive barbarity exemplified in certain existing peoples that have not yet emerged from it. For this school of thought, the mythological "oddities" of the ancient Greeks could not be attributed to a wayward development of language but rather to a particular stage in the social and intellectual evolution of mankind — a stage that all peoples live through and from which those that were called archaic had not yet emerged. Myth is no longer a "pathological condition of language" but a vestige of savagery that can be defined as the savage state of thought. This leads to an insistence upon those features which distinguish savage thought from our own civilized intelligence and a determination to establish between the two types of mentality, a distance that, in the case of Lévy-Bruhl, becomes a veritable gulf. Tylor had defined savage thought by its animism; Frazer had seen sympathetic magic as its main characteristic, and finally Lévy-Bruhl relegated it to a kind of ghetto, confining it within a "prelogical" stage just as a schizophrenic, whose madness is in many respects related to the primitive mentality, is shut up in an asylum. Altogether ruled by affectivity, unfamiliar with the principle of non-contradiction, insensible to causal sequence, barely able to distinguish subject from object, and governed by a law of participation that assimilates the most diverse things together, the savage thought that is at work in myth is not merely different from our own conceptual system; insofar as it is prelogical and mystical, it constitutes its contrary and reverse just as madness is not simply different from reason but is its precise opposite.[29]

In thus laying the emphasis on the emotions and passions that control the behavior and thought of primitive peoples, the anthropologists of the English school tend to see ritual as the most important aspect of religion. Myth is considered to be of secondary importance. It is the reflection in language of the religious ritual, which is the only thing that is really important from the point of view of the needs of the group, and for which it provides an oral justification and commentary. The way to explain a myth is to discover the ritual to which it corresponds. Apart from this, the theory of evolutionism does not simply draw constantly upon the idea of a primitive survival. It also fosters the use of comparativism between different civilizations and religions on a global scale. Rituals, divine figures, and episodes taken from myth belonging to very different frameworks are lifted right out of their religious, cultural, and social context. Their distinctive features are disregarded and they are assimilated together in vast categories under such headings as mana, totem, fertility cults, mother goddesses, and spirit of vegetation — categories that are sufficiently general and vague to be applied all over the place, without being rigorously pertinent anywhere. In the end Tylor and Lang's disciples, too, resort to explanations of a naturalistic nature although these take a different form from those of the school of comparative mythology. It is not the sun and the storms that archaic religions experience in the bedrock of natural reality but man's relations with the earth from which he draws his subsistence. The life and death of vegetation, the return of the forces of spring and, for ancient Greece, the *eniautos daimon* form, through the rites of renewal that they occasion, the original nucleus around which pantheons and mythologies are believed to revolve.

229

C. Myth and Literary History: Historical Philology

By opening up traditional Greek scholarship to linguistics and anthropology, both these schools of interpretation, each in its own way and within its own limitations, gave new impetus to the study of myth. The new German school of philology opposed them both. In this school, at about the same time — the end of the nineteenth and beginning of the twentieth century — philology turned in on itself and also manifested a desire to take over the study of classical mythology. While it certainly contributed toward the collection of evidence and the construction of research tools that are still indispensable today, it nevertheless, in its presentation of the facts, imposed a general view and methodology so narrowly positivist that the fundamental problems of myth, in the case of the Greeks, were pushed aside. One of its leaders, Otto Gruppe, gave a clear account of its spirit and techniques.[30] The method adopted is historical and genetic. Its purpose is to establish the exact credentials of a myth — that is, its origin and the way it developed — using the tools of philology and chronography. Where does it come from, where did it first appear, when did it become established, what successive forms did it take, what is known of its first attested version which must be considered as its archetype?

By rejecting all research specifically directed toward elucidating the myth's meaning, this reduction of the analysis of myth to a chronological and typographical inquiry ultimately leads to the assimilation of myth to history. If the archetype of a myth makes its appearance at a particular point in place and time it is assumed to reflect a particular historical happening such as tribal migration, strife between cities, the overthrow of a dynasty, and so on. At the extreme this becomes Euhemerism. Thus Jean Bérard has no compunction in declaring: "One of the results of the research carried out since the beginning of this century into the study of ancient religions has been to bring to light the substratum of historical reality that often underlies legend." Yet is it not a fact that the essential interest of a myth stems precisely from the extraordinary distance that separates the event we sometimes believe we can place at its origin from the cycle of stories as they have come down to us?

The second aspect of the work of the philological school is linked with this failure to recognize myth's own specific character. It is the purely literary nature of its analysis of the texts. The various versions of a myth are studied from the point of view of the type of literature, the *genre* of composition and the personality of the writers who used them. Thus Carl Robert devotes himself to the development and transformation of myths in literature and in art.[31] Ultimately, myth is considered to result from the same type of analysis as aesthetic, poetic, or intellectual creations and to be the same kind of phenomenon. According, to Ulrich von Wilamowitz-Möllendorf,[32] the noblest and most authentic manifestations of religion are to be found in the works of the great writers and philosophers.

The historical positivism of this school is the essential directing element in Martin P. Nilsson's work, which represents the epitome and model of the history of religion and mythology in Greece.[33] The works of the Swedish scholar, whose authority continues to exert a heavy influence on the development of studies in this field, are conditioned by a sharply defined attitude of mind and a distinctive intellectual approach both to the myths themselves and to the religious data. The study of Greek religion is not approached in such a way as to discern the basic structure of the organization of the pantheon, the various forms of grouping by which the divine powers are associated together or opposed to each other, or the articulations of the theological system. Its purpose is to reveal the fundamentally composite, syncretic, heterogeneous nature of classical religion, which is regarded not as an organized whole but as a collection of gods associated together more as the result of historical chance than through any internal logic. A gallery of disparate portraits is thus presented in what might just as well be alphabetical order, as in a dictionary. In this disjointed perspective the individual characteristics of each of these divine figures seem to bear little relation to each other and they are ascribed to a process of fusion between elements of different origins that happen by chance to have come together. Thus, for Nilsson, the Greek Dionysus is the result of a fusion between an Asiatic spirit of vegetation and an orgiastic cult devoted to a Thracian deity. But the fundamental question remains the status of the Greek Dionysus in the archaic and classical periods, the position he holds in a religious consciousness that was quite unaware of his possible double origin. The important points are the functions of this god and his religion within the global system to which he must have belonged for a very long time (a fact that diminishes the relative significance of the problems concerning his origins) since his name already appears on tablets from Mycenaean Pylos and, in any case, festivals in his name certainly predated the Ionian colonization of Asia Minor.

The same disparate character is attributed to mythology as a whole. The theory is that it comprises three radically separate basic strata: the first, causal or etiological explanations; the second, history's contribution to legend; and the third, "imaginary" elements that the historian of myth is unable to explain in terms of an actual event. Because he fails to detect in them any reflection of reality, he assumes them to result from the "free play of the imagination" (to use an expression of Nilsson's). He sees them as a gratuitous fantasy whose vivid creations express a body of popular beliefs and peasant superstitions still very close to the earth "which is the source of all religion and the origin even of the great gods."[34]

The concept of a pantheon with barely any structure, an eclectic collection of many unconnected elements, and that of a mythology that is an amalgam of random material are closely linked. Thus Edouard Will writes that Greek religion presents "an astonishing collection of contradictions and paradoxes which it is difficult to resolve on the basis of local myths. It seems clear that it is this infinite diversity within Greek religion as a whole, this confusion that affects all the local pantheons and religious systems, that accounts for the absence of any great systematic texts of the type that have come down to us from India or Iran."[35]

According to the bias and logic of this kind of traditional phi-lology then, any attempt to decipher Greek religion and mythology seems doomed to failure. How can one hope to find any order in what appears, by its very nature, to be a muddled rag-bag? When classical scholarship turns in on itself in this way it emphasizes the paradox inherent from the start in the opposition between *logos* and *muthos* as expressed by the ancient writers: namely, that the same people, the same civilization held to be the embodi-ment of the virtues of intellectual clarity, rigor, and order could have lived in a sort of chaos where their religion and mythology were concerned.

D. THE INTELLECTUAL HORIZON OF MYTHOLOGICAL STUDIES

The three currents of thought that mark the beginnings of a mod-ern science of mythology certainly rival one another and occa-sionally engage in bitter polemic, but their discussions are aired, so to speak, within closed walls, within the framework of an intel-lectual space that confines them all equally. We can define the outlines of this framework and the limitations it imposes upon all three currents of thought despite their profound theoretical and methodological differences.

1. In different, even contrary forms, the point of view adopted is always fundamentally a genetic one, research being always directed toward discovering "origins." Whether it is different stages in the evolution of language, the successive points in social and intellectual development, or the historical transformations a particular theme may have undergone, the principle of expla-nation is always the same, namely in terms of a primitive state or an original archetype.

2. There is, as yet, no sign of the idea that religion and myths form an organized system whose coherence and complicated work-ings it is important to grasp. Each myth, each version, and each deity are studied in isolation. For example, the method of pro-

233

cedure adopted in Farnell's classic work, *The Cults of the Greek States*, is to study each god in turn, together with the mythology connected with him, as if a pantheon, a totality of individual entities, could be cut into separate slices.

3. The method of tackling myth is reductionist. Instead of seeing it as a specific form of expression, a language to be decoded, these writers explain it in terms now of an accident, an aberration in the development of language, now of a ritual practice, now of a historical event. If ever myth is lucky enough to be considered something more than the realities that underlie it and onto which it is grafted, this additional dimension is then dismissed as unimportant, the result of a kind of gratuitous game, an unnecessary fantasy of no intrinsic significance.

4. In default of any appropriate linguistic and sociological analysis, the notion of the religious symbol is used in a purely literary, metaphorical way. Either the mythical symbol is connected with the original, primitive roots that all religion is believed to express (the forces of nature, man's relation to the earth, the life and death of vegetation) or else it is reduced to one of the "imaginative fantasies" of the poets and philosophers.

5. Restricted to this framework, the study of the mythical thought of the Greeks oscillates between two extremes: Either an attempt is made to restrict it to a primitive mentality of unvarying quality and invariably opposed to our own (that is to say, a mentality obsessed with animism or sympathetic magic, a prelogical type of thought) – or, alternatively, our own categories of thought are applied to it as if the "common sense" of contemporary Greek scholarship was, like Cartesian reason, the most universally distributed commodity in the world. In neither case can the inquiry be truly historical or recognize what it is that distinguishes Greek thought from other forms of mythical expression any more than it can give any general synchronic account of the overall structure of such systems of thought.

III. *Myth Today*

During the period between the wars the horizon of mythological studies was transformed and a new problematic emerged. The
changes took many forms, depending on different points of view
and originating in a number of different disciplines, such as the
philosophy of epistemology, psychology, sociology, ethnology, the
history of religions, and linguistics. However, all these studies had
one feature in common: They all took myth seriously, accepting
it as an undeniable dimension in human experience. The narrow
outlook of the positivism of the preceding century was rejected
together with its naïve belief in the inevitable progress of societies from the shadows of superstition toward the light of reason.
A fuller knowledge of other cultures occasioned a reappraisal of
the particular form of rationality adopted and developed by the
West. There was a new interest in discovering the authentic and
essential nature of that shadowy part of man that is hidden from
him. This new attitude was eventually to lead, in various ways,
to the rehabilitation of myth. Its "absurdity" was no longer de-
nounced as a logical scandal; rather, it was considered as a challenge scientific intelligence would have to take up if this other
form of intelligence represented by myth was to be understood
and incorporated into anthropological knowledge.

If we adopt a classification suggested by Edmund Leach, it will
perhaps be possible to distinguish the essential guidelines of these
different methods of approach. They sometimes overlap and
become confused but they resulted in the elaboration of the three
main theories around which the study of myth revolves today,
namely symbolism, functionalism, and structuralism.

A. SYMBOLISM AND FUNCTIONALISM

Following Creuzer[36] and Schelling,[37] one of the main features of
the modern inquiry into the meaning and significance of myths
is that mythical symbolism is recognized as a mode of expression
that is different from conceptual thought. Ernst Cassirer is certainly the scholar who has developed this line of analysis farthest

and most systematically. However, the concept of the symbol provides, as it were, the main thread of thought for Freud's and Jung's psychology of the subconscious, for the religious phenomenology of such writers as Van der Leeuw[38] and Walter F. Otto,[39] and for the overtly hermeneutical orientation of historians of religion such as Mircea Eliade[40] and philosophers such as Paul Ricoeur.[41] So despite the sometimes contrary directions in which they lead, all these different approaches to myth are linked together by one theme. We may thus attempt to define the common characteristics that these different points of view derive from their use of the notion of the symbol.

The symbol differs from the sign used in conceptual language in a number of ways. The sign's relationship to what it signifies is an arbitrary one (or, to put it more precisely, using the terminology of the linguists, the sign is twofold; there are two sides to it: what signifies and what is signified, and the link between the two is — at least when each sign is considered in isolation — entirely arbitrary). The sign refers to something outside itself as to a known object (or referent). A sign can only signify if it is related to other signs, in other words if it is part of a general system. Within this structured framework that which at one level is signified may, at another, higher, level function as a signifier. The sign is determinate, circumscribed; it lends itself to certain precise operations; at the extreme, in technical and scientific language, it is simple, univocal, transparent. It is defined by the series of operations in which it can be used, by the logic behind these operations, by the rules that govern their combinations.

In contrast, there is something "natural" and "concrete" about the symbol; it belongs, in part, to what it expresses. According to the symbolists this natural link between the symbol and what it embodies results from the fact that the symbol does not refer to some object outside itself, as in the relationship between a "knowing" subject and a known object. In this sense the mythical symbol may be described as "tauto-gorical": It does not represent something else but stands on its own as a declaration of

236

itself. It is not knowledge of another object but a presence in itself. Thus it does not belong to the order of intellectual comprehension, as the sign does, but rather to that of affectivity and desire in which the fundamental reactions and deepest aspirations are not only lived subjectively within each individual but are also projected and objectivized externally in forms created by the imagination, in mythical representations whose basic structures (or archetypes, in the Jungian sense) are believed to be as consistent and as universal as those of logical thought. To be sure, this idea of symbolism can lead to two contrary interpretations of myth according to whether the symbol is judged to be on a higher or a lower level than the concept. If lower it is assimilated, as by Freud, with other forms of the "symptomatic" expression of unconscious desires; it is connected with the products of the affective impulses as manifested in the imagery of dreams, and the fantasies of certain neuroses that are occasioned by the condensation, displacement, and symbolical representation of the objects of the libido. Alternatively, the symbol may be placed above the concept (and here it is stressed that it is only valid when applied to knowledge of the phenomenal world). In this case, as with Jung and Kerenyi, Van der Leeuw, Otto and Eliade, it is associated with the effort to translate that which, in the intimate experience of the *psuchē*, or collective unconscious, cannot be contained within the limits of the concept and eludes the categories of understanding: Such things cannot, strictly speaking, be known, but can nevertheless be "thought" and recognized through forms of expression that convey man's aspirations toward an unconditioned state, the absolute, the infinite, totality — that is to say, to use the language of religious phenomenology, his intimations of the sacred. The question of whether the symbol is considered to be on a higher or a lower level than conceptual thought depends upon an author's personal philosophy. It does not, however, affect the necessary conditions for a concrete analysis of myths that follow from a symbolist reading of them. The symbol is defined as fluid, diffuse, indeterminate, complex, syncretic. In contrast to the sign, ideally univocal, the symbol is polysemic; it can become charged with a limitless number of new expressive meanings. Signs and categories of signs can be defined precisely; they each have a distinctive function; they are employed in regular combinations. In contrast, symbols possess a fluidity and freedom that enable them to shift from one form to another and to amalgamate the most diverse domains within one dynamic structure. They can efface the boundaries that normally separate the different sectors of reality and convey in the reflection of a network of mutual relationships the reciprocal effects and the interpenetration of human and social factors, natural forces, and supernatural Powers. Concepts, in contrast, isolate these different entities, giving them precise definitions in order to arrange them in separate categories. The sign has no meaning outside the system to which it belongs. But a true symbol can stand on its own by reason of its own internal dynamic, its ability to evolve indefinitely, its capacity to express one aspect of human experience as an echo of everything there is in the universe. It is this elasticity of the symbol that equips it to convey — in a form always necessarily limited — that which is beyond limitation, namely totality and the infinite. Thus the symbol is never at rest, never in a state of equilibrium. It possesses a constant impulse aiming toward something beyond what it immediately expresses. This inner tension that impels myth to reach indefinitely beyond itself qualifies it to express the sacred, the divine. At the same time it explains the permanent vitality of myths, the way that they constantly become charged with new meanings and absorb commentaries, glosses, and new interpretations that open them up to new dimensions of reality yet to be explored or rediscovered.

This view of the symbol has the merit of bringing home the problem of mythical language and its specific relation to the meaning of the stories. However, it accepts as self-evident a whole series of assumptions that are, to put it mildly, questionable. Is it really the exclusive function of myth, of all myths, to aim at expressing the sacred, the divine, that which is free from all conditioning, in terms of symbols? Such a theory assumes myth and religion — religion in the spiritual sense — to be one and the same thing. And many students of myth would not accept this assumption expressed in this form.[42] Furthermore, for the various disciplines currently engaged in the study of myth — psychology, sociology, linguistics — this concept of the symbol raises more problems than it solves. Is there really any justification for drawing such a sharp contrast between the language of myth, which is symbolical and imagistic, and other, conceptual languages that use signs? Myth uses the common language of everyday even if it does use it in a different way. It would be easy to demonstrate the many continuities between symbols and signs and to show how equivocal and uncertain the use of the term symbol (mathematical symbol, for instance) may still be. Above all, in connection with the more specific problems of myth, it will be objected that when a symbolist attitude is adopted the work of patiently decoding the myth's structure by analysis is replaced by an immediate, intuitive interpretation that, to specialists, always seems gratuitous and, more often than not, positively mistaken. To declare that the symbols myth deploys are constant and carry universal archetypal meanings is totally to neglect the cultural, sociological, and historical context. There is a real danger of being misled by the so-called familiarity of symbols and of drawing incorrect or anachronistic conclusions. Jung claimed that his collection of archetypal symbols — the earth mother, the wise old man, the divine child, the sun, the *animus* and the *anima*, the Self, the cross, the mandala, etc. — are to be found universally, but his claim does not, to say the least, carry conviction. Besides, linguistic studies have shown that there are profound phonological, morphological, and syntactical differences between different groups of languages. So how, without a vestige of proof, is it possible to accept the idea of a single symbolical language conceived, not as a system operating on several levels, but as a universal vocabulary the meaning of whose components could be determined just by correlating them term for term?

239

The functionalists, and chief among them Malinowski,[43] thus had no difficulty in drawing attention to the wide gap between the interpretations of a symbolist kind and the role myths actually play in the social and institutional context of the peoples among whom they have remained alive. For the anthropologist working in the field, myth is just one part, one fragmentary aspect of the much wider scene of social life seen as a complex system of institutions, values, beliefs, and modes of behavior. Considered from this point of view myth no longer appears as the bearer of a "metaphysical" truth, a religious revelation or even of a simple abstract explanation. It contains no theories and transmits no spiritual teaching. It is integrally linked with ritual – oral narration and formal action representing the two inseparable sides of a single symbolical form of expression. Its role is to reinforce the social cohesion or functional unity of a group by presenting and justifying the traditional order of its institutions and modes of conduct in a codified form that is agreeable to listen to and easy to remember and transmit from one generation to the next. Myth thus satisfies two needs in the life of the group. The first is the general need for regularity, stability, and long-term consistency in various kinds of human society. Second, it makes it possible, within a particular society, for individuals to adjust their reactions to each other in accordance with the customary procedures and rules, to accept the same norms of behavior and to respect the social hierarchies.

Opposed as they are, functionalism and symbolism can be seen as the two sides of a single picture. Each conceals or neglects the features recognized and revealed by the other. The interest of the symbolists is focused on myth in its particular form as a story but they do not call upon its cultural context to help them to understand it. They restrict themselves to a consideration of the myth itself, the text as such, studying not the system of which it is a part, only the characteristics of the vocabulary taken in isolation.[44] The functionalists, in contrast, do indeed seek to discover the system that makes the myth intelligible, but instead of seeking it in the visible or hidden structure of the text, that is, in the myth itself, they find it elsewhere, in the sociocultural context that provides the framework to the stories, in other words in the ways in which the myth is embedded in social life. Thus, the specific nature of myth and its own particular significance are lost on the functionalists. For them, myth can tell us no more than social life itself does; and so, in their view, there is nothing more to be said about it except that, like every other element in the social system, it makes it possible for the life of the group to function. This teleological optimism no more gives a satisfactory explanation of mental and social phenomena than it does of biological facts. As Lévi-Strauss points out: "To say that a society functions is a truism; but to say that everything, in a society, functions is an absurdity."[45]

B. A NEW APPROACH: FROM MAUSS TO DUMÉZIL

A new approach is evident in the works of Marcel Mauss, Marcel Granet, and Louis Gernet, an anthropologist, a sinologist, and a Greek scholar, all three associated with the French school of sociology. Together they modified Durkheim's theories so as to take account, in the study of myth, of the contributions of history, linguistics, and psychology. Mauss' criticism of certain theses of Wundt, produced as early as 1908, is of the greatest importance in this respect.[46] Wundt saw myth as less objective, less connected with social conditions and constraints than language, because it is affected by the fluctuating emotions of the social group as a whole. Mauss was not satisfied with objecting, according to orthodox Durkheimian theory, that myth has an institutional character, pointing out the constraints on its themes even when they appear most gratuitous and the fact that myth represents a norm for the group. He goes on to compare myth with language, describing it as a system of symbols that makes communication within a particular group possible. Once rescued from the sphere of affective confusion and the spontaneity of fantasy in which Wundt situated it, the mythical symbol can be defined in terms of, on the one hand, the social conditions that affect it and, on the other, the rules of linguistics. Myth is no vague expression of individual feelings or popular emotions. It is an institutionalized system of symbols, a codified verbal behavior that, like language, conveys various modes of classifying facts — by coordinating, grouping, and opposing them, various ways of recognizing both resemblances and differences, in short, ways of organizing experience. Thought takes shape by expressing itself symbolically in and through myth as it does in and through a language: It comes into being even as it communicates. This collection of classificatory norms and mental categories conveyed in myth creates, as it were, the general intellectual atmosphere of archaic societies, and governs their ethical and economic attitudes as much as their strictly religious practices. In this sense it can be said that, for Mauss, even though the individual characteristics of different mythical systems are connected to their own particular sociohistorical conditions, every symbolical mythical system conveys a "global" message, that is, a reflection of the total man.

In his study of the legendary world of ancient China, Granet made no secret of his debt to Mauss.[47] If he writes that, in the case of a civilization such as that of China, legend is in a sense truer than history, it is because he detects in it the same fundamental features of thought for which language is both the vehicle and the instrument: the spatial and temporal frameworks, the relation between microcosm and macrocosm, a logical organization of thought and a concept of the universe constantly governed by the polarity between the great opposed principles of yin and yang. Granet uses legend to discover the social facts and intellectual structures that, together, constitute the institutionalized basis of the Chinese mentality.

Gernet's research in the field of Greek studies is comparable in that it too recognizes the interdependent nature of mythical symbols, institutional practices, linguistic data, and mental frameworks. His thesis of 1917 entitled *Recherches sur le développement de la pensée juridique et morale en Gréce*, still strongly marked by the influence of Durkheim, is — even at this early date — subtitled "A Semantic Study." This inquiry into the way that religious procedures, with the mythical symbolism connected with them, developed into a juridical system was perhaps the very first attempt to produce a structural semantic analysis.[48] The meanings of particular terms, their use at different times in history, the initially mythical significance of words such as *dikē, hubris, aidos*, etc., and the subsequent specialized meanings they acquired in their semantic evolution, the syntactical constructions in which they are used, the appearance of new words derived from old roots, the relationships between them based on similarity and contrast – in sum, the analysis of a semantic field and the transformations it undergoes leads on to a study of the representations and customs of a social group. There is no break between the linguistic, institutional, and conceptual domains. When mythical concepts and themes are discovered they are consistently and simultaneously studied from these three points of view. To this extent myth enjoys a rehabilitation. It has a meaning, and a specific one, but the fact that it means something *per se* does not cut it off from other linguistic factors or intellectual structures any more than from its social context. It is not a confusion of emotions, an individual fantasy, a gratuitous product of the imagination, or an obscure revelation of secret knowledge. It refers one to the institutional and mental system that it, in its own particular way, expresses. Three characteristics define Gernet's conception of myth and the way he analyzes it: (1) Like Mauss and Granet, he sees myth as an expression of the "total social situation," peculiar to types of society in which the economic, political, ethical, and aesthetic categories have not yet become distinguished and are all, as it were, contained symbolically in myth. In the case of the Greeks, the differentiation of functions that was to appear in time was not at first apparent. The various functions are still "more or less conflated" in myth. Mythical thought "tends to be total, it embraces economics, religion, politics, law and aesthetics all at once."[49] One of its fundamental characteristics then is that it is polyvalent and polysemic. (2) According to Gernet, myth is a kind of language:

243

Taking heed of the lesson provided for us by the linguists, we ought to take account both of the connections between different elements or moments in a single story and also of the associations through which an episode, a theme or an image can convey the same meaning. Connections and associations can help us to understand but we must not be impatient.[50]

(3) The language of myth draws upon concrete images rather than abstract ideas although there is no radical break between images and ideas, only differences in the level of abstraction. Within a given society the interrelationships between different combinations of images are governed by certain rules, so when a later Greek author takes a mythical model and transforms it he is still not completely free to recompose it as he will. Even without realizing it, he "works along the lines of the legendary imagination." "The traditional associations continue to operate even in an imagination which now works merely to give pleasure." True, a story told by the mythographers "is always, to some degree, a reconstruction but the way it is fitted together does not depend entirely on the discretion of the narrator or on the literary sources: it reflects a tradition even in the connections that the mythographer may himself have invented."[51]

Georges Dumézil takes a step further in the same direction. In the eyes of certain critics he has appeared to be resuming the studies in comparative Indo-European mythology so discredited by the excesses of Müller and his disciples. But this is because they have entirely misunderstood the orientation of his work. In reality, Dumézil radically deflects the course of these studies, combining in an examination of the history of religions both comparative philology of the kind pursued by Meillet and Benveniste and the historical sociology of Mauss and Granet. By making a rigorous use of the combination of these disciplines it is possible to regroup the different religious systems of Indo-European peoples within a single field of study. Here, beneath the significant differences in general orientation and pattern – what Dumézil calls the different "ideological fields" — a comparative analysis reveals profound structural analogies. These similarities may be summed up as follows: (1) There is a truly intellectual significance to the model of tripartite functions that represents the keystone in the structure of the various Indo-European pantheons and mythologies. These three functions are sovereignty, seen both as magic and violent and also as law-giving and pacific; warrior power and physical strength; and fertility, the source of nourishment and prosperity for the human group. The fact is that the agreement in this respect between one religious system and another is not merely one of language or theology. It reflects a complex and coherent body of concepts. (2) A religious system implies not so much a product of the imagination (even if this be governed by certain rules) but rather what we may call an ideology. This ideology not only influences ritual and myths; it also determines the type of discourse in literary genres that appear to be quite different, such as epic poetry and the annals of Roman history. So, to the extent that he is seeking to discover structures of thought, the comparative mythologist may find what he is looking for in literary works. Now, however, the relationship is reversed. He proceeds from the religious ideology to the literary compositions instead of seeking to treat religious phenomena and mythical traditions in a literary way. Thus the problems of the transformations or transpositions that occur between the appearance of the myths as such and the creation of epics or novels are posed in quite different terms. (3) The structures that the comparativist seeks to reveal are mental structures: They are concerned with the great frameworks of thought — ways of representing both the human and the divine universe and the organization of society, maintaining a balance between its necessary constituents. They do not relate to the historical events or even the social factors that they are sometimes thought to express directly or simply to reflect. The comparative mythologist does not attempt to recreate history or to reconstruct the primitive state of societies. There may be marked distortions and discontinuities separating the ideology that inspires the mythical traditions of a group and its actual social organization. Thus, in analyzing a society it is necessary to take account of all its many aspects, each one of which has its own particular features and develops relatively autonomously with its own dynamic and logic and its own type of temporality. The permanence or longevity of linguistic features, religious ideologies, and mythical traditions may stand in sharp contrast to the rapid and violent succession of political or military events and the varying rhythm of change in a society's institutions.

Georges Dumézil thus clears the way for an analysis that at every level respects myth's own specific features, that approaches it from within, considering the corpus of texts as an objective world that must be studied as itself and for itself. In such an analysis the writer refers to a myth's context in order to reveal or illuminate the semantic values of certain elements in the story, not so as to reduce the myth as a whole to an order of reality that may be separate from and alien to it, whether it involves emotive drives, ritual practices, historical facts, social structures, or man's experience of the absolute.

C. The Structuralism of Lévi-Strauss

It fell to Claude Lévi-Strauss, after the Second World War, to undertake this exploration in a systematic way, taking the lead in the theoretical reflection on problems of myth and the concrete analysis of a vast body of American-Indian mythology in the oral tradition. In four successive volumes he applies the principles and methods of structural analysis to the domain of mythology, and his work represents both a measure of continuity with earlier studies and, at the same time, a break and a new point of departure.

There is a measure of continuity in the sense that myth is regarded, as it was by Mauss, as a system of communication whose categories and structures it is the mythologist's task to understand. As in Gernet's work and even more in Dumézil's, a precise textual analysis, which is alert to the internal connections between the different elements of the story and the associations that link all the episodes and different versions together, is used to discover the intellectual framework of the myth, an overall network of interconnected concepts, a coherent apparatus of oppositions.

His work also marks a break, in the sense that, since Bachelard, one can talk of an epistemological break, and one that operates at several levels. From now on the model used in deciphering myth is drawn from linguistics — structural linguistics, to be precise — which studies language as opposed to speech, that is, the rules governing language, its formal framework, not the particular utterances of different individuals. In a similar manner Claude Lévi-Strauss makes a distinction, in myth, between the ordinary sense of a story as it is directly expressed in the narration, a sense that may appear fantastical, futile, or even totally absurd, and another, hidden sense that is not conscious as the former is. It is this second, non-narrative meaning that the mythologist aims to discover just as the linguist seeks the abiding structure of the language behind the flow of words. Myth is not simply a story that unfolds its syntagmatic sequence along the diachronic axis of an irreversible time, in the same way as one word follows another in the discourse of a speaker. It is also, just as language is, an ordered arrangement of different elements that together form a synchronic system, a permanent order that constitutes the semantic space from which the story is produced, although those employing myth are no more conscious of this than they are of the phonological and syntactical rules that they automatically obey when they speak in a particular language. So there are two levels at which a myth can be read. One is the manifest, narrative level. The other is a deeper level that can be reached by means of an analysis that finds among the "elements" that constitute the story (short phrases, originally termed "mythemes" by Lévi-Strauss, that condense its essential episodes into a simple relationship) oppositions and homologies that do not depend upon the narrative order, that is to say upon their position and function in the linear chain of the story. To get this permanent structure underlying the text to

247

emerge, the phrases expressing these relationships, or mythemes, are arranged along two axes, one horizontal following the narrative order of the story, the other vertical. Along the latter all the mythemes that can be classified together by reason of similarity of theme are regrouped in columns. Thus, in the myth of Oedipus chosen by Lévi-Strauss as a universally familiar example to illustrate his method of procedure, the total body of mythemes is arranged into four separate columns. The first contains those that, in one form or another, express an overrating of blood relations (Cadmos abandons everything in order to find his sister; Oedipus marries his mother; Antigone buries her brother Polyneices despite his betrayal and the order that his corpse be denied burial). The second contains those that convey an underrating or devaluation of these same blood relations (Oedipus kills his father, curses his sons; the brothers Polyneices and Eteocles kill each other). The third column is for the mythemes that deny man's autochthony, his genealogical relationship to the earth (Cadmos kills the chthonic dragon; Oedipus triumphs over the Sphinx). In the fourth column are those mythemes that, in contrast, express the idea that man is rooted like a plant in the maternal soil (Oedipus' swollen foot, and all the abnormalities in the legs or gait of the line of the Labdacids). The arrangement of the mythemes into columns makes their true meaning emerge because it shows them not as isolated elements but as groups comprising types of relationship that are opposed or that correspond to each other. Thus it becomes apparent that although the first and second, and the third and fourth columns are opposed to each other, this double opposition also encompasses a formal homology: The relationship of the fourth to the third column is as the first to the second. This proportional relationship that constitutes the structure of the myth turns the myth into a kind of logical tool, making it possible to mediate between exclusive terms of contradictory situations. Thus, in the example of the Oedipus myth, we have on the one hand a belief in the autochthony of man (attested in the myths concerning his emergence from Mother Earth) and, on the other, his birth from the union of a man and a woman (necessary to the entire sociological code of filiation). It would, then, appear that what underlies the myth and is implied in the basic structure of the text when it is seen as arranged into four columns is, as it were, a logical problem: Blood relations are first overrated then underrated; autochthony is first denied then affirmed. Explicitly formulated, the question conveyed by the structure of the myth could perhaps run as follows: Is like born from like (man from man) or from something other (man from the earth)? By suggesting that "the overrating of blood relations is to the underrating of blood relations as the attempt to escape autochthony is to the impossibility to succeed in it," the mythical structure, at the same time as it places the terms used in the story in their relationships of mutual exclusion or mutual implication, stresses the impossibility of coming down definitively on one side or the other. It thereby expresses the consequent need to maintain a mediatory balance between statements that are incompatible to each other but each of which, when taken in isolation, splits into two and endlessly oscillates between the two opposite poles of, one the one hand, excessive affirmation, and on the other over-radical negation.

Given that Lévi-Strauss is not a specialist in Greek mythology, his choice of the myth of Oedipus to illustrate his method seems somewhat gratuitous. He himself refers to it as a "street pedlar's choice": It is a promotional "demonstration" like that of a pedlar in the marketplace who wants to make it easy for his public to grasp the method of using the instruments he is trying to sell and their advantages. However, although this promotional exercise may have its advantages from the point of view of clarity, it is not without its disadvantages. In the first place it may suggest that it is possible to decipher a myth even without a knowledge in depth of the civilization that produced it, and that it need be set in no context other than that provided by itself. Second, the process of separating out the different episodes and that of classifying the mythemes in the myth's matrix according to similarity of theme cannot fail to strike the Greek scholar as equally arbitrary. By this procedure (which is based upon, but not justified by, certain remarks made by Marie Delcourt) Cadmos' murder of the dragon and Oedipus' triumph over the Sphinx are forced — or at least edged — into the same category involving a denial of autochthony, and Oedipus' swollen foot and the lameness of the Labdacids into the symmetrically opposite category involving an original rooting in the earth. Finally, and above all, interpreting Lévi-Strauss' text literally and crediting it with a universal application, most readers have believed that the inference is that any and every myth can be used as a logical tool of mediation between contradictions that, in life, are insoluble, and that this mediatory role is the exclusive and invariable function of mythology in the eyes of the structuralist.

Now, in the same year as he published *Anthropologie Structurale*, which contained his study of Oedipus, Lévi-Strauss was pursuing in *Le geste d'Asdiwal*, no longer a promotional examination of a myth chosen *ad hoc*, but a rigorous demonstration of his methods of decipherment as applied to a number of versions of a myth of the Tsimshian Indians of British Columbia, whose social and material conditions of life are, thanks to the anthropologists, now very well-known. In this text, which we must take as our point of departure since here Lévi-Strauss is working in his own field, the myth is divided into different segments, each segment has attributed to it a semantic significance not directly determined by the narrative itself, and these meanings are then arranged along a series of axes representing the many different levels on which they simultaneously operate. And in this instance all these operations that are to reveal the structure of the myth, that is to say, the network of oppositions and parallelisms that coordinate many different codes at the same time, are only made possible by a precise and exhaustive knowledge of the myth's cultural and ethnographical context. The myth's semantic framework and the basis for the significant oppositions operative at various levels within it are provided by many different factors: geography, both physical and human, ecology, seasonal migrations of population, technical and economic circumstances, social structures, institutions, kinship relations, and religious beliefs and practices; and it is all of these that make it possible to discover the many codes — geographical, techno-economic, sociological and cosmological — used to convey the myth's message. Similarly, in *Mythologiques*, Lévi-Strauss collected, analyzed, and interpreted a mass of data on the flora and fauna, the astronomy, the technology, the clothing and ornaments, etc., contained in the myths of the American Indians. Without this painstaking catalogue showing how plants, animals, objects, events, and human groups are classified in these societies, it would have been impossible to establish the semantic links that determine the interrelationships between the major protagonists in the myths — the lynx, the owl, the snake, the anteater, the jaguar, honey, tobacco, the moon, the Pleiades...not to mention those between the son, the nephew, the parents, and the uncle.[52]

Meanwhile, compared with *Le geste, Mythologiques* represents, if not a new departure, at least a more decided orientation toward the problems of the relationships between different myths. To be sure, Lévi-Strauss at the outset stressed the fact that it is in the nature of myth to produce variants of a single story. The diversity of these versions is not an obstacle to be removed by seeking out a single prototype, one authentic version, in order to dismiss all the rest as derivative and of no consequence. For a mythologist every version is of equal value. The same mental equipment is at work in each and it is more often than not by comparing many different versions, through their differences, in fact, that one can discover a common pattern and make out the structure of the myth. But *Mythologiques* goes even further. The inquiry concerns the whole corpus of myths and perhaps looks even further toward the totality of actual and possible myths, seeing these as creations of the mind resulting from a pattern of transformations, governed by certain rules of permutation that, in principle at least, can be subjected to logico-mathematical analysis. It has been pointed out that Lévi-Strauss presents, as it were, two theories of myth, the one superposed upon the other.[53] According to the first, all myths emerge from two levels of analysis and are governed by two sets of rules: First, at the level of the myth's deep structure, it emerges from a system of interlocking codes; second, at the level of the linguistic expression, from the narrative form adopted by this logical structure in the telling of the story. According to the second theory, myth is discourse organized in such a way that general rules can be applied to the transformations it may undergo, the whole body of myths being the product of the interplay of these transformations. In this sense it could be said that it is not so much a case of men thinking their myths but rather of the myths thinking themselves.

Lévi-Strauss forestalled and rejected this accusation of theoretical ambiguity. He emphasized that the division of a myth into superposable segments that are shown to be variations on a single theme, and the superposition of an entire myth over others that are considered to be transformations of a single model, are simply two sides to or two stages in a single operation:

> The other procedure, which is complementary to the first, consists in superposing a syntagmatic sequence in its totality – in other words a complete myth – on other myths or segments of myths. It follows, then, that on both occasions we are replacing a syntagmatic sequence by a paradigmatic sequence; the difference is that whereas in the first case the paradigmatic whole is removed from a the sequence, in the second it is the sequence that is incorporated into it. But whether the whole is made up of parts of the sequence, or whether the sequence itself is included as a part, the principle remains the same. Two syntagmatic sequences, or fragments of the same sequence which, considered in isolation, contain no definite meaning, acquire a meaning simply from the fact that they are polar opposites.

It is an open question whether one accepts this point of view or rejects it, questioning the relevance in the case of myth of the structuralist model of the two axes, one paradigmatic and the other syntagmatic (or, more generally, questioning the validity of a pure and simple transference of linguistic schemata to the structures of myth — which is not a language in itself but a way of using an already constituted mode of speech). Nevertheless, one must recognize that following Lévi-Strauss the situation is no longer the same either from a theoretical point of view or so far as the concrete work of decipherment is concerned; his work marks a turning point and a new departure. For his adversaries as for his disciples and those working along parallel lines, mythological research now not only confronts new questions; it is no longer possible to pose even the old problems in the same terms.

IV. *Interpretations and Problems of Myth*

The first category of questions concerns the relation between, on the one hand, the narrative level of the text, its immediate linguistic sense, and on the other its structural architecture, its mythical meaning. How are these two levels articulated? There would seem to be two alternatives. One may accept that there are rigorous implications between the two levels; the problem then is (1) how to determine the rules that make it possible to pass from the structure to the narrative, and (2) how to fit these rules into the organization of the general linguistic model to which we have referred. Alternatively, one might assume there to be an arbitrary element in the composition of the stories, that is in the way in which the texture of discourse relates to the underlying structure — which would explain why there may be an indefinite number of variants. In the latter case one seeks to distinguish in the text only those elements pertaining to the underlying code that are part of the permanent logical structure of the myth, paying no attention to the narrative composition that, in these circumstances, is considered to be without any intrinsic significance. However, at this point the linguists are bound to protest. They will point out that a myth, like any other story, is governed by strict narrative rules which one should attempt to define and analyze formally. For the very reason that the story unfolds within a linear time it implies an initial situation that, by the end of the narrative, has undergone a transformation. The transformation comes about through the performance — or actions — of the actors or "subjects" who are endowed with qualities or characteristics that are adapted to the situations and that put them in a position to accomplish these actions or suffer their consequences. It is possible to draw up a formal table of the types of performances and the modalities of change that are implied in the mythical narrative and so one can propose a kind of general logic for this type of story.[54] To this point a mythologist will add that since the narrative form is one of the essential characteristics of myth, any decipherment that swept it aside, disrupting or destroying the narrative structures in order to fasten upon the mythical structure, would be failing to interpret the myth in all its dimensions. Indeed, a philosopher such as Ricoeur goes even further: While accepting that Lévi-Strauss' method represents a necessary stage in the process of uncovering the myth's deep semantic meaning which eludes a surface reading, he denies that it is a method capable of exhausting the full meaning of myths.[55] As Lévi-Strauss sees it myth needs to be not understood but decoded. It is not a question of getting at the meaning of a message by deciphering it on the basis of a known code but of using a particular message, in itself insignificant or absurd, to find the secret code that underlies it and that occasioned its expression. By thus denying that myth has a message to transmit, one denies its capacity to say anything, to formulate any statement, be it true or false, about the world, the gods, or man. It is assumed that, in itself, no myth has or indeed can have anything to say on any aspect of reality. It is only when considered all together, as a body, that myths bring into play rules of structural transformation similar to those that govern the organization of other structured systems, for instance matrimonial alliances, the exchanges between social groups, or relations of political dominance or subordination.

When posed in this way, so as to reveal its full implications, this discussion that today lies at the heart of the problems concerning myth raises a series of other, closely connected issues. If all myths have the same meaning, the structures one discovers in them are based upon a logic of categories inherent in the organization of the mind; the world and man appear in myth only as the means for discourse; they represent the material that "is the instrument of meaning, not its object."[56] Thus, the device of mythology has the role of a formal framework, an instrument of thought. But this immediately raises the question of whether this framework or instrument represented by the device of symbolism cannot also be used to express and transmit, in a narrative form different from the abstract pronouncements of the philosopher or the sage, a knowledge of reality or a vision of the world – what Georges Dumézil would call an ideology. Through its syntactical and semantic organization the language employed by myth in itself represents a way of arranging reality, a kind of classification and setting in order of the world, a preliminary logical arrangement, in sum an instrument of thought. It is nevertheless also used, in communication, to transmit messages and to say something to others; through Aristotle's thought this unconscious linguistic equipment even accedes to the status of theoretical knowledge. The example we have already used of a work such as Hesiod's, in which traditional mythological material is rethought and reorganized, testifies to such a use of mythical symbolism for the purpose of setting out a body of teaching, of communicating knowledge concerning the divine order in the form of theogonical, cosmogonical, or anthropogonical stories. So we ought to distinguish between the many different forms and levels of mythical expression for which the methods of decoding may be similar but will not be identical.

We should note in this respect that Lévi-Strauss works on a body of oral stories that affords a very large number of variants. The nature of the material itself calls for a systematic comparison between the various stories to distinguish the formal features that reappear from one myth to another, whether the relationships involved are those of homology, inversion, or permutation. At the same time it excludes an exhaustive philological analysis of each of the various versions. The problem is quite different in the case of a great written work with a strong and elaborate structure such as the *Theogony* or the *Works and Days*. Here it is not a question of selecting as most important those elements that can also be found, in a more or less altered form, in other versions. Instead, the scholar must attempt an exhaustive analysis of the myth in all the detail of its textual form. Strictly speaking, every single episode and term used should be accounted for. On one level the inquiry should focus upon the narrative as it appears from an analysis of the mode of composition, the syntactical relationships, and the temporal and consequential connections that are inherent in the story. But it is not enough to work out how the various episodes interconnect within the texture of the narrative. It is also necessary to shed light upon what the linguists would call the grammar of the story, that is, the logic behind the narrative, by revealing the model upon which the interplay of actions and reactions is constructed, the dynamic force behind the changes that compose the web of the plot as the tale unfolds. It is then necessary to pass on to a second type of analysis aimed this time at the semantic content, and to distinguish the various levels of meaning within the strata of the text. This can be done by establishing the many different networks of oppositions and homologies that connect all the details in the myth (places, times, objects, agents, or subjects, performances or actions, initial positions held and situations reversed). The problem then is to define the match between the formal framework constituted by the grammar of the story and the concrete semantic content that is present at many different levels. It should be noted, furthermore, that, like certain syntactical elements in language, the "grammar" of the story may include semantic aspects while the semantic content itself follows a certain order of logical relations as a result of the multiplicity of correspondences, polysemy, and ambiguity. This internal study of the text presupposes that, in order to reveal all the levels of meaning of the various terms together with all their mutual implications or exclusions, one also examines other texts — close variants and similar groups of different myths that present similar semantic configurations. However, for the myth to be completely decoded yet a third operation is necessary. By considering a wider corpus of material to which it is related, the cultural context of the myth can be determined. In this way it is possible to explore the semantic space within which the story, in its own particular form, was both produced and understood: This comprises categories of thought, classificatory frameworks, the selection and codifying of reality, and major systems of oppositions.[57] It is by reference to this framework of categories and to the logical combinations it gives rise to that the modern interpreter can give a full interpretation of myth, carefully locating it in its rightful place in the context of a mental and social history.

Such a procedure might make it possible to suggest certain solutions to some of the difficulties that we have indicated and also lead to the formulation of a number of new problems. We would not, as Paul Ricoeur does, assume there to be a discontinuity in the domain of myth, only one part of which is suited to Lévi-Straussian structural analysis while the other proves intractable — namely, the Semitic, Greek, and Indo-European sector (to which our civilization belongs). Rather, we would point out that mythical thought everywhere is composed of many levels and that the evidence that we possess, whichever cultural sector it belongs to, does not always come from the same level. Ricoeur noted that it was not just by chance that Lévi-Strauss' examples all come from the geographical area in which anthropologists of the last generation identified the presence of totemism: He suggested that these were peoples who excel at the mental procedure of making distinctions and classifications of every kind ranging from the area of natural phenomena to that of kinship or exchange relationships, and that this emphasis on taxonomy is reflected in their myths.

257

The question that then arises is whether the structural approach has not discovered in the sector where totemism has been found a type of myth in which oppositions and correlations, whose function it is to convey distinctions, are more important than the semantic content. The implication is that precisely the opposite is the case at the other end of the spectrum of mythologies, namely in the Semitic, Greek, and Indo-European traditions. Here, the relative weakness of the syntactical and classificatory organization stands in contrast to the semantic richness that affords endless reinterpretations and the renewal of meanings, as social and historical contexts change. This would account for a new opposition that has been suggested between the two forms of mythology: the different ways they relate to time and history. In the case of the "cold" societies in which the dimension of time is not stressed, myths, like institutions, are synchronically extremely coherent but diachronically fragile, since every new factor or change threatens to upset the earlier equilibrium. In contrast, at the other end of the spectrum myth is adapted to a temporal perspective since it is forever open to reinterpretation. Here, one's interpretation should therefore take this diachronic dimension into account.

We may well wonder whether it is really possible today to maintain this opposition between cold societies frozen in immobility, and hot ones at grips with history. All societies to a greater or lesser degree experience changes that their myths reflect, integrating or digesting them in their own particular ways. Certainly it is true that a mythical tradition such as that of the Greeks has always lent itself to being recast and reinterpreted. However, the many variants of a single myth and the transformations, even the inversions that sometimes turn one myth into another among the peoples studied by Lévi-Strauss, bear witness to a similar situation: The myths are all related to each other and the appearance of a new version or myth is always connected with the myths that already existed before, myths that were current in that particular group, or which belonged to neighboring peoples. When our evidence is of a kind that it is possible to date, and the myths therefore contain indications of historical depth, we call them variations; when we come upon them all together, all collected at a single time, we call them variants. But from the point of view of their mythical thought there is no difference between the two.

For this reason a more useful distinction would seem to be between oral and written traditions. The myths from oral cultures have been collected by anthropologists without any historical perspective, in bulk, usually in fragmentary and dispersed order, just as they have come to hand. The only way to deal with them seems to be as Lévi-Strauss does. And the framework of categories, the network of codes that he discovers is of a similar type to those to be found, in a different genre, in the tales and stories of folklore. In written literature, alongside data similar to and on the same level as oral myth, we also find grand general systematized constructions the sum total of whose different parts integrates into one unified message. This conveys an interpretation of the universe and provides an answer to those same problems that, in yet another mode, philosophy in its turn attempts to pose and resolve. This would suggest both a continuity and also a series of breaks between oral tales, myth or rather the various different levels of myth, and philosophy.

But the real difficulties lie elsewhere. The first is well-known and we may formulate it as follows: What is the link between the semantic space revealed by structural analysis as the myth's intellectual framework, and the sociohistorical context in which the myth was produced? What, from the point of view of the practical task of decoding, is the relationship between on the one hand a synchronic study where every detail is explained in terms of the network of relationships that make it a part of the system and, on the other, a diachronic inquiry in which all the details that appear in different temporal contexts are explained in terms of how they relate to those that preceded them in earlier versions? No doubt the answer would lie in showing that no details can be considered in isolation, whether in a historical inquiry or in a synchronic analysis. What are always revealed are structures linked

259

more or less closely with others, and the versions that are found to vary at different times turn out to be new renderings, more or less extensive as the case may be, of the structures that lie beneath the very systems that are the object of a structural study.

The second is less familiar. Myth is not only characterized by its polysemy and by the interlocking of its many different codes. In the unfolding of its narrative and the selection of the semantic fields it uses, it brings into play shifts, slides, tensions, and oscillations between the very terms that are distinguished or opposed in its categorical framework; it is as if, while being mutually exclusive these terms at the same time in some way imply one another. Thus myth brings into operation a form of logic that we may describe, in contrast to the logic of non-contradiction of the philosophers, as a logic of the ambiguous, the equivocal, a logic of polarity. How is one to formulate, even formalize, the balancing operations that can turn one term into its contrary while yet, from other points of view, keeping the two far apart? Ultimately, the mythologist has to admit to a certain inadequacy as he is forced to turn to the linguists, logicians, and mathematicians in the hope that they may provide him with the tool that he lacks, namely the structural model of another kind of logic: not the binary logic of yes or no but a logic different from that of the *logos*.

Notes

Note to Introduction

1. L. Gernet, *Anthropologie de la Grèce ancienne*, Paris, 1968, pp. 93-137.

Notes to Chapter I

1. The French version of this text was first published in *Eirene, Studia Graeca et Latina*, IV, 1965, pp. 5-19.

2. C. Parain, "Les caractères spécifiques de la lutte des classes dans l'Antiquité classique," *La Pensée*, no. 108, April 1963.

3. K. Marx, *Capital*, Vol. I, ch. 2, p. 316, Lawrence & Wishart, 1974.

4. K. Marx, *Grundrisse*. See the section on "Forms which precede capitalist production" (English translation by Martin Nicolaus published by the Pelican Marx Library, 1973).

5. A.J.V. Fine, "Horoi: Studies in Mortgage, Real Security and Land Tenure in Ancient Greece," *Hesperia*, suppl. IX, 1951; L. Gernet, "Horoi," *Studi in onore di Ugo Enrico Paoli*, 1955, pp. 345-53; "Choses visibles et choses invisibles," *Revue Philosophique*, 1956, p. 83; G. Thomson, "On Greek Land Tenure," *Studies Robinson*, 2, pp. 840-57; N.G.L. Hammond, "Land Tenure in Attica and Solon's seisachtheia," *The Journal of Hellenic Studies*, 81, 1961, pp. 76-98; J. Pecirka, "Land Tenure and the Development of the Athenian Polis," *Geras, Studies presented to George Thomson*, Prague, 1963, pp. 183-201; D. Asheri, "Laws of Inheritance, Distribution of Land and Political Constitutions in Ancient Greece," *Historia*, 12, 1963, pp. 1-21; M.I. Finley, "The Alienability of Land in Ancient Greece," *Eirene*, VII, 1968, pp. 25-32; also in Finley, *The Use and Abuse of History*, London, 1975.

6. *Grundrisse*, p. 479.

7. *ibid*. pp. 475-6.

8. *ibid*. p. 476.

9. The limited scale of production for the market throughout antiquity (and especially in archaic times) seems to us to have been disregarded by some Marxists who have, in our opinion, overestimated the spread of exchange value in Greek social life and the hold that the category of commodities had on their minds. It may be useful to quote some texts: "But the production of commodities does not become the normal, dominant type of production until capitalist production serves as its basis" (*Capital*, Vol. 2, p. 30); "In the ancient Asiatic and other ancient modes of production, we find that the conversion of products into commodities...holds a subordinate place which, however, increases in importance as the primitive communities approach ever nearer and nearer to their dissolution" (*Capital*, Vol. 1, p. 83); "Had we gone further, and enquired under what circumstances all, or even the majority of products take the form of commodities, we should have found that this can only happen with production of a very specific kind, capitalist production" (*Capital*, Vol. 1, p. 166); "It is only from this moment (the capitalist period) that the produce of labour universally becomes a commodity" (*Capital*, Vol. 1, p. 167 n); "Aristotle is aware of the fact that the different things measured by money are entirely incommensurable magnitudes. What he seeks is the oneness of commodities as exchange values, and since he lived in ancient Greece it was impossible for him to find it" (*A Contribution to the Critique of Political Economy*, translated into English by S.W. Ryazanskaya, edited by Maurice Dobb; published by Lawrence & Wishart, 1971); "There was, however, an important fact which prevented Aristotle from seeing that to attribute value to commodities is merely a mode of expressing all labour as equal human labour, and consequently as labour of equal quality. Greek society was founded upon slavery and had, therefore, for its natural basis, the inequality of men and of their natural labour powers. The secret of the expression of value, namely that all kinds of labour are equal and equivalent because, and in so far as, they are human labour in general, cannot be deciphered until the notion of human equality has already acquired the fixity of a popular prejudice. This, however, is possible only in a society in which the great mass of the produce of labour takes the form of commodities, in which, consequently, the dominant relation between man and man is that of owners of commodities. The

brilliancy of Aristotle's genius is shown by this alone, that he discovered, in the expression of the value of commodities, a relation of equality. The peculiar conditions of the society in which he lived alone prevented him from discovering what 'in truth' was at the bottom of this equality" (*Capital*, Vol. 1, pp. 65-6). Cf. also pages 338, 344 and 346 of the *Introduction à une critique de l'Economie politique*, translated into French by Molitor.

10. *Grundrisse*, pp. 494-5.

11. Cf. E. Will, "Trois quarts de siècle de recherches sur l'économie antique," *Annales, E.S.C.*, 1954, pp. 7-22.

12. M.I. Finley, *Studies in Land and Credit in Ancient Athens, 500-200 BC.*, 1952, p. 77.

13. *Capital*, Vol. 1, pp. 85-6.

14. Cf. J. Pecirka, *op. cit.* pp. 194 ff.

15. Cf. L. Gernet, *Droit et société en Grèce ancienne*, Paris, 1955; particularly: "Le droit de la vente et la notion du contrat en Grèce d'après M. Pringsheim," and "Sur L'obligation contractuelle dans la vente hellénique," pp. 201-36.

16. L. Gernet, "Choses visibles et choses invisibles," *Anthropologie de la Grèce antique*, Paris, 1968, p. 410.

17. Cf. the study by Karl Polanyi, "Aristotle discovers economy," in *Trade and Market in the Early Empires*, Glencoe, 1957, pp. 44-94.

18. In Antiquity labor power was not a commodity; there was no labor market, only a market for slaves, which is entirely different. "The slave," wrote Marx, "does not sell his labour power to the owners of slaves any more than the bullock sells his labour to the peasant. The slave is sold, including his labour power, once and for all to his owner." In this sense, the slave like the bullock or like a tool, remains, in the performance of his productive duties, outside the general system of social exchange just as he is, as far as civic life is concerned, outside society. Not only is the labor power of the slave not a commodity, but the product of his labor may not be either if, for example, it is directly consumed by his owner. For the product to become a commodity, the owner must decide to sell it in the market. But, even in this case, the labor of the slave, not being a commodity, does not assume the abstract form of a *general rule*. It is not an "overall equivalent" in the context of the circulation of commodities as a whole: It is a particular "service" rendered by the slave to his owner. To borrow Marx's own terms in *Capital*: "Here the particular and natural form of labour and not, as in

a society based on the production of commodities, its general abstract form, is the immediate social form of labour" (Vol. 1, p. 82). The formulation Marx applied to statute labor *(corvée)* in the Middle Ages is completely valid for slave labor. "It was the distinct labour of the individual in its original form, the particular features of his labour and not its universal aspect that formed the social ties at that time" (*A Contribution to the Critique of Political Economy*, London, Lawrence & Wishart, 1971, p. 33).

19. Claude Mossé, *La fin de la démocratie athénienne*, Paris, 1962.

20. "As money of account and in the form of coins money assumes a local and political character, it uses different national languages and wears different national uniforms. Coined money circulated therefore in the *internal* sphere of circulation of commodities, which is circumscribed by the boundaries of a given community and separated from the *universal* circulation of the world of commodities" (*A Contribution to the Critique of Political Economy*, p. 107 [translation slightly modified]). On the role and significance of the coinages of the city-states, cf. E. Will, "De l'aspect éthique de l'origine grecque de la monnaie," *Revue Historique*, 1954, pp. 209 ff.; "Réflexions et hypothèses sur les origines du monnayage," *Revue Numismatique*, 1955, pp. 5-23; also C.M. Kraay, "Hoards, small change and the origin of coinage," *The Journal of Hellenic Studies*, 1964, pp. 76-91.

21. "Credit money belongs to a more advanced stage of the social process of production and conforms to very different laws" from money in circulation (*A Contribution to the Critique of Political Economy*, p. 116).

22. "Just as in theory gold and silver as money are universal commodities, so world money is the appropriate form of existence of the universal commodity...They are realised as embodiments of universal labour time in the degree that the interchange of the products of concrete labour becomes worldwide...As money develops into international money, so the commodity owner becomes a cosmopolitan" (*ibid.* pp. 151-2).

23. *ibid.* pp. 132-3; see also pp. 125 ff. and p. 134, where Marx notes that the role played by hoarding was all the greater because "exchange value had not yet penetrated all relations of production."

24. "In countries which have purely metallic currency or are at an early stage of development and production, hoards are extremely fragmented and scattered throughout the country, whereas in advanced bourgeois countries they

are concentrated in the reservoirs of banks" (*ibid.* p. 137).

25. "The never-ending augmentation of exchange-value, which the miser strives after, by seeking to save his money from circulation, is attained by the more acute capitalist by constantly throwing it afresh into circulation" (*Capital*, Vol. 1, p. 151).

26. "...and although at certain stages of production the commodity owner hides his treasures, he is compelled to show to other commodity-owners that he is a rich man, wherever he can safely do so. He bedecks himself and his house with gold" (*Contribution to the Critique of Political Economy*, p. 134).

NOTES TO CHAPTER II

1. This article was first published as the introduction to the collective volume, *Problèmes de la guerre en Grèce ancienne*, edited by J.-P. Vernant, Mouton, Paris and The Hague, 1968.

2. G. Glotz, *La Solidarité de la famille dans le droit criminel en Grèce*, Paris, 1904, p. 92.

3. Cf. Aristotle, *Poetics*, 1453b 19-22.

4. Aristotle, *Nicomachean Ethics*, 1161b 27-30: "Parents love their children because they recognise themselves in them (for since they come from the parents they are in a certain way other selves; they are, however, other since they exist apart from them)...; brothers love each other because they have their origin from the same beings. The identity of their relations to these makes them identical to each other...They are therefore in a sense the same being even though they exist as separate individuals." And, more generally, the definition of the *philos* as an *alter ego*: "ἔστιν ὁ φίλος ἄλλος αὐτός," ibid. 1166a.

5. Cf. the remarks of E. Benveniste, "Don et échange dans le vocabulaire indo-européen," *L'Année sociologique*, 3rd series, 1951 (1948-9), pp. 13-14 on the subject of the Latin *hostis*. This ambiguity of *xenos* is particularly noticeable in a term such as *doruxenos*, which is the subject of the seventeenth of Plutarch's *Greek Questions*. In ancient times the people of Megara did not yet form a single city; they lived in villages, divided into five different groups. It sometimes happened that these waged war against each other — a war which they waged ἡμέρως καὶ συγγενικῶς. Whoever had captured a prisoner took him home, offered him salt and invited him to table, and then sent him freely back to his own home. For his part, the prisoner never failed to pay his ransom and remained forever

the *philos* of his captor. For this reason he was not known as *dorialatos*, prisoner of the lance, but as *doruxenos*, guest of the lance. As W.R. Halliday notes in his *Commentary to the Greek Questions* (Oxford, 1928, p. 98), *doruxenos* is used in Attic tragedy with the different meaning of: ally in war.

6. *Republic*, V, 470bc; *Letters*, VII, 322a; cf. also *Iseaus*, IV, 18.

7. *Alcestis*, 532-3, 646.

8. Pindar, *Nemeans*, IX, 39.

9. Cf. in Aristophanes, *Lysistrata*, 203, the κύλιξ φιλοτησία used in a parody of an international pact, together with the remarks of G. Glotz, *op. cit.* p. 157.

10. Cf. F. Vian, *Les Origines de Thèbes, Cadmos et les Spartes*, Paris, 1963, p. 118 ff.

11. On ritual battles, cf. H. Usener, *Archiv für Religionswissenschaft*, 7 (1904), p. 297 ff.; *Kleine Schriften*, Leipzig, 1913, IV, p. 432 ff.; M.P. Nilsson, *Griechische Feste von religiöser Bedeutung*, Leipzig, 1906, pp. 402-8 and 413-7.

12. Cf. L. Gernet, *Le Génie grec dans la religion*, Paris, 1932, pp. 52-4.

13. During the *Katagōgia* festival at Ephesus, amid an atmosphere of carnival license, fights with cudgels took place between the masked participants; all the town squares flowed with blood (*Acts of Timotheus*, ed. Usener, Progr. Bonn, 1877, p. 11, 1; Photius, *Bibl.*, Cod. 254). On the seventh of Artemision, at Antioch, the festival held in honor of the goddess reached its culmination "with blood-shed in the course of fist fights; there were as many fighters as there were *phulai* or tribes in the city, one fighter for each tribe...." One may compare the theme of a fight between women, and a women's Ares in the *Hubristica* at Argos.

14. *Lithobolia* of Troezene in honor of Damia and Auxesia: Pausanias, II, 32, 2; on the *balletus* of Eleusis: *Homeric Hymn to Demeter*, 265 ff.; Hesychius, s.v. βαλλήτος; Athenaeus, 406 and 407c.

15. Pausanias, III, 14, 8; 20, 8.

16. Livy, 40, 6; cf. M.P. Nilsson, *op. cit.* pp. 494-5. Livy (40, 7) stresses the significance of the rite as an expression of unity and reconciliation that, by allowing rivalries to be worked out in the form of a game, acts as a kind of *katharsis*; at the end of the ritual battle the two sides were normally supposed to gather to feast together (*benigna invitatio*) and to dispel any lingering aggression in friendly jests (*hilaritas juvenalis, jocosa dicta*). The deep significance of the ritual is revealed in Demetrios' remark: "*Quin comisatum ad fratrem imus et iram eius, si qua ex certamine resident, simplicitate et hilaritate nostra lenimus?*"

17. Hesychius s.v. *Ξανθικά*; cf. Suda (= Polybius XXII, 10, 17), s.v. *ἐναγίζων*: "*ἐναγίζουσι οὖν τῷ Ξανθῷ οἱ Μακεδόνες καὶ καθαρμὸν ποιοῦσι σὺν ἵπποι ὡπλισμένοις.*"

On this Macedonian month, the correct form of which is *Ξανθικός*, and which falls in early spring at the beginning of the military season, cf. Jean N. Kalleris, *Les anciens Macédoniens. Étude linguistique et historique*, I, pp. 237-8. Plutarch (*Life of Alexander*, 31) is clearly writing of the same ritual of the *Xanthica* or *Xandica*. The episode shows that the ritual battle serves as a trial and an omen. Of the two camps into which the fighting men are divided, one is supposed to represent Alexander, the other his enemy Darius. It is necessary that, without actually cheating, the "good" side should be victorious. The comparison with the data from Sparta is all the more striking in that the battle of the ephebes at the Platanistas is preceded by a fight between two wild boars each of which represents one of the *moira*. The outcome of this fight between the two animals foreshadows the victory to be won by one of the two sides.

18. Cf. "La Tradition de l'hoplite athénien," *Problèmes de le guerre en Grèce ancienne*, pp. 161-81.

19. L. Gernet, "Frairies antiques," *Anthropologie de la Grèce antique*, pp. 21-61, and especially pp. 36-45. "Structures sociales et rites d'adolescence dans la Grèce antique," *Revue des Études grecques*, 1944, Vol. LVII, pp. 242-8.

20. On the cult of Artemis Korythalia who is a kourotrophe deity, cf. M.P. Nilsson, *op. cit.* pp. 182-9.

21. Cf. Diodorus Siculus, III, 69-70.

22. Aeschylus, *Eumenides*, 292; Pausanias, I, 14, 6; VIII, 26, 6; IX, 33, 7; Schol. Apoll. Rhod., I, 109; Diodorus Siculus, V, 72.

23. Herodotus, IV, 180 and 189. On the relation between the Libyan data and the story of Athena, cf. F. Vian, *La Guerre des géants, le mythe avant l'époque hellénistique*, Paris, 1952, pp. 265-79.

24. Aeschylus, *Seven against Thebes*, 529-44; Euripides, *Phoenician Women*, 145-50; 1153-61.

25. Plutarch, *Life of Lycurgus*, 15, 5. It seems that in Argos the woman had to wear a false beard on her wedding night, to sleep with her husband. On the exchange of clothing and its meaning, cf. Marie Delcourt, *Hermaphrodite: Mythes et rites de la bisexualité dans l'Antiquité classique*, Paris, 1958.

26. Thucydides, II, 39, 1 and 4.

27. Even in the fourth century, in Aeneas the Tactician's *Siegecraft*, secrecy

only plays a part on a tactical, operational level. It is seen as a cunning trick of war, not a general characteristic of warfare as such.

28. J. de Romilly, *Histoire et raison chez Thucydide*, Paris, 1956, pp. 148-74.

29. "La Phalange: Problèmes et controverses," in *Problèmes de la guerre en Grèce ancienne*, pp. 119-42.

30. "La Fonction guerrière dans la mythologie grecque," *ibid*. pp. 53-68.

31. *ibid*. pp. 183-202.

32. Cf. Y. Garlan, "Fortifications et histoire grecque," *ibid*. pp. 245-60.

33. Cf. Angelo Brelich, *Guerre, agoni e culti nella Grecia arcaica*, Bonn, 1961.

34. Herodotus, I, 82; V, 1; Diogenes Laertius, I, 74; Strabo, 357.

35. *Problèmes de la guerre en Grèce ancienne*, pp. 207-20.

36. *ibid*. pp. 231-43.

37. *ibid*. pp. 261-87.

38. M. Lejeune, "La civilisation mycéenne et la guerre," *Problèmes de la guerre en Grèce ancienne*, pp. 31-51; G.S. Kirk, "War and the Warrior in the Homeric Poems," pp. 93-117.

39. *ibid*. pp. 69-91.

40. *ibid*. pp. 53-68.

41. *ibid*. pp. 119-42.

42. *ibid*. pp. 143-60.

43. *ibid*. pp. 161-81.

44. It is hardly necessary, at this point, to draw attention to the work of G. Dumézil and in particular, as regards our present problem, to *Aspects de la fonction guerrière chez les Indo-Européans*, Paris, 1956.

45. *Problèmes de la guerre en Grèce ancienne, op. cit.* appendix. For the Hittite data, see Albrecht Goetze, "Warfare in Asia Minor," *Iraq*, Vol. XXV, 2, 1963, pp. 124-30.

46. "Le Rôle politique des armées dans le monde grec à l'époque classique," *Problèmes de la guerre en Grèce ancienne*, pp. 221-9.

NOTES TO CHAPTER III

1. First published in *La Parola del Passato*, Rome, 1973, pp. 51-79.

2. *Against Stephanos*, II, 18; *Against Leochares*, 49.

3. Cf. the remarks of H.J. Wolff on the differences of meaning between ekdidonai or ekdidosthai, on the one hand, and apodidosthai on the other;

"Marriage Law and Family Organisation in Ancient Athens," *Traditio*, II, 1944, p. 48.

4. On the rules governing the dowry, cf. L. Gernet, "Observations sur le mariage en Grèce," *Revue d'histoire du droit français*, 1954, pp. 472-3; and in particular the text of the discussion which followed L. Gernet's paper given at the Institut de Droit romain on 17th April 1953. A typed record of this text can be found in the archives of the Institut, in the University of Paris.

5. Isaeus, III; *Succession of Pyrrhos*, 39.

6. *Against Neera*, 16-17.

7. *ibid.* 118 and 13; *Against Leochares*, 49.

8. *Against Neera*, 118.

9. *ibid.* 122.

10. *Gorgias*, 464b.

11. *Against Aristocrates*, 53; cf. also Lysias, I, *On the Murder of Eratosthenes*, 30-1 and Plutarch, *Life of Solon*, 23.

12. On the exclusion of the *nothoi* from the *anchisteia*, cf. Isaeus, VI, *Succession of Philoctemon*, 47; Pseudo-Demosthenes, XLIII, *Against Macartatos*, 51 and LVII, *Against Euboulides*, 30; Athenaeus, 577b. For an interpretation of the facts, cf. H.J. Wolff, *l.c.*, p. 75 f.; also W. Erdmann, *Die Ehe im alten Griechenland*, Munich, 1934, p. 363 f.; W. R. Lacey, *The Family in Classical Greece*, London, 1968, p. 280 f.; A.R. Harrison, *The Law of Athens, The Family and Property*, Oxford, 1968, p. 61 f.

13. *Lives of the Philosophers*, 2, 26. Cf. J. Pépin, *Aristote. De la noblesse* (fragment 3) in the collective volume *Aristote. Fragments et témoignages*, Paris, pp. 116-33.

14. Plutarch, *Life of Pericles*, 37, 5. Timotheus, the Athenian general, son of Canon, may have been the beneficiary of the same right. According to Athenaeus, 577a-b, his mother was a courtesan of Thracian origin.

15. Aristotle, *Politics*, I, 3, 2.

16. E. Benveniste, *Vocabulaire des institutions indo-européennes*, Paris, 1969, Vol. 1, chap. iv: "L'expression du mariage," pp. 239-44.

17. L. Gernet, "Aspects mythiques de la valeur en Grèce," *Journal de Psychologie*, 1948, pp. 415-62; *Anthropologie de la Grèce antique*, Paris, 1968, pp. 93-137.

18. *Constitution of Athens*, IV, 2.

19. *ibid.*, XIII, 5. Cf. H.J. Wolff, *op. cit.* p. 87.

20. Cf. Isaeus, *Succession of Philoctemon*, 47, with the formula "ἀγχιστεία ἱερῶν

καὶ ὁσίων"; cf. also Pseudo-Demosthenes, *Against Macartatus*, 51: "*νόθῳ δὲμηδὲ νόθημὴ εἶναι ἀγχιστείαν μηθ᾽ἱερῶν μηθ᾽ὁσίων...*."

21. Dittenberger, *Sylloge* (3rd ed.), 1213 B; cf. H.J. Wolff, *l.c.*, p. 89.

22. Plutarch, *Life of Solon*, 22, 4.

23. "The key to the entire system of Athenian marriage lies in the legal position of the *nothoi* and the way they are opposed to the *gnesioi*" (*l.c.*, p. 75).

24. Cf. in Demosthenes, XLIV, *Against Leochares*, 49, the definition of the *gnēsios* as someone who, being the issue of a marriage through *enguē*, is son by blood, *gonō gegonōs*.

25. It would seem that this is how we should explain the "ideology" of marriage during the classical period, in particular the strongly emphasized opposition between the wife and the concubine both in practice and in religious representations. The wife is seen from the point of view of her child-bearing function and is associated with the cereal-producing earth of Demeter; the concubine, together with the *hetaira*, is associated with the domain of erotic seduction presided over by Aphrodite and represented, in the myth of Adonis, as incapable of giving rise to authentic and lasting fruits. Erotic pleasure and legitimate marriage are classified into categories of thought which are the more firmly separated from one another precisely because, in social practice, the status of the *pallakē* remains in many respects equivocal, oscillating between the courtesan with whom she may often be confused and the wife from whom she is often not clearly distinguished from an institutional point of view. Cf. on this problem, M. Detienne, *The Gardens of Adonis: Spices in Greek Mythology* translated by J. Lloyd, Hassocks, 1977. In our introduction to this book, we wrote: "One might formulate the hypothesis that religious thought was all the more insistent in consecrating the unique significance of marriage by opposing it systematically to erotic seduction since, in default of an unequivocal legal definition, the distinction between concubine and legitimate spouse remained in the fifth and fourth centuries somewhat hazy and uncertain." (Cf. *infra*, p. [166].)

26. Cf. *Iliad*, IX, 146 and 288-90: Agamemnon promises Achilles that, over and above the presents to make reparation for the wrong he has done him, he will give him one of his own daughters "*ἀνάεδνον*," exempting Achilles, as husband, from offering any *hedna*, while Agamemnon will, notwithstanding give him many "*μείλια*" gifts in token of his gratitude; also *Iliad*, XIII, 365 ff.: Othryoneus asks for Priam's daughter without *hedna*, ("*ἀνάεδνον*"), promising

instead to perform some great exploit. Priam accepts.

27. *Iliad*, I, 114.

28. *ibid*. IX, 336 and 340.

29. *ibid*. XIX, 291 f.

30. *ibid*. XXII, 48.

31. *ibid*. VIII, 302 f.

32. *ibid*. XI, 101 f.

33. *ibid*. XVI, 737 f.; cf. also II, 726-8; XIII, 693; XV, 332: on Medon, the bastard son of Oileus, the brother of Ajax. On the bastard Teucros, brought up in his father's house, *Iliad*, VIII, 284; on the bastard Padaios whom the wife, to please her husband, brings up carefully, treating him as an equal with her own children, cf. *Iliad*, VI, 69-71.

34. *ibid*. XIII, 171 f.

35. *Odyssey*, IV, 3-15.

36. *ibid*. XIV, 199 f.

37. *ibid*. I, 429 f.

38. Herodotus, I, 60; Aristotle, *Constitution of Athens*, 14, 4; cf. L. Gernet, "Mariage de tyrans," in *Hommage à Lucien Febvre* (Paris, 1954), pp. 52-3 = *Anthropologie de la Grèce antique*, pp. 358-9.

39. L. Gernet, *op. cit.* pp. 344-59.

40. Apollodorus, *Bibl.*, III, 7, 5-6. Gernet writes: "We know of at least one hero, Alcmaeon, who was certainly bigamously married."

41. Xenophon, *Polity of the Lacedaemonians*, I, 7-8; Plutarch, *Life of Lycurgus*, 15, 13.

42. Even though, as P. Vidal-Naquet rightly notes, "Economie et société dans la Grèce ancienne: l'oeuvre de Moses I. Finley," *Archives européennes de sociologie*, VI, 1965, p. 119, the expression is supported by the authority of Aristotle, *Politics*, II, 1268 b 40, "in the past the Greeks... used to buy their wives from each other [τάς γυναîκας ἐωνοûντο παρ'ἀλλήλων]."

43. "Marriage, Sale and Gift in the Homeric World," in *Revue internationale des droits de l'Antiquité*, 3rd series, II, 1955, pp. 167-94.

44. L. Gernet, "Notes de lexicologie juridique" in *Mélanges Boisacq* (Brussels, 1937), pp. 396-8; *Observations sur le mariage en Grèce* (typescript of the discussion, Institut de Droit romain, University of Paris).

45. Herodotus, VI, 126-30; cf. L. Gernet, "Mariages de tyrans," *Anthropologie*

de la Grèce antique, pp. 365-7.

46. It is in this text of Herodotus that we find for the first time the term *enguē* with the verbs in active and passive forms: *enguan* is used of the father engaging his daughter; *enguasthai* of the future husband accepting the engagement. It is significant that Cleisthenes engaged his daughter "according to Athenian law" by declaring: "ἐγγυῶ παῖδα τὴν ἐμὴν Ἀγγαρίστην νόμοισι Ἀθηναίων." It perhaps suggests that the ἐγγύη was already included in Solon's laws on marriage. It certainly implies that Agariste is engaged to be married to Megacles so that she shall go and live with him in Athens as *gunē enguētē* and their children will be Athenian. The fact that it is specifically noted suggests that the case could have been otherwise, and that when the marriage competition was over the chosen son-in-law might have been installed in the house of his father-in-law (as were many of Priam's sons-in-law) or, as in the case of the Argive marriage of Peisistratos, the sons might have remained, together with their mother, in the house of their maternal grandfather as citizens of Corinth, not of Athens.

47. *Life of Theseus*, 13, 4.

48. Cf. L. Gernet, "Mariages de tyrans," *Anthropologie de la Grèce antique*, p. 350 f.

49. *Olympians*, VI, 120 and 130.

50. Cf. for example Pindar, *Olympians*, IX, 95.

51. On the importance of this lineage that provided its daughters as wives, cf. L. Gernet, "Mariages de tyrans," *Anthropologie de la Grèce antique*, pp. 351 and 353.

52. Apollodorus, I, 9, 8 and I, 9, 11.

53. *ibid*. III, 14, 18.

54. *Iliad*, XI, 221 f.; other instances: Perseis, the daughter of Ocean, gives birth to Circe and Aietes by Helios (Hesiod, *Theogony*, 956 f.); Aietes marries the Oceanid, Iduia, the sister of his mother (*ibid*. 352-6). Actaeon, son of Aristaeos and Autonoe, the daughter of Cadmos, desires to marry Semele, his maternal aunt (Acousilaos, fr. 33 Jacoby). According to one version, Telephos, whose mother Auge is a daughter of Laomedon, marries another of the latter's daughters.

55. Herodotus, XI, 122.

56. *Iphigenia at Aulis*, 49 f.

57. Apollodorus, I, 7, 9. These mythical facts could be compared to the text of one of the laws of Charondas, reported by Diodorus Siculus, XVII, 18:

It allows a woman to leave her husband and cohabit as wife with whomever she chooses (ἀπολύειν τὸν ἄνδρα καὶ συνοικεῖν ᾧ ἂν βούληται).

58. Cf. *Iliad*, VI, 190 f.: The king of Lycia, having in vain attempted to bring about the death of Bellerophon, who has come to his land from faraway Argos, gives him his daughter, at the same time sharing his royal honors with him and presenting him with a vast domain in central Lycia. His intention is to "retain" (cf. line 192: κατέρυκε) the young man through this marriage. Similarly, when Alkinous suggests to Odysseus, who has only just landed on the island, that he should marry Nausicaa, he does so in the hope of seeing his son-in-law settle down to dwell (cf. μένων) in Phaeacia, where the king would provide him with a house and riches (*Odyssey*, VII, 313-15).

59. On this double aspect of the woman in marriage, cf. J.-P. Vernant, *Mythe et pensée chez les Grecs* (4th ed., Paris, 1971), Vol. I, pp. 139-41.

60. For an interpretation of this myth, cf. G. Dumézil, *Les trois fonctions dans quelques traditions grecques, eventail de l'histoire vivante (Hommage à Lucien Febvre)*, II, 1954, pp. 25-32, reprinted in *Mythe et epopée*, I, pp. 580-6. To the evidence presented by G. Dumézil one may add the article by Collouthos, *L'enlèvement d'Hélène*, which both in form and in substance brings new evidence to support his thesis.

61. Euripides, *Iphigenia at Aulis*, 1300 f. Mme Elena Cassin drew our attention to this difference between Athena and Aphrodite on the one hand and Hera on the other, and fully realized its importance in respect of the relation between marital status and sovereignty.

62. Cf. W.K. Lacey, "Homeric ἕδνα and Penelope's κύριος," *Journal of Hellenic Studies*, 1966, pp. 55-65.

63. *Odyssey*, I, 277-8.

64. *ibid*. II, 53.

65. *ibid*. II, 114-15 and 195-7.

66. *ibid*. II, 132; cf. XX, 343-4.

67. *ibid*. II, 223 f.; cf. XVI, 73.

68. *ibid*. XX, 341.

69. *ibid*. XVI, 387-92 and XX, 334.

70. *ibid*. II, 335-6; VI, 384-6; cf. also XVII, 80.

71. In a quite different social and historical context, this link between the woman and her house also appears extremely clearly in the difference the Gortyn

Law establishes between two cases: "If the slave goes to the free woman and marries her, their children will be free, but if the free woman goes to the slave and marries him, their children will be slaves" (inscr. Cret. IV, 72, col. VI, 56; col. VII f.).

72. *Odyssey*, XXI, 115-16.

NOTE TO CHAPTER IV

1. These two parallel studies were first produced by J. Gernet and J.-P. Vernant in November 1963 and published in the *Bulletin de l'Association Guillaume Budé*, Paris, 1964, 3, pp. 308-25. We should like to express our warmest thanks to Jacques Gernet for having allowed us to include the text of his comments on China.

NOTE TO CHAPTER V

1. An earlier version of this text appeared in *La naissance des dieux*, Editions Rationalistes, Paris, 1966, pp. 55-78.

NOTES TO CHAPTER VI

1. This text has already appeared in *L'Année sociologique*, 1953-1954, Paris, pp. 331-52.

2. L. Moulinier, *Le pur et l'impur dans la pensée et la sensibilité des Grecs jusqu'à la fin du IVe siècle avant J.-C.*, Paris, Klincksieck, 1952.

3. *ibid.*, p. 28.

4. He writes (p. 26): "Homer's heroes are devoted to hygiene."

5. Hesiod, *Works*, 724-60; Moulinier, pp. 33-7.

6. Aeschylus, *Eumenides*, 238-9; cf. Moulinier, p. 183.

7. Antiphon, *Choreutes*; cf. Moulinier, p. 192.

8. Antiphon, *Herodes*, 82-3.

9. Eugen Fehrle, *Die kullische Keuschheit im Altertum*, 1910.

10. Moulinier, p. 296.

11. Are they, in effect, really so positivist and simple even for us? Why are grease and cosmetics on the face of a woman not regarded as uncleanliness?

12. *Odyssey*, XXII, 439 and 480. On the religious meanings of the term *kakon* and its derivatives, cf. L. Gernet, *Recherches sur le développement de la pensée juridique et morale en Grèce*, pp. 241-2 and 245.

13. *Iliad*, XXIV, 480 ff.; Moulinier, p. 31 ff.

14. *Iliad*, XIX, 267.

15. Moulinier, pp. 34, 64-70, 162-4.

16. *ibid*. 163 and note 13.

17. Moulinier writes: "The Selli must be very strange people not to wash their feet" (p. 28). Another ritual obligation for the Selli is to sleep lying on the bare ground (Sophocles, *Trachiniae*, 1166), a rule that is neither more nor less strange than the first. It would seem that the two rules reflect the same symbolism. It is true that if one accepts that "the defilement is the dirt itself," one cannot help but find a religious injunction to keep one's feet dirty "very strange."

18. Even if, as has been demonstrated, Hestia, in certain aspects, is particularly related to sexual life.

19. Moulinier (pp. 260-70) bases his remarks upon a number of questionable points made by Rohde. L. Gernet, however, points out very clearly that the *daimones* "do not have individual personae"; "a δαίμων is conceived as an impersonal divine being"; "the Keres or Erinyes (associated with the δαίμων, *Od.*, II, 134-5) are not so much individual 'spirits' but rather manifestations of this divine being, particularly when it is seen as unpropitious." *Recherches*, pp. 316 and 317.

20. L. Gernet, *Recherches*, p. 317.

21. *ibid.*, p. 321.

22. P. Chantraine and O. Masson: "Sur quelques termes du vocabulaire religieux des Grecs: la valeur du mot ἄγος et de ses dérivés," *Sprachgeschichte und Wortbedeutung*, Festschrift Albert Debrunner, 1954.

23. Cf. Moulinier, p. 16.

24. Chantraine and Masson, *op. cit.*, and Moulinier, p. 250 ff.

25. *Persae*, 628.

26. Moulinier, p. 272 ff.

27. *ibid*.

28. Cf. L. Gernet, *Le Génie grec*, p. 230.

NOTE TO CHAPTER VII

1. This text was originally published as the Introduction to Marcel Detienne's *The Gardens of Adonis: Spices in Greek Mythology*. Translated by J. Lloyd. Hassocks, 1977.

NOTE TO CHAPTER VIII

1. This study has appeared in *Quaderni Urbinati di Cultura Classica*, University of Urbino.

NOTES TO CHAPTER IX

1. This study could not have been written without Marcel Detienne's researches on the history, or prehistory, of a science of myth. I have drawn extensively upon his findings, benefited from my discussions with him and made use of two of his as yet unpublished articles. I should like to take this opportunity to thank him for all the help he has given me.

In a slightly different form this text is due to appear in the Italian and English editions of the *Encyclopaedia of the Twentieth Century*, Instituto della Enciclopedia Italiana, Roma, as an article entitled "Myth."

2. Cf. A. Parry, "Thucydides' use of abstract language," *Language as Action*, Yale French Studies, 1970, 45, pp. 3-20.

3. Cf. E. Benveniste, "Catégories de pensée et de langue," *Les Etudes Philosophiques*, 1958, 4, pp. 419-29.

4. Cf. B. Gentili and G. Cerri, "Strutture comunicative del discorso storico nel pensiero storiografico dei Greci," *Il Verri*, 2, 1973, pp. 53-78.

5. Thucydides, II, 22, 4. For a commentary on this text, cf. B. Gentili and G. Gerri, *l.c.*

6. Polybius, II, 56, 7-12.

7. Pindar, *Olympians*, I, 59.

8. *ibid.*, 82.

9. A. Jolles, *Einfache Formen. Legende, Sage, Mythe, Rätsel, Spruch, Kasus, Memorabile, Märchen, Witz*, Tübingen, 1930; translated into French by A.M. Buguet under the title: *Formes simples*, Paris, 1972.

10. On all these points, cf. M. Detienne, "Mythes grecs et analyse structurale," soon to appear in *Quaderni Urbinati*.

11. H. Frankel, *Dichtung und Philosophie des frühen Griechentums*, Munich, 1962.

12. P. Walcot, "The Composition of the Works and Days," *Revue des Etudes grecs*, 1961, pp. 4-7; H. Schwabl, *Hesiods Theogonie. Eine unitarische Analyse*, Vienna, 1966.

13. Cf. P. Walcot, *Hesiod and the Near East*, Cardiff, 1966.

14. Cf. M. Detienne, *Crise agraire et attitude religieuse chez Hésiode*, Bruxelles, 1963.

15. Cf. F. Buffiere, *Les mythes d'Homère et la pensée grecque*, Paris, 1956; J. Pépin, *Mythe et allégorie. Les origines grecques et les constatations judeochrétiennes*, Paris, 1958.

16. Cf. B. Bravo, *Philologie, histoire, philologie de l'histoire*, Warsaw, 1968.

17. J.-F. Lafitau, *Moeurs des sauvages americains comparées aux moeurs des premiers temps*, 4 vols., Paris, 1724; De Brosses, *Du culte des dieux fétiches ou parallèle de l'ancienne religion de l'Egypte avec la religion actuelle de la Négritie* (no place indication), 1760.

18. We are here following M. Detienne and borrowing from his study entitled: *Mythe et language* for the references to A. Lang and M. Müller.

19. A. Lang, *La mythologie*, Paris, 1880, p. 20.

20. M. Müller, *Nouvelles leçons sur la science du langage*, translated into French by G. Harris and G. Perrot, Paris, 1968, p. 115.

21. A. Lang, *op. cit.*, p. 63.

22. L. Preller, *Griechische Mythologie*, 2 vols. (4th ed. by C. Robert, Berlin, 1894).

23. A.H. Krappe, *Mythologie universelle*, Paris, 1930; *La genèse des mythes*, Paris, 1938.

24. P. Decharme, *Mythologie de la Grèce antique*, Paris, 1884.

25. A. Kuhn, *Mythologische Studien*, 1886.

26. *op. cit.*, p. 27.

27. E.B. Tylor, *Primitive Culture: Researches into the Development of Mythology, Philosophy, Religion, Language, Art and Custom*, London, 1903. A. Lang, *Mythology*, 1880; *The Making of Religion*, London, 1909 (1st ed. 1898).

28. J.G. Frazer, *The Golden Bough: A Study in Magic and Religion*, 12 vols., London, 1911-15.

29. Cf. I. Meyerson, *Les fonctions psychologiques et les oeuvres*, Paris, 1948, p. 128.

30. O. Gruppe, "Geschichte der klassischen Mythologie und Religionsgeschichte, während des Mittelalters im Abendland und während der Neuzeit," in *Lexicon der griechischen und römischen Mythologie*, by W.H. Roscher, Supplement, Leipzig, 1921. By the same author, *Griechische Mythologie und Religionsgeschichte*, Munich, 1906.

31. C. Roberts, *Die griechische Heldensage*, 2 vols., Berlin, 1920-1.

32. U. von Wilamowitz-Möllendorf, *Der Glaube der Hellenen*, 2 vols., Bâle and Stuttgart, 1959.

33. M.P. Nilsson, *Geschichte der griechischen Religion*, 2 vols., Munich, 1967 (I), 1961 (II).

34. M.P. Nilsson, *La religion populaire dans la Grèce ancienne*, translated into French by F. Durif, Paris, 1954, p. 33.

35. E. Will, "Bulletin historique," in *Revue historique*, 1967, p. 452.

36. F. Creuzer, *Symbolik und Mythologie der alten Völker, besonders der Griechen, Vorträgen und Entwurfen*, 4 vols., Leipzig and Darmstadt, 1810-12.

37. F. W. J. Schelling, *Introduction à la philosophie de la mythologie*, translated into French by S. Jankelevitch, 2 vols., Paris, 1945-6.

38. Van Der Leeuw, *La religion dans son essence et ses manifestations, Phénoménologie de la religion*, translated into French by J. Marty, Paris, 1948.

39. W.F. Otto, *Die Götter Griechenlands. Das Bild des Göttlichen im Spiegel des griechischen Geistes*, Frankfurt am M., 1947.

40. M. Eliade, *Traité d'histoire des religions*, Paris, 1949; *Aspects du mythe*, Paris, 1963; *La nostalgie des origines. Méthodologie et histoire des religions*, Paris, 1971.

41. P. Ricoeur, "Structure et Hermeneutique," *Esprit*, 1963, n.s. 11, pp. 596-627; the article "Mythe" in *Encyclopaedia Universalis*.

42. Cf. G.S. Kirk, *Myth: Its Meanings and Functions in Ancient and Other Cultures*, Cambridge, Berkeley and Los Angeles, 1970, in particular p. 8 ff.

43. B. Malinowski, *Argonauts of the Western Pacific*, New York and London, 1922; *Myth in Primitive Psychology*, London, 1926.

44. Cf. D. Sperber, "Le Structuralisme en anthropologie" in *Qu'est-ce que le structuralisme?*, Paris, 1968, pp. 169-238.

45. *Structural Anthropology*, translated by C. Jacobson, New York & London, 1963, p. 13.

46. M. Mauss, *Oeuvres*, vol. II: *Représentations collectives et diversité des civilisations*, Paris, 1969, pp. 195-242.

47. M. Granet, *Danses et légendes de la Chine ancienne*, 2 vols., Paris, 1926 (and 1959); *La pensée chinoise*, Paris, 1934; *La religion des Chinois*, 1951.

48. Cf. S.C. Humphreys, "The Work of Louis Gernet," *History and Theory*, vol. X, 2, 1971, p. 183.

49. L. Gernet, *Anthropologie de la Grèce antique*, Paris, 1968, p. 131.

50. *ibid.*, p. 100.

51. *ibid.*, p. 120.

52. Cf. M. Godelier, "Mythe et Histoire," Annales E.S.S.C., Special no. of *History and Structure*, 1971, p. 543.

53. D. Sperber, *op. cit.*, p. 204 ff.

54. Cf. Claude Brémond, *Logique du recit*, Paris, 1973.

55. P. Ricoeur, "Mythe," article, *Encyclopaedia Universalis*.

56. C. Lévi-Strauss, *The Raw and the Cooked*, translated by J. & D. Weightman, London, 1969, p. 341.

57. Cf. in particular M. Detienne, *The Gardens of Adonis: Spices in Greek Mythology*, translated by J. Lloyd, Hassocks, 1977; and *supra*, "The Myth of Prometheus in Hesiod."

DATE DUE
